Collecting & Restoring
HORSE~DRAWN VEHICLES

Collecting & Restoring
HORSE-DRAWN VEHICLES

Donald J. Smith

 Patrick Stephens, Cambridge

First published in 1981

British Library Cataloguing in Publication Data

Smith, Donald John
    Collecting and restoring horse-drawn vehicles.
    1. Horse-drawn vehicles—Collectors and
    collecting
    I. Title
    688.6   TS2020

    ISBN 0 85059 429 4

Text photoset in 10 on 11 pt English Times
by Manuset Limited, Baldock, Herts.
Printed in Great Britain on 100 gsm matt
coated cartridge by St Edmundsbury Press,
Bury St Edmunds, Suffolk, and bound by
Weatherby Woolnough, Wellingborough,
Northants, for the publishers Patrick Stephens
Limited, Bar Hill, Cambridge, CB3 8EL,
England.

Frontispiece *An LGOC
'garden seat' omnibus at
Newington Green, Stoke
Newington, on the Victoria-
Stoke Newington route c 1907*
(B.B. Murdock).

Contents

Acknowledgements

The author wishes to acknowledge the help and advice of the following: Mrs M. Sanders Watney, R. Brereton Esq, E. Cripps Esq, J. Watmough Esq (Editor of *Horse and Driving*), B. Murdock Esq, M.H. Brindley Esq, K. Bennett Esq. M. Williams Esq, The Curator and Staff of the Museum of English Rural Life at The University of Reading, The Curator and Staff of Hereford and Worcester County Museum, The Curator and Staff of Birmingham Museum of Science and Technology.

Introduction

During recent years there has been widespread interest in the use and preservation of horse-drawn vehicles. It now seems incredible that from the late 1930s this form of transport was being phased out of national life, partly for unsound economic reasons, but often to appease a whim of fashion. Apart from a brief respite during the Second World War, when a number of horses were retained to save imported fuel, the draught horse—together with both commercial vehicles and pleasure carriages—seemed doomed to premature extinction. Now that the wheel has literally turned full circle, there has been a remarkable change in the climate of opinion at all levels. In the world of leisure large numbers of people are reacting against the mundane standards of mass entertainment, seeking more individual and challenging recreations, of which driving horse-drawn vehicles is one of many exciting alternatives. Those who collect and restore old carriages for their own sake are motivated by as many ideas and theories as collectors of antique furniture or first editions, with perhaps a dash of nostalgia which accompanies any form of revival. For others an impending world fuel crisis has played an important role; time and motion experts having proved considerable savings when using horses for short-range deliveries. But, apart from purely financial considerations, it is also worth taking into account the eye-catching publicity of horse teams in city streets and at public shows.

The following pages are intended as a basic guide for those wishing to restore, collect, drive or model horse-drawn vehicles, or merely admire and appreciate craftsmanship not only of a bygone era but of a living tradition. As with most traditions, it is necessary to introduce an element of history, if only for the recognition of types and full understanding of both practical function and aesthetic design. There are explanations not only of different types and styles of vehicles but also of their function, acquisition and use, with further notes on horses, harness and showing.

The first difficulty to overcome, especially for the novice, is understanding the names and descriptions used for vehicles and their components, some of which have different meanings in past ages or in different parts of the English-speaking world. The earliest forms of wheeled vehicles were carts or wagons, both of equal importance according to terrain and the needs of local communities. Even the chariot is a form of cart. While carts were two-wheeled, wagons had four wheels, irrespective of size or capacity. It is generally considered that carts were better suited for highland districts with narrow tracks and passes, while wagons were associated with rolling plains or sheltered valleys. There are notable exceptions and areas of compromise, where both wagons and carts were used, but several historians have divided Europe into either cart or wagon countries, carts dominating in the south, while the plains and forests of the north and east (with the exception of north-western Scandinavia) would be wagon country. It is believed, however, that both carts and wagons, especially the latter, arrived from the steppes of Central Asia with the westward migration of formerly nomadic tribes.

Britain may be termed a microcosm of Europe with both cart and wagon areas, at least until the late 19th century, although on some hill farms the sledge, or wheelless drag, was long-used (where even the two-wheeled vehicle was unsafe) in steeply sloping fields. The wagon was almost unknown in Scotland— on the majority of farms and holdings—until the 1900s. In parts of Wales, Cornwall and the Pennines, the vehicles most widely used were the wain or gambo, being low-slung carts which were cheap to construct and easy to repair and maintain.

With the passage of time, both carts and wagons acquired many improvements. The main advantage of the cart was for tipping, while for smaller loads, with a single horse, it had obvious advantages over the lumbering wagon. The latter, however, had greater overall capacity and durability, and was also better suited for the development of braking systems, which were never entirely successful on carts.

Wagons, originally spelt 'waggons', were noted for their wider distribution throughout farming and trading communities and for greater diversity of regional designs. Being much larger than carts, and bearing greater loads, they were frequently drawn by a team or pair of horses rather than by a single animal. In ancient times wagons were considered vehicles of wealth and ceremony, symbolic of riches and the fertile lowlands. From them large numbers of other vehicles have descended, used for both pleasure and commerce, including the stage coach or wagon, also the state coaches of rulers and aristocrats, and so on right down to the mechanically propelled vehicles of the modern age. An ancestral memory frequently associates the wagon with all that is solid, firmly established yet at the same time progressive (at least in the material sense), so that carts were often despised as cheap and tawdry. Much depends on outlook, exact rules being hard to follow, although even today the term cart may be used only in contempt or derision. A borderland of controversy exists concerning many lighter vehicles running on two wheels, termed cars by some and carts by others, especially relating to the governess car, jaunting car and ralli or rally car. In the latter connection 'car' is a common noun in its own right, deriving from the Latin *carrus* meaning a form of chariot but, according to some authorities, being a much heavier, perhaps four-wheeled, vehicle of ancient Gaul. It is wrong to assume that 'car' is merely a shortened form of either cart or carriage, although from the mid-19th century a wide range of so-called village or rustic carts have been termed cars, at least in more fashionable circles. The dogcart (either the two- or four-wheeled) has always been a cart and seldom, if ever, termed a car or carriage. It may be further noted that a horse car was also of a type of four-wheeled tramcar—drawn on channel rails by a horse or pair of horses—terms used in both Britain and America.

It is a further complication that certain light, four-wheeled vehicles, having the outward appearance of carriages or carts were also known as road wagons—

these being mainly used for the training and exercise of light harness horses, especially in North America, where such types were not always hooded or covered. The term wagon, in this sense, was often synonymous with a version of the American buggy, although usually of the cheaper kind with commercial connotations, the owner-driver using his vehicle for business purposes rather than for pleasure driving. By the same token, a cart in Europe was often a degraded carriage used with trade or professional needs as a primary consideration.

The term coach is now related to an enclosed or headed vehicle on four wheels, which may be either public or private, the main survivors in regular use being associated with royal or state ceremonial, although some vehicles (resembling the former stage coach) are known as drags and driven in certain four-in-hand show classes by amateur whips (drivers). On a coach the roof or upper part of the vehicle is a fixture integral with the bodywork. Springing or suspension, for which the modern coach is renowned, began to develop during the second half of the 17th century.

The term carriage derived from the Latin *carruca*, a type of small phaeton or pleasure vehicle, but developed—from the mid-19th century—as a medium-heavy vehicle in its own right. In one sense all vehicles are carriages, whatever their size, shape or purpose, including the timber-carriage and guncarriage which bear only the slightest resemblance to later driving carriages of European culture. In another sense 'carriage' also denotes a shortened form of under-carriage, fore-carriage or hind-carriage, being the carrying gear beneath the body of a vehicle. The modern English interpretation of the word, at least in more conservative circles, relates to a four-wheeled vehicle, usually open but often with a falling hood, sometimes drawn by a single horse but more frequently by a pair or team of horses. There were a few two-wheeled vehicles also included in the list of carriages (in this category), mainly of superior type, the only examples above dispute being the two-horsed curricle and the single-horsed cabriolet, both of the early 19th century.

Buggies were at first round-backed, two-wheeled vehicles of English origin, frequently hooded and drawn by a single horse or pony. The term in this connection was mainly used during the late 18th and early 19th centuries, although revived during the late Victorian era. In America the buggy was a square or tray-shaped vehicle, although early types had rounded corners, carried on four equirotal wheels (all wheels being the same size). This latter develop-ment, in the United States, became the most popular owner-driven carriage or vehicle in the world, remaining in vogue from the 1830s to the 1940s, the Model T Ford of the 1920s being little more than a mechanical buggy.

The dray was a heavy type of open, flat-topped wagon without side planks or supports, apart from (in some cases) removable stakes or stanchions. In North America those widely used in city haulage were known as transfer drays, usually pulled by large teams of heavy horses. Some were sprung wagons but the majority were dead-axle types, drawn at a slow pace through dense traffic.

The lorry or lurry was a type of dray used for local and commercial delivery purposes, especially by the railway cartage services. It could be described as a light dray, especially when drawn by a single horse and having removable side stakes. In England the vehicle used for delivering domestic coal was a form of lorry, also known as a rulley or trolley, although earlier types, in the London area, were noted for their high-curved frontboards and distinctive spindle sides.

The London-Watford parcel mail van, exhibited in the Penny Post Jubilee celebrations procession in 1890 (B.B. Murdock).

Both were wrongly termed coal carts, just as other four-wheeled vehicles for collecting ashes and refuse were known as dust carts.

The float or floater was often a medium to heavy dray with fairly high sides, usually with cranked axles and a low platform for easy loading. It was popular for the carriage of certain livestock, especially prize cattle at shows (both as a two- and four-wheeled type), also for loading crates, casks and barrels. In America the term float usually meant a heavy dray, a name widely used in this connection by the Studebaker Company of wagon and carriage builders. A decorative float was also used in carnivals and street parades as a show wagon, or for advertising purposes. Towards the end of the 19th century two-wheeled floats were used by farmers and country folk for marketing and general purposes, some—with seats removed—even appearing in the hayfield. They were also used for taking milk churns to the nearest railhead, being easy for rear loading through an outward opening door, only slightly above road level. For this reason they also gained popularity with city dairymen for milk rounds, until displaced by a larger, four-wheeled box wagon or van.

The name truck, sometimes used in Britain during the 18th century, derives from the Latin *trochus* for 'hoop'—some types having a canvas top supported by hoops. The use of this word survived in colonial America for both two- and four-wheeled heavy goods vehicles, the loading platform often sloping in a rearward direction for ease of use.

The term trap relates to a small, cheaply made, pony-drawn vehicle, with either two or four wheels, but usually the former. It was a description widely used from the mid-19th century, although now considered a slang expression.

Some vehicles had strictly local names, a tub cart in the Midlands and Lancashire often being a tub or trap, while in the north-east especially north of the Tyne, it was a 'Digby' and in the west country a 'jingle'. In the Yorkshire Dales a type of market cart was often termed a 'shandry'.

The majority of early vehicles were made by specialist craftsmen, many of whom were also wheelwrights, making and repairing wheels as the main part of their livelihood, but also constructing complete vehicles to order. The wheelwright and wagon builder were country or village craftsmen, although at a later period more elaborate vehicles were made by town-based firms, often specialising in certain types of wagon, coach or carriage. Such concerns would

'The Gondola of London'—a typical Hansom in London with passengers descending. The date is 1901, the exact location unknown (B.B. Murdock).

have workshops employing many craftsmen following a number of different trades rather than a few all-rounders able to work in wood or metal. It also became the normal routine for such parts as axles and brakes to be made by outside concerns which merely supplied vehicle builders, taking no part in assembly. By the mid-19th century many farm wagons and carts were being produced in urban factories by methods akin to mass-production, rural crafts-manship having begun its slow decline. Factory-made wagons were exhibited at agricultural shows and fairs while the would-be purchasers were bombarded with leaflets, catalogues, newspaper advertisements and the attentions of trained travellers or salesmen. The makers of cheap carts and carriages had nothing to learn from Henry Ford of Detroit, with his celebrated production line methods. Factories for making such vehicles, often obtainable through cash-on-delivery or hire-purchase schemes, were multi-storied blocks (especially in America), each vehicle starting as a heap of raw materials on the top floor and not completed until reaching a loading bay at the rear entrance. While the sizes and proportions of European types were likely to be more varied, from type to type and maker to maker, American production was keyed to a far wider range of standardisation, for which reason leading dimensions of the more outstanding American types have been recorded in a further chapter.

It may be of interest to note that many inventions wrongly attributed to the manufacture of the automobile and the bicycle were introduced for or by carriage makers, including tubular metal frames, wire-spoked wheels, pneumatic tyres and ball-bearing hubs. The process was, however, sometimes reversed, especially in the United States, with the auto-top buggy and its folding roof, similar to that of a touring car (automobile).

The author's drawings, which illustrate much of this book, are intended as artistic impressions and are not drawn to scale.

Chapter 1

Early developments

Ancient civilisations

The wheel is of prehistoric and unrecorded origins, although wheeled vehicles or carriages—as we know them—are thought to have developed in either ancient China or India. The first vehicles were ox-carts descended from slides or sledges with an A-shaped framework of crude timbers, long before 3,000 BC. The slide or sledge, one end resting on human shoulders or the body of a domestic animal, would have a basketwork container at the opposite end, lashed with hide thongs or grass ropes, under which crude disc-wheels or rollers might be fitted. The draught pole or thills (shafts) for harnessing either a single beast of burden or a pair of animals, would be attached by means of a yoke across neck and shoulders. Oxen were frequently used in early civilisations for both draught and agricultural purposes, mainly ploughing. They worked in pairs or teams and the neck yoke was better suited to their conformation than later collars and side shafts.

The wagon or four-wheeled vehicle came after the development of the cart, depending on a double A or H frame, both models and remains of which have been found in ancient burial places. The use of two- or four-wheeled units related to terrain and other local conditions, although more imposing wagons may have been kept for ceremonial purposes even by those using carts for mundane tasks.

In Ancient Egypt most internal communications were by river craft. The chariot and other wheeled vehicles, apart from crude trollies, appear to have developed after the invasion of the Hyksos or Shepherd Kings, about 1,500 BC. These nomadic warriors, by whom the Egyptians were ruled for over a hundred

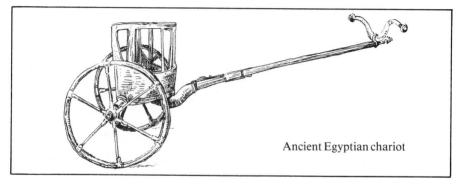

Ancient Egyptian chariot

years, brought the chariot and domestic horse, which were also used and developed in many other civilisations of the ancient world, from the north-east. Early chariots were made of wood with tyres of hardened leather, the latter held in place by copper springs. The first evidence of metal tyres was discovered in royal tombs of the Sumerian civilisation at Ur and dated back to about 3,000 BC. Chariot harness was adapted from the ox-yoke, with an additional form of neckband or breastband, which later developed as either the neck or breast collar of European civilisation.

The Greeks and Romans

Evidence of both two- and four-wheeled vehicles, many of them chariots, has been found in Crete, dating from before 1,800 BC. These types were eventually taken to other Greek islands and the mainland, and were widely used—especially in warfare—during the Mycenean period. Greek chariots were much larger than those of the Egyptians, Sumerians, Assyrians and other peoples of the Near and Middle East. They were usually driven to a pair of horses harnessed on either side of a draught pole, but later by three and four horses abreast. Construction was of wood and leather but the spoked wheels, unlike the wooden wheels of the Egyptians, were often of bronze. There were races for the larger four-horse types at the early Olympic Games. The first four-horse vehicle is said to have been driven by the warrior-king Erectheus of Athens. With the four-horse team, known to the Romans as a *quadriga*, the strongest horses were harnessed to the centre pole or yoke, while the other horses were attached to the front of the vehicle by ropes. The yoke-pole was bent to suit the conformation of the animals to which it was attached, while most vehicles were drawn by means of curricle-type gear in which leather-bound arms from the yoke rested on the saddle pads of the harnessed pair. Greek chariots had only one pole or yoke, whatever the size of their team, while Lydian chariots (from Asia Minor) used a pole for each horse, up to three horses, from which side shafts may have developed. Reins on the war chariot passed over and through a grooved ball on the pole which improved control through greater purchase.

A type of wagon or dray, usually drawn by oxen, was used by the Ancient Greeks for mainly agricultural purposes. There were also ceremonial cars and pleasure vehicles but use of the latter was not encouraged, partly on account of the badly made roads, but mainly because they were thought to foster laziness and self-indulgence. High-ranking ladies travelled for short distances in a closed car or carriage, hung on the outside with long curtains, known as the *apene*, while there are also records of lighter, two-wheeled gigs. In most cases, however, young and healthy people were expected to walk on foot or ride on horseback. Chariot racing, apart from pleasure driving, was encouraged as its risks and competitive element were excellent both for character building and military training.

The Etruscans of Northern Italy made considerable use of chariots, taking their designs from the earlier Greek models, although many of their vehicles—for both war and peace—were of solid bronze. These types, often richly moulded and having nine-spoked wheels, were further noted for a high front-board and low-slung bodywork, the latter for safety in cornering at speed. They were further copied and refined by the Romans, with whom chariot racing was one of the most popular pastimes and spectator sports.

The Roman chariot, widely used in all aspects of national life, was mainly

Assyrian chariot

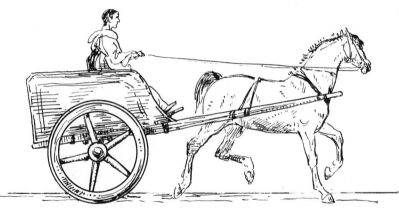

The *Cisium*

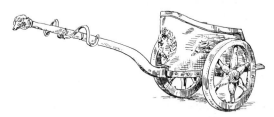

Roman chariot

Early British chariot

responsible for an interest in road making and other facets of civil engineering. This led to the expansion of an empire in three continents and control over subject races which ensured comparative peace and prosperity for a number of centuries.

The Roman war chariot or *currus*, was the first vehicle to use the new roads, large numbers of which were laid-out from about 300 BC. It was soon followed by a wide range of both two- and four-wheeled vehicles, although some may have been restricted to cities and built-up areas. There were equivalents of many later types connected with almost every phase of public and private life from a long-distance sleeping carriage or *carruca dormitoria* to the *essedum* or fashionable carriage, which later developed from a two-wheeled gig with cross seats, entered at the front. The smaller *cisium*, drawn by a single horse, was for light, swift work and made use of suspension in the form of leather straps or thoroughbraces. Vehicles in the Roman province of Thrace on the shores of the Black Sea, also used a form of suspension resembling a slung hammock on wheels. Most larger vehicles, however, were of the lumbering, dead-axle type, often drawn by teams of mules or oxen, which although slower were hardier and better able to withstand extremes of climate and temperature.

The first Roman vehicle, apart from the *currus*, was the dray or *plaustrum* with either spoked or disc-wheels, drawn by oxen and mainly used in farm work or on large estates. It may be noted that the first disc-wheel appeared as little more than a cross-section of a log, but a more sophisticated, later version was made from three or more flat sections joined by overlap and rounded at the rims or edges. A crude form of crosswise seating fitted to the *plaustrum* was gradually refined to a *sella curulis* in which governors or magistrates toured the provinces to administer justice and inspect public works. In the early days of Roman civilisation carriages with comfortable seats and protective canopies were limited to the use of administrators, the high-ranking priesthood and other members of the ruling classes. Lesser officials used a lighter, two-wheeled carriage or *carpentum* which could be further adapted as a ceremonial or bridal car. The later baggage wagon, also used as a military vehicle, was the four-wheeled and basket-shaped *arecera*, as depicted on Trajan's Column of Victory. Heavier versions for both goods and passengers, often drawn by oxen, were known as *raeda*.

As the Roman Empire increased in power and affluence, citizens of all classes yearned for luxury and refinement, so that carriages eventually became adjuncts of fashion or display. Dashing young men drove about in the *cisium* or *essedum*, many of which were eventually hired to the public, working over stages between posting houses and from what amounted to cab ranks. The public *essedum* was later fitted with a rear platform for luggage and known as a *birotum*. Fashionable ladies preferred a *carruca* or four-wheeled *pilentum,* the latter having an embroidered canopy supported by tapering columns or uprights. These were originally seen only in ceremonial processions, but were eventually owned by private citizens and as much in evidence as the modern car or taxi-cab.

In the Celtic lands of Western Europe various types of chariot and carriages were already known before the Roman conquest. Both Britain and Gaul had their versions of the *currus* and *essedum*, drawn by two or more native ponies, often driven with great skill. The British chariot could be fitted with a cross seat on which the warrior rested until reaching the battle zone. The driver frequently urged-on his horses or ponies from a crouching position on the draught pole, allowing more room for the warrior to select and aim his missiles. Like the *essedum,* the average British chariot was bow-shaped, enclosed at the back and entered through the front. A larger, much heavier chariot which may have been copied from the Romans and known as the *corvina*, was sometimes used in later years.

The Mediaeval period

With the decline of the Roman Empire, Europe deteriorated into smaller, often warring, kingdoms, in turn comprising feudal estates which became self-sufficient both as a necessity and chosen policy, between which communications were discouraged if not actually forbidden. Where towns or cities were necessary for administration and a limited amount of trade, these were built on rivers or estuaries, connected by water-borne traffic, as in the days of Ancient Egypt. The Roman system of roads was often badly neglected, remaining tracks and bridleways menaced by outlaws and often impassible in bad weather through lack of drainage. The few people venturing abroad, including pilgrims and merchants, travelled overland only where they were some distance from the coast or navigable rivers, riding or walking in convoy for company and protection. As in the time of the Ancient Greeks there was a return to Spartan standards, in which wheeled vehicles, apart from a few heavy wagons, were frowned upon and most people preferred to ride horses, asses or mules or walk on foot, according to means and inclination. While the nobles and warrior-knights rode horses, priests and lawyers rode mules and asses. Ladies rode small, well-broken horses, often of Spanish origin, known as jennets, while yeomen and folk of substance but humbler stock rode coblike animals which might also serve for pack or draught work. On the field of battle swift chariots and small horses had been ousted by armoured cavalry on large horses which were able to carry great weights. A few military vehicles were still used, with clumsy disc-wheels, both as supply wagons and as carriages for the slings, giant catapults and other siege-engines then in use.

Between inland ports, where there were neither rivers, lakes nor estuaries, merchandise was carried in panniers on the backs of horses or ponies, especially in the north of England. Pack horse trains were used on an increasing scale until the late 18th century, when they were finally replaced by vehicles on improved

Mediaeval cart

Mediaeval long wagon

roads, also by increased numbers of boats and barges over a network of new canals and improved river navigations. The few wagons used throughout the Middle Ages were of crude construction, parts bound together with leather thongs or ropes and the wheel rims having iron studs rather than tyres, although these latter were eventually replaced by strips or strakes of iron held down by smaller studs. A few vehicles had canvas covers supported by hoops, but most were open, having basketwork sides on stakes or spindles, rather than a solid framework with planks. Draught was by means of a wagon pole but often with the addition of a doubletree and swingletrees or draught bars at the platform or rearward end, many vehicles having at least one horse ridden by a mounted driver or postillion.

Towards the end of the Mediaeval period, with the growing commercial wealth of cities and great increases in the population, feudal power with its loyalties, restraints and superstitions began to wane. Material and worldly standards replaced spiritual values, with a greater need for personal comfort and prosperity. The hammock wagon, as used in Ancient Thrace, was revived for a short period during the 12th century, while during the reigns of Edward II and Edward III there was a four-wheeled vehicle, similar to an earlier Roman type, known as a long wagon or whirlicote. This was drawn by several horses in tandem or one-behind-the-other, at least one of which was in the charge of a postillion. The typical whirlicote was long and narrow on large equirotal wheels, its hood richly embroidered and mounted on semi-circular hoops. Yet with such large wheels it was difficult to turn or change direction and many vehicles of this period seemed less advanced than the Roman wagon, the latter having smaller front wheels and a fore-carriage able to turn in limited lock. A solution to this problem came many years later with the introduction of cut-under or arched parts of the bodywork, also the use of iron arches or cranes, the latter so-named as they resembled the curved necks of wading birds. For a temporary period, however, cranes and cut-under also meant separation of the box or driving seat from the rest of the vehicle.

Chapter 2

Coaches, carriages and owner-driven vehicles

The true coach, as opposed to an elaborate covered wagon, was invented in Eastern Europe, taking its name from the Hungarian town of Kocs. This in turn was partly influenced by the construction of German agricultural and military wagons, especially in the use of a strong under-perch or beam forming a connection between fore- and hind-carriages. A vehicle of this type, although perhaps suspended on leather thoroughbraces, was presented to the Queen of France by the King of Hungary in 1457. The use of primitive coaches, some of which were little better than carrying boxes on wheeled platforms, spread throughout Europe, especially the central-eastern parts of Hungary, Austria and Germany, and also to the Netherlands and Flanders, but were much later in reaching Britain and France.

Several early coaches came to Britain during the 1550s, imported from Holland and Germany. The first to be made and designed on English soil was ordered by the Earl of Rutland and constructed by Walter Rippon in 1555. In France coaches had been discouraged and later banned by royal decree, during the early 14th century, and even by 1560 there were only a dozen vehicles of this type in the whole country, three of which were in Paris. In 1580, during the reign of Elizabeth I, Henry Fitzallen, Earl of Arundel, brought a new coach from Germany which was greatly admired by members of the court circle. Elizabeth was the first English monarch to make regular use of coaches, usually

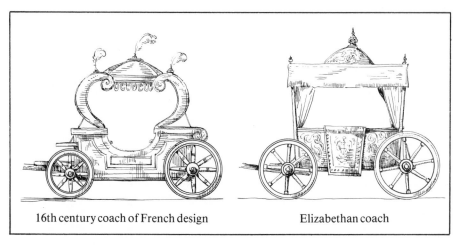

16th century coach of French design   Elizabethan coach

Nobleman's coach, late 17th century

designed for her by a Dutch coach builder named Boonen. The first coach to appear in Spain was owned by Charles Pubest a steward in the service of Charles V. It first travelled abroad in 1546, causing such interest that whole townships lined its route in wonder and curiosity. At a slightly later period there are records of the Queen of Naples riding in a light coach or carriage—the bodywork of which had been decorated with the heraldic lillies of France, by way of compliment—to meet Charles of Anjou. It was from Naples that pleasure coaches and such vehicles gradually spread throughout both the Italian mainland and the island of Sicily. Small, fairly light coaches of the 16th century were known as Pomeranians.

During the early part of the 17th century greater attention than hitherto was paid to interior comfort and trim. The first coach with glass windows was brought from Italy to France in 1620, as up to that period window apertures had been protected by leather curtains only. Although first used in other countries, glass windows for vehicles—both fixed and droplights—were the invention of a Frenchman named Bassompierre. Finely tooled and often perfumed leather was used throughout the century, both for interior trim and to decorate or protect exterior panels. The Infanta of Spain and Consort of the Emperor Ferdinand rode in a leather-lined, glass coach as early as 1631, but there were many vehicles with open or partly covered window spaces until the early 18th century, although gradually declining in numbers from the 1640s.

The royal or princely families of Germany were among the first distinguished and discerning patrons of coaches and coaching. The Duke of Hanover, Ernest Augustus, had at least 50 gilt coaches in his stables by the 1670s, each of which was drawn by a team of six horses.

Although 17th century roads may have been paved and surfaced in some towns and near their approaches, in the depths of the country they were almost impassable during winter and dust-choked, with sun-baked ruts, in summer. A large number of routes were unsafe for all-weather driving until improvements in civil engineering and the introduction of turnpike trusts a century later. Potholes could often break wheels and axles while after heavy rain the mire would be axle-deep. Those driving produce and market wagons to various trading centres complained that narrower wheel rims of coaches increased the depth and danger of ruts, while coachmen always expected right of way for their high-born, wealthy and socially important passengers. To the average wagoner, and to many horsemen and pedestrians, the new-fangled coaches were a curse of the highways, termed 'stinking hell carts'. Before the advent of reasonable springing they were hellish enough for their occupants and mainly used for the sake of fashion and display, long journeys being avoided whenever possible and undertaken in short stages.

From 1605 there were numerous hackney coaches in London, often discarded and patched-up vehicles of wealthier folk, rescued from the scrapheap by their new owners. They were drawn by two or three horses apiece and could be hired for short distances or by the hour, so that even the less well-off could catch a glimpse of luxury and display, although far removed from imagined comfort. Hired for under a pound a day they were popular enough to cause traffic jams and became a public nuisance, also causing great unemployment among city watermen. In 1635 hackney coaches were banned from the city by law, but some were later re-introduced for long-term hire and distances of not less than three miles. Fifty hackney coachmen were registered in 1637 to ply either for long or short distances, but owners were not allowed to keep more than twelve coach horses at a given time. The first cab rank in England was outside an inn or hostelry in the Strand, known as the Maypole, where a Captain Bailey and three drivers employed by him stood, with four coaches. There is some dispute as to the meaning of the word hackney, which may derive either from the part of London where it was first used or from a French word *haquenée* for vulgar or commonplace, also meaning a third-rate horse from a livery stable.

A turning point in the history of coaches came with the first use of steel springs during the mid-17th century, although it is difficult to establish exactly when or where they were introduced or by whom they were invented. Eduard Knapp of London has been credited with a patent registered early in the century, while the French lay rival claims for the experiments of a clock-maker named Daleme, although so-called Daleme springing of combined steel springs and leather straps was not widely used until the early 18th century. Until the late 1660s the more progressive design of coach had its bodywork hung between corner pillars by means of short leather braces, a type known to have been widely used in the household of Louis XIV. These were replaced, a few years later, by elbow springs of the Daleme type and eventually by laminated whip and S springs, the latter noted for S curves from the supporting corner pillars. The familiar C springs, shaped in the form of a letter C, but also known as scroll springs, came during the second half of the 18th century, remaining popular for over a hundred years. Steel springs of the laminated or leaf type not only made a vehicle more comfortable, but able to withstand greater shocks and enabled the makers to use designs with lighter weights and materials. From the second half of the 17th century the coach began to loose its boxlike, ungainly appearance, acquiring by slow degrees a new-found elegance.

The characteristic design of the Berlin, or Berline, first appeared during the 1660s and has been attributed to several individuals but in later years to Phillip de Chiese, employed as a civil engineer by the Duke of Brandenburg. The first vehicle of this type had two under-perches in parallel or a double-perch, high enough at the fore-end to allow the front wheels to lock through 90 degrees. It may be noted that with the normal under-perch wheels rarely locked through

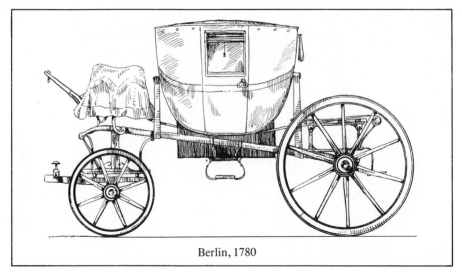

Berlin, 1780

more than 45 degrees, often much less. It was first used in Berlin, from which its name derives, but was neglected after a short period, although restored to favour in Germany, Britain and France about a hundred years later. Sideways motion of the body was checked by short straps connecting with the double-perch at each of four corners. A coupé or cut down version was known as a Half Berlin or Habbeline, while a narrow type for two people facing each other was a Vis-à-Vis.

In later years the cumbersome state or town coach was less frequently used than a smaller and neater state chariot or town chariot, sometimes known as a half coach.

Chariots

The chariot was a smaller version of the coach, originally square and near-upright but later appearing with generous curves. Although the 18th century version had little enough in common with the hunting and war chariots of antiquity, it was smaller and faster than the average coach, seating two passengers facing forwards. Town and state chariots were almost identical, while the earlier posting or travelling chariot was essentially for long distances and cross-country driving. All of these types could be driven either to a team or pair of horses, usually from a high box-seat with a fringed hammer cloth—the latter being for both ornament and protection. The travelling chariot, however, might have its box removed and the horses driven by postillions, hired with their teams at posting houses or inns. Suspension was by means of S or whip-springs, on earlier types, but later C springs were used. With the dress chariot, which might be driven to Court or society functions, footmen in full dress livery rode on a rear platform or dummy board, between the springs. They wore plumed cocked hats, tailcoats thick with gold lace, plush knee breeches and shoes with silver buckles, carrying wands or staves with which to clear the way or hold back a crowd. When the vehicle was travelling at speed they hung on by means of straps fixed almost at roof level. Passengers of the chariot shared a crosswise seat inside, opposite a large glass panel or windscreen. Folding steps let down on either side, lowered by the footmen.

Above *A town or dress chariot of about 1850, now in the Leicester Transport Museum.*

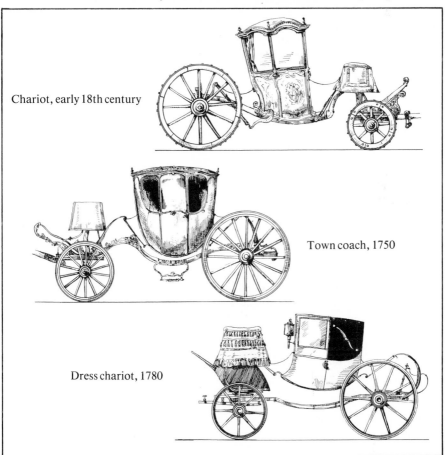

Chariot, early 18th century

Town coach, 1750

Dress chariot, 1780

A state chariot or dress chariot (Science Museum, Crown copyright).

A distinctive feature of the travelling or posting chariot was the sword case at the rear of the bodywork—suspended horizontally—originally made to contain dress swords but later holding various odds and ends. The rear platform, and sometimes the space normally occupied by the box-seat, would be taken up by large trunks, well strapped down. With the travelling coach or chariot servants were often sent ahead, with extra luggage, in a high square vehicle known as a fourgon.

Old and unwanted chariots were converted into vehicles for public hire on long-distance routes, known as post chaises, working from inns and posting houses, each drawn by a pair of swift horses but sometimes by a team of four. They were painted a bright yellow and known as 'yellow bounders' on account of their colour and speed. The postboys in charge, often middle aged or even elderly men, sometimes drove from the box but were usually postillions, wearing jockey caps or low-crowned top hats and waist-length shell jackets. By

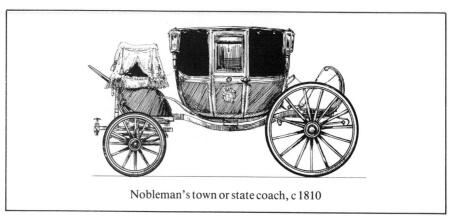

Nobleman's town or state coach, c 1810

Post chaise

tradition there was a great deal of rivalry between postboys and the drivers of stage coaches. Both were made redundant by the advent of the steam railways, although cheaper and greatly improved stage coaches outlasted the majority of post chaises, which were also more expensive, very few of which were seen after the early 1840s.

Chaise and phaeton

For lighter coaches and carriages the use of cranes and cut-under were found to be ideal, especially for sporting phaetons of the late 18th century, driven on increasingly busy roads. Early types, however, retained the perch for additional strength and stability.

During the second half of the 18th century there was an increase in driving for pleasure encouraged by contemporary road improvements. Within a few years Britain changed from having some of the worst roads in Europe to possessing by far the best, for which such far-sighted engineers and planners as General Wade (in Scotland), Metcalf (Blind Jack), McAdam, and later Telford, were mainly responsible. This partly related to the Jacobite rebellions and threats of foreign invasion to support or exploit them, the movement of British troops and their baggage wagons being greatly hampered by the conditions into which so many of the highways and trunk roads had fallen.

Smaller and lighter owner-driven carriages were much favoured from the 1760s onwards. The main two-wheeled type was the chaise, not to be confused with the post chaise or posting chariot. In England this was drawn by a single horse with a turn of speed, although the prototypes were often heavy and clumsy, having a low centre of gravity and the driving seat being too far back for the comfort of the horse, thus straining its hind-quarters. The continental chaise, however, deriving from a refinement of the caretta or pleasure cart of southern Italy, was of much lighter framework and more pleasing design. This was popular on both sides of the English Channel during the 1770s and 1780s, having an underframe or double-perch on thoroughbraces, similar to the Berlin.

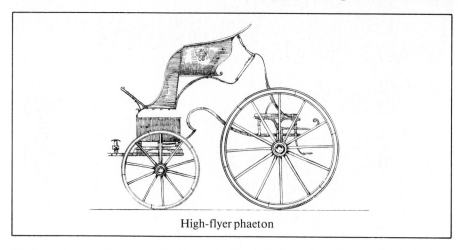

High-flyer phaeton

Bodywork was elegant, almost shell-like, with straight shafts of lancewood. Side panels were painted with attractive designs in the rococo manner, similar to the Fresian Sjees (to be mentioned in a later chapter). It was mounted by means of a hoop-like step or metal ring at the rearward end of the shafts. It was usually large enough for a driver and single passenger, side-by-side.

The four-wheeled driving phaeton, named after the legendary driver of the sun-chariot, was also known as a 'high-flyer' on account of its high-mounted driving seat for either one or two persons, on large carrying wheels. Towards the end of the century the wheel diameters were as much as five feet at the front and six feet to eight feet at the back. Phaetons were usually driven to a pair of horses, although there were a few smaller and single-horse types, but sometimes to a team of four or six. With six horses the leaders were controlled by a postillion. These were the favourite vehicles of the younger sporting set, then known as bucks and Corinthians, including the Prince Regent, later George IV. There were also a few notable women drivers including Lady Lade and the notorious Lady Archer, the latter said to be, 'as renowned for her skill with the whip as for the cosmetic powers she exercised upon her complexion'.

Cocking carts

Nearing the turn of the century there was a craze among the more daring to drive a high-mounted, two-wheeled vehicle, its seat directly above a slatted under-boot, known as a cocking cart. This was driven to a single horse or tandem (one horse behind the other), often at furious speeds. The under-boot was used to carry fighting cocks to a match or main. An American cocking cart, introduced during the late 19th century, was driven to three horses abreast, with two draught poles, one on each side of the centre horse. An Irish version of about 1800 was known as the 'suicide gig', having an even higher driving seat with a high rear seat for the groom. Merely climbing into these vehicles, much less driving them, required nerve and agility.

Curricles

During the 1800s many owner-driven vehicles tended to be slung much lower and nearer the road than those of the previous decade. They were safer and easier to mount than the high-flyer or cocking cart, but still capable of high

A curricle (Science Museum, Crown copyright).

speed when drawn by the right horses. By this time the Prince Regent had become portly and, although still a leader of fashion, would have found it awkward and undignified even attempting to enter anything higher or less stable. The curricle was a popular two-wheeled carriage of the late Regency period, originating in Italy some years earlier, where it was in direct line of descent from the Roman chariot. It remained popular in England for about fifty years and was revived during the 1890s. A curricle was drawn by a pair of well-matched horses, its centre or draught pole having T-shaped crossbars with rollers which rested on the pad saddles of both animals. Traces from the neck collars also linked with horizontal swingletrees or draught bars at the rear end of the pole, which was the main source of connection and draught power. The crossbars at back level were mainly to balance the pair in action. A groom known as a tiger rode on a seat mounted between the rear springs, this being a youth or mature man of dwarfish stature. They were known as tigers as they frequently wore stripped waistcoats as part of their livery. Large and powerful horses were often used, the short, slight build of the tiger seeming to emphasise their strength and height.

Cabriolets

The cabriolet was slightly later than the curricle but soon became its chief rival. It was driven to a single horse, of great height and power. This was essentially a hooded vehicle with upward curving shafts and a high dashboard at the front. As with the curricle, the tiger tended to be small but nimble and was forced to stand on the rear platform, there being no rear seats on this type. As the cabriolet travelled at great speed the horse usually carried a warning bell on its neck collar. Among the distinguished patrons of this vehicle were Count d'Orsay, an exiled French nobleman living in London (known as the Last of the Dandies), and the novelist Charles Dickens. The Duke of Wellington favoured the curricle.

The whisky

This was a small, light, two-wheeled vehicle, almost a form of gig. Its lines

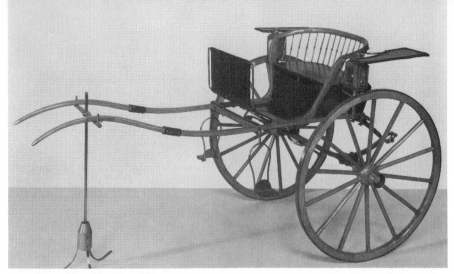

Above *A Stanhope gig of about 1840* (Science Museum, Crown copyright).

Left *A hooded buggy of about 1880* (Science Museum, Crown copyright).

Below *A Tilbury* (Science Museum, Crown copyright).

resembled the earlier continental chaise, but on a much smaller scale. The shafts were usually straight and the external bodywork was sometimes covered in a pattern of decorative canework (a caned whisky). Drawn by a small, swift horse or pony. It was popular from about 1810 to 1820.

Gigs

Early gigs were light, sporting vehicles, driven to a single horse, but towards the end of the 18th century their name was synonymous with anything cheap or roughly made. They were taxed very low and sometimes cost less than £12 to make, which worked out at only a few shillings per annum to the revenue, although marked on the side panels with the undignified slogan 'Tax Cart'. The name gig is said to derive from 'whirligig', meaning an inconsiderable thing or trifle. Later types such as the Dennett, Stanhope, Tilbury, Liverpool and Lawton gigs were of a much higher standard of construction and far more elegant than their predecessors. Several of these are still driven in both harness classes at shows and cross-country or combined events.

The Dennett was designed about 1814 by a coach builder named Bennett, and may have been driven by three sisters, all stage dancers popular in London about that period, named Dennett. It made use of three patent springs in combination, two lengthways and one crossways, named after each sister. This was an early example of so-called platform springing or suspension.

The Stanhope of about 1816 was made to the designs of the Hon Fitzroy Stanhope. It was hung on four springs and considered safer and easier to drive than the Dennett, also more comfortable. Much heavier than the Dennett it sometimes had a folding hood, while its driving seat was stick- or rib-backed like a Windsor chair.

The Tilbury was named after its maker and designer, a London carriage builder who also assisted in constructing the first Stanhope. It was mounted on six under-springs and, although usually driven without a hood, was one of the heaviest two-wheeled vehicles of its type, on account of the extra ironwork needed for the suspension. Safe and comfortable on the roughest mountain roads, large numbers were exported to Spain and Portugal.

Lawton and Liverpool gigs were introduced in about 1830 and are very similar to each other. They were square-sided with plain, straight back-rests rather than rounded or stick backs. Both were refinements or up-dated versions of the Tilbury; the Lawton was named after its designer, while the Liverpool was first driven in the town (later a city) of that name. The Liverpool gig always has a distinctive top rail or iron and mudguards (splashers) above the wheels. Lawton is the trade name of the maker even more than the name of a special gig or type of vehicle.

Low-fronted gigs of an even later period had either well-fronts or cab-fronts for easy access, especially useful for older people and the less agile. These had low front platforms while, with the cab-type, shafts were fixed by means of brackets in front of the dashboard, rather than forming part of the bodywork.

All gigs were enclosed at the rear and could be for either town or country driving. They were frequently used by well-to-do farmers and businessmen, representing a cross-section of the middle classes, known as the 'gigmanity'.

Open carriages

These were usually lighter and less formal than coaches or even chariots, open

A canoe-type landau (Science Museum, Crown copyright).

or semi-open with falling hoods. Apart from the curricle and the cabriolet they usually ran on four wheels. With notable exceptions, they were drawn by a pair of horses or a larger team and may be divided between travelling and town carriages, there being variations of both types. The landau and the barouche were among the earliest and most outstanding types, dating from the closing years of the 18th century, but remaining popular for well over a hundred years. A large version of the landau, known as a state landau, is still used for ceremonial purposes from the Royal Mews, especially for the drive down the course during Ascot Week.

It may be noted that all open carriages were greatly improved in design, structure and comfort by the introduction of elliptical leaf springs, invented or rationalised by an Englishman named Obadiah Elliot in 1804. This enabled builders to dispense with the heavy under-perch, lowering the centre of gravity, also improving the underlock and allowing the bodywork, in many cases, to be self-supporting. The landau was of German origin and seated four passengers facing each other, two per side. Early types were either square-shaped or deeply rounded, with hoods which would not lie totally flat, while later versions had shallow canoe-shaped bodywork and fully collapsible hoods. The five-glass landau could have the fore-part, directly behind the box-seat, protected by raised glass windows. Other types had double hoods which might be raised at either end and joined in the centre, if desired, to make an enclosed carriage. A smaller type of coupé, but with a landau-style hood, was known as a landaulette. All types were normally driven from a box-seat, although the state landau appearing in royal processions is drawn by a team of six horses in the charge of postillions, minus the box. Such types also had a rear seat for footmen.

The barouche was originally a French carriage, seating two people facing forward, its passengers protected by a half-hood raised from the rear. There were usually rear seats for two footmen, as with the state landau. The calèche or calash was also French and at first almost identical with the barouche but slightly larger, seating two people facing forward with two carriage attendants further back. It was perhaps of even sturdier construction than the barouche or landau, frequently used for long-distance work. A later, eight-spring, calèche was large enough to seat four passengers and two footmen. This latter had complex suspension with both elliptical and C springs, also retaining the full under-perch.

The britschka, dating from about 1818, was a semi-enclosed travelling carriage of Eastern Europe, developed from a Polish wagon. It normally seated two passengers facing forwards, enclosed at the front by glass panels and a windscreen. In summer a knee flap could be opened for the use of two extra passengers, facing in the opposite direction. Used by a single person for long-distance travel, the bodywork, with its flat underside, could be turned into a sleeping compartment. A hooded rear seat was large enough for two or three carriage servants. The engineer Isambard Kingdom Brunel lived in a britschka for several weeks while surveying the main line of the Great Western Railway between London and Bristol. A smaller version of the britschka, popular in France, was the dormeuse. Such vehicles were often used by ambassadors for continental travel, carrying the diplomatic bag and having an armed escort.

Smaller carriages

One of the most interesting of these was the droshky, a light Russian vehicle brought to Western Europe during the period of the Napoleonic Wars. It had both an under-perch and C springs, being driven to either one or two horses from a low box-seat. In Russia it was frequently drawn by three horses abreast known as a troika, the centre horse trotting between shafts and doing most of the work, while the two outer horses, their traces decorated with bells, cantered for show, their necks arched and inclined outwards or sideways. A later, more refined version of the droshky, its rear bodywork only a few inches above the axletree, was constructed by David Davies of Albany Street, London, and was known as the pilentum. The droshky and the pilentum had falling half-hoods but were usually driven with the hoods down, the two passengers facing forwards, swathed in bearskin rugs.

The 'sociable' of the 1850s and '60s, popular until the end of the century, seated four passengers, or two facing each other on opposite seats. It was an open vehicle although sometimes having a rear or half-hood, mainly driven from a low box-seat, but sometimes by an occupant of the rear seat, its box removed. Square and angular in shape it somewhat resembled a small version of the original or square landau, a later type of the 1880s being known as the sociable-landau. A smaller version of this vehicle, driven to a pony, small cob or pair of ponies was the Parisian, very low and much favoured by lady drivers and elderly passengers. It often seated two adults and two children facing each other, and was driven from the rear seat. The village phaeton of the 1890s, also deemed suitable for the less agile driver, was a low-slung, square-shaped vehicle without doors, seating six—two facing backwards at the rear—with an under-boot for hand luggage.

Broughams

The Brougham, named after its designer, was introduced during the 1830s, appearing in several versions. Lord Brougham and Vaux was a busy man who lived without ceremony but needed a small, light vehicle for town use, having the comfort of a coach and the handiness of a cab. It was enclosed or headed and driven by a coachman, with room for two passengers facing forwards. The square front panel of clear glass made it resemble a smaller version of the town

chariot. The prototype was cumbersome for its size and almost cartlike, produced by Sharp and Bland, a firm better known for its heavy road vehicles. A later and much lighter version, by Robinson and Cook, proved a far greater success, nearer Lord Brougham's original intentions. At a later period a bow-fronted Brougham with a curved windscreen made its appearance, also a type seating four, better known as a Clarence. The larger, roomier versions were produced by Laurie and Marner and, although designed as modest family coaches, became the fore-runners of the four-wheeled cab or growler. A more ornate and better appointed Clarence was known as the Sovereign. The Brougham was the last of the original, coachman-driven vehicles to be designed in Britain.

Victorias

These were fashionable carriages of the open type, but usually having a rearward half-hood. They were up-dated versions of a similar carriage known as a milord, widely used on the Continent. There were both square and round types, driven from a box-seat, having a forward facing passenger seat for two. Being easy to enter they were ideal for society ladies with flowing skirts, widely used by them for afternoon driving. A less elegant or panel-boot Victoria had a folding seat behind the box for a rearward facing passenger.

Introduced from Paris by the then Prince of Wales, later Edward VII, this vehicle was greatly favoured by his mother, Queen Victoria, after whom the British version was eventually named. Victorias were driven either to a single horse between shafts or, less frequently, to a pair, the latter harnessed to a carriage pole. When the box was removed it became a jockey carriage, its single horse ridden by a postillion known as a jockey. There were many of the latter type at seaside resorts during the 1890s, especially Scarborough.

Later phaetons

Owner-driven phaetons of the 18th century were essentially sporting vehicles, presented with style and dash. Although replaced by lower, two-wheeled carriages such as the curricle and cabriolet, they were revived during the second and third decades of the 19th century both as much lower pony-drawn vehicles

and as a larger and heavier type (used for exercising coach horses), but with a return to former elegance in the spider phaeton of the 1880s. Some of the types known as village phaetons are more correctly termed light family carriages, while the true phaeton was merely a speed or exercise machine. All types were usually owner-driven. During the 1830s there was a short-lived equirotal phaeton, invented by W. Bridges Adams, one of which was ordered by the Duke of Wellington. This latter was the combination of a gig body at the front with a cabriolet at the rear, on large wheels of equal height (front and rear) which made it almost impossible to overturn.

The almost miniature pony phaeton was low enough to have its step only a few inches above ground level. From the early 1820s it was driven by George IV (formerly the Prince Regent), by this time too stiff and stout for either curricle or cabriolet. When driven by ladies it was often followed by a male escort or mounted groom. Wheels were 22 ins in diameter at the front and 33 ins at the rear, with prominent splashers or mudguards, while the dashboard was fairly high and many drivers used an enveloping leather apron.

The park phaeton of about 1834 was a larger version of the pony phaeton, sometimes—but not always—having a rear seat for a groom. It was a fine-

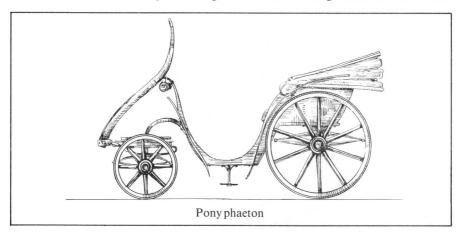

Pony phaeton

Above *A mail phaeton* (Science Museum, Crown copyright). **Below** *A Stanhope phaeton* (Science Museum, Crown copyright).

weather vehicle for leisure driving, seldom appearing with hood or protective apron. Usually accompanied by a mounted escort.

Mail phaetons of the mid-1820s and later periods resembled the detached front half of a mail coach, although four-wheeled vehicles in their own right. They were used either for training or exercising coach horses or for the delivery of mails in remote areas. There was a fairly high box-seat at the front with a falling hood, and a lower rear seat for a groom, the latter reached by iron steps through a side door. An even larger type, for two extra passengers, seating five in all, was the Beaufort phaeton. Both were considered suitable only for strong, active men, shunned by the novice and faint-hearted.

A much lighter vehicle, of the same type as the mail paheton was the demi-mail phaeton of 1832, with a rib-backed driving seat. There was also a T-cart phaeton, designed by an officer in the Brigade of Guards, having a much larger and wider seat at the front than the groom's rear seat, so that—seen from above—it resembled a letter T. The Stanhope phaeton was designed and frequently driven by the inventor of the Stanhope gig, being a scaled-down version of the mail phaeton drawn by a single horse. The driving seat of the Stanhope phaeton was rounded and rib-backed, while the rear seat had a plain back-rest. Shafts were detachable, connected to open-ended futchells or brackets of the fore-carriage, for greater ease of storage.

The spider phaeton, much favoured by Lord Lonsdale, had a Tilbury-type body, mounted on iron arches, above elliptical springs, with a small seat for the groom between the large rear wheels. It was much nearer to the 18th century versions of the phaeton than other vehicles of the period, considered ideal for showing-off the paces of a smart, well-bred horse.

Wagonettes and brakes

Four-wheeled wagonettes and brakes (the latter also spelt 'breaks') are still used to a limited extent (especially on the island of Sark, where motorcars are forbidden), but may be considered in a slightly different category from most owner-driven vehicles. While some were privately driven, they were usually in the hands of professional coachmen and either regular or specially-hired employees. They could be used for anything from a family party to a sight-seeing tour or school outing, while some were kept for meeting trains at the nearest station.

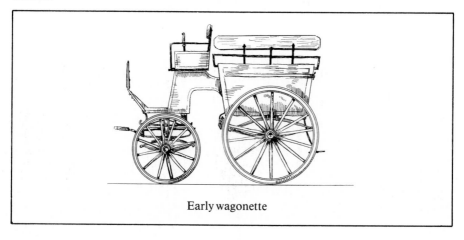

Early wagonette

Above and above right *Wagonettes seen at Dodington Carriage Museum* (K. Bennett) *and the Science Museum* (Crown copyright).

The wagonette of 1842 is the earliest vehicle of this type, built by the firm of Amersham to the designs of Lord Curzon. Three years later an improved and much smarter version was constructed for Queen Victoria, designed by the Prince Consort. Interior seating was longitudinal and inward facing, with a raised driving seat at the front end, having a plain back-rest. Some types had removable seating which could be taken out when the floor space was needed for luggage. Most were driven to a single horse or pair of horses, although the much larger Lonsdale wagonette could be harnessed to a four-in-hand (four-horse) team. The Brougham-wagonette seated six to eight, being a semi-open or convertible type and considered the cheapest form of passenger vehicle for its size, costing in the region of 90 guineas and being cheaper than the ordinary Brougham or Clarence. Like the real Brougham this was sometimes bow-fronted.

The charabanc was a French vehicle used for attending race meetings and other sporting events, driven by either amateur or professional coachmen. The first example to appear in Britain was a gift from Louis Phillipe, King of the French, to Queen Victoria. It was driven to a four-in-hand team and had crosswise seating for seven, including the driver, with a groom's seat at the rear. All seats were at the same level but those in the centre were usually vis-à-vis, or facing each other. A slatted under-compartment or boot, for sporting dogs, was under both front and rear ends of the vehicle. There was an arched cut-under of the bodywork for full-lock, while seating was reached by both rear and side steps.

Brakes were much larger and heavier versions of the wagonette, dating from the 1860s. They were used as sight-seeing vehicles, as luggage vans and to train or exercise coach horses. Several are still kept at the Royal Mews for this purpose, appearing as stand-ins for more precious coaches and carriages at dress rehearsals for state ceremonial. The more elegant versions were sometimes headed with a light canopy and known as carriage brakes. A more popular version was the shooting brake, having a slatted under-compartment—at the fore-end—for shooting-dogs. The larger or body brake had longitudinal seating like a wagonette, entered by means of an iron step and rear door. The latter

were often used, with the seats removed, to convey luggage and items of furniture between town and country houses in the days when people of social standing would have both town houses and a country seat, with perhaps the odd hunting or shooting box. Brakes were also used, experimentally, to convey infantry troops on field days and at manoeuvres.

The skeleton brake was merely a framework and platform with a high-perched driving seat, used for training young horses and breaking them to harness work. The novice was hitched to pole gear in company with an older or more experienced horse, while the groom on the rear platform rode in a standing position, ready to jump off and run to the head of the novice at the first signs of trouble.

Below *A carriage brake or station omnibus—this vehicle was owned by the Great Western Railway at Ilfracombe c 1900* (GWR official photograph).

Charabanc   Body brake

Two-wheeled dogcart   Manchester market cart

Float c 1890

Types still in use

While many of the vehicles previously described in this chapter are either defunct or rarely seen, except in museums, those considered in the following section are comparatively modern (or revivals) and still used for regular showing or pleasure driving. Some, including the dogcart, date back to the early 1800s, but the majority represent the second half of the 19th century and are still being made to order, while in the case of the governess car and tub cart large numbers were being produced until the end of the Second World War. Another popular survivor for modern use is the Liverpool gig, previously mentioned.

The dogcart appears as both two and four-wheeled versions, although the authentic and original type is two-wheeled. Formerly used for taking gun dogs on shooting expeditions, its ancestors were so-called shooting gigs and phaetons, near relations to the cocking cart, although modern versions are smaller and lower than earlier types. It was revived after about twenty years, during the mid-1840s, especially for country driving, when certain vehicles of this height and type were exempt from the heavy tax liabilities on most pleasure carriages. The under-boot (with side slats) was useful not only for dogs but on many practical errands about a farm or small estate. The two-wheeled dogcart was usually driven to a single horse but frequently as a tandem, at least for show purposes. Show dogcarts eventually appeared (having little or no connection with the canine race) on which the slats were either dummies or merely painted. A further characteristic of the dogcart was the back-to-back seating (dos-à-dos), for three passengers and a driver, the rear passengers having their feet supported on a tailboard with letting-down chains. Some in this category had adjustable and sliding bodywork which could be moved backwards and forwards on parallel brackets to improve the driving position. The almost equally popular dogcart-phaeton or four-wheeled dogcart, was sometimes large enough to carry six, including the driver, often drawn by a pair of horses harnessed to a pole. A special show dogcart with an adjustable seat was also known as a tandem cart, some of this type having the front or driver's seat much higher than the rear seat.

From the 1840s onwards there was a wide range of vehicles, mainly two-wheeled and similar to the early dogcart, also elligible for tax exemptions, safe to drive and easy to store and maintain. These included the Worthing cart, Leamington cart, Worcester cart, Whitechaple cart and perhaps a hundred others, mostly named after their place of origin and with only minor differences of design and construction.

Ralli or rally cars, less frequently known as carts, were introduced in 1885, although not widely used until their revival during the 1890s, at least ten years later. They were similar to a small version of the dogcart with back-to-back seating, but even lower, driven to a large pony or cob, there being—as with many British vehicles—both large and small versions. Curved panels inclined gracefully above the wheels on either side, while the shafts fitted inside rather than outside or under the bodywork. Some of the smaller versions were for a driver and single passenger only, on the same seat. During their early days most of these vehicles were manufactured by the firm of C.S. Windover and Company, the rights of whom were contested through the patent laws in a notable court case. To the general public they became known as 'clothes baskets', a name coined by a correspondent employed by *The Daily Telegraph* in reporting the case.

About 1850 a range of so-called market carts appeared, heavier than a gig or most two-wheeled types previously mentioned. They had a cross seat or bench for two, but were mainly for carrying goods or the produce of the small country tradesman. Perhaps the best known of these was the Manchester market cart, produced in fairly large numbers until the early 1920s. Some were able to carry nearly a ton dead weight, although neat and colourful enough not to be confused with ordinary trade vehicles. The sides of the bodywork would be panelled on a heavy oak framework. Most had a small toeboard rather than a high foot or dashboard. Springs were semi-elliptical and the shafts straight rather than curved.

The float, also mentioned in an earlier chapter, was mainly used, like the market cart, by small traders and farmers. It had a rear door and crosswise seating, well back in the interior. There were several versions in larger and smaller sizes. Like the ralli car, the shafts were often inside the bodywork, although sometimes bracketed to the front boards or framework as with the cab-

A governess car in the Hereford and Worcester Museum (M.H. Brindley).

fronted gig. Most had low platforms with large semi-elliptical side springs and cranked axles. They also had holes bored in the floor to assist in cleaning out and washing down. In busy traffic conditions, especially on milk rounds, the float was driven from a standing position, giving the driver a better view ahead. They were introduced during the 1890s but not used by dairy companies until the 1900s.

The governess car was mainly designed for taking children for joy-rides and picnics, in the care of a nursery governess or willing aunt. It was introduced about 1900 and considered very safe, being low, usually rounded and almost impossible to overturn. It had cranked axles and either plain or spindle sides, while a few were of basketwork and some even headed. In most cases they were harnessed to a sedate pony or even a donkey. Seating was round the inside perimeter of the bodywork, rather than crosswise, entered through a rear door. It could be driven from either side but sitting on the skew and not square-on to the direction of travel, which was its chief snag, although the pony almost drove itself. Accommodation for the legs of the driver was to be found in a concave section of the side cushions and their supports. The feet of the passengers dangled in the tub, or well, at the bottom of the car, road clearance being attained by the cranked axles. Allowance for seating and back rests was in the form of a ledge or outward overhang at the sides of the well. A larger version of this vehicle was known as the tubcart, both types having splashers or mudguards. Many floats, governess cars and tubcarts were left in the natural colour of their woodwork, or grained and varnished, although most had painted wheels.

State coaches

The state coaches of royal and imperial families still make limited appearances on ceremonial occasions. They usually seat four passengers vis-à-vis, with an ample box-seat and rear platform for standing footmen. They are elaborate versions of larger, once fashionable town coaches used by the nobility of their day, some of the older types still preserved dating back to the mid-18th century. Apart from museum pieces they are the oldest road vehicles to survive intact.

The oldest state and ceremonial coaches in Britain are those used by the Speaker of the House of Commons and the Lord Mayor of London. Both are drawn by heavy horses at a slow walk, now heavyweight shires hired from the stables of Whitbread the brewers. They have small front wheels, with high box-seats, elaborate hammer cloths, deep but low-slung bodywork and heavy under-perches with very little road clearance. The horses are escorted by walking grooms while the near-side forehorse of each team, especially on the Lord Mayor's coach, may be ridden by a postillion. The Lord Mayor's vehicle dates from 1757. Perhaps the most important state coach is the Royal coach of England, also known as the Golden Coach, exhibited to the public at the Royal Mews, Buckingham Palace. This was ordered for the wedding of George III in 1761, a year after his coronation, but not completed until 1762. Like the majority of vehicles of this type it has elaborate painting and gilding, the side panels being the work of a famous Italian painter, Cipriani. The royal coach was formerly driven from the box to a team of Hanoverian cream horses, but the driving seat was removed during the short reign of Edward VII, so that crowds lining the streets would have a better view of the occupants. The coach is now drawn by grey horses (the Windsor Greys), decked in colourful state harness and ridden by postillions. The interior of the coach is lit by means of electric battery lamps.

Coronation state coach, 1761

State coach c 1820

Several other coaches used by the British Royal Family are similar to a type of vehicle known as the state coach, or four-seater town coach, often replaced by the smaller dress chariot during the first half of the 19th century. Some, however, were still being made for, and used by, wealthier families right up to the 1890s. They were driven from the box to well-matched pairs, or teams of four horses, appearing only on very special occasions. Lamps often appeared on all four corners of the bodywork. The large, square windows allowed plenty of opportunity for the occupants to see and be seen. The majority were mounted on C springs but also retained the under-perch.

In several countries which are now republican, state coaches no longer appear on the streets but may be viewed in museums and at former royal or imperial palaces. These include coaches formerly owned by the House of Hapsburg in Vienna, royal and imperial carriages at the Musée de Compiègne in France, Papal coaches at the Vatican and state coaches of the Portuguese royal household at a carriage museum near Lisbon.

Chapter 3

Public transport vehicles

Stage coaches and stage wagons

A regular service of public transport vehicles, mainly stage wagons, appears to have started during the early 17th century, long before the Civil War. The earliest types were in the form of heavy wagons topped by canvas covers on hoops or tilts, the interiors fitted with a limited number of rough benches. They also carried boxes and bales of merchandise and were frequently open-ended. Their eight-horse teams moved at about two miles per hour controlled by teamsters walking alongside cracking whips but, in later years, riding nimble ponies. The first type of stage wagon, a few dating back to the late 16th century, were enlarged versions of the baggage wagon of the Low Countries, known as the Flanders wagon, also used for military transport. Their capacity was in the region of 4 tons, but later vehicles—some better known as carriers' wagons—were up to 8 tons. Broad wheels eventually shod with iron strakes or strips, helped to grind down hard ruts, a wider tread also proved better for soft going, although many vehicles only ran during the more reliable months of spring and summer. These were dead-axle wagons and, in certain conditions, the jolting was so bad that passengers preferred to walk rather than ride, for at least part of the way. Even after the introduction of better organised stage and mail coach services, stage wagons continued to operate for nearly two hundred years and were known, towards the end, as 'the poor man's stage coach'. Slow and lumbering, they were much cheaper than stage coaches but unlikely to crash or overturn, the main danger being from fire when the badly greased axle-arms tended to overheat or a pipe smoker allowed his glowing ash to blow against the tinder-dry covering. Long after the coming of the main line railways, a type of carriers' wagon plied between remote villages—mainly for parcels and goods—but taking a few passengers by arrangment.

Stage coaches of an improved type connected the larger towns and cities from the mid-17th century, although a regular coach service is known to have run between Edinburgh and Leith as early as 1610. All services were greatly hampered by the lack of good roads and improved by the eventual use of better surfacing methods and materials. Early coaches resembled a large, gentleman's town coach or Berlin, although later types had a heavier, single under-perch. The box-seat was high and wide, shared by driver and guard, while luggage was stowed on the roof or a platform at the rear of the bodywork. During the early 18th century some coaches had a basketwork compartment or rumble at the

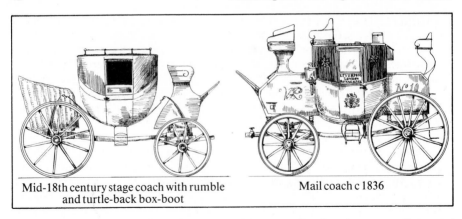

Mid-18th century stage coach with rumble
and turtle-back box-boot

Mail coach c 1836

rear, for passengers unable to afford inside seats. Steel springs were first used on a London to Shrewsbury coach in 1774.

In 1784 John Palmer of Bath invented a system of mail delivery, to be sponsored by the government, based on enlarged and improved stage coaches. These were to replace the unsatisfactory service of mail or postboys, who formerly rode between towns with bags of letters and parcels but were often decoyed and robbed, especially in remote areas. Mail coaches, as they were termed, were among the first large vehicles to use C springs. They were turned out in the royal livery of red, black and gold, having the royal arms and cyphers painted on their doors and side panels. The guard eventually sat on a rear seat with the mails and valuables under his feet in a locker, his feet and legs wrapped in a bearskin rug. He guarded the mails with pistols and blunderbuss, each coach having a small armoury of weapons. A limited number of passengers and parcels were carried at higher than ordinary rates, but the service was always as swift, safe and comfortable as possible. From the 1800s there were a number of outside or gammon seats, named after a Mr Gammon by whom a bill for their introduction was guided through Parliament. By this period the under-perch was equally strong but lighter in weight and appearance, while suspension was balanced on an arrangement of transverse and longitudinal springs—at either end—joined by D links. This was known as Telegraph or mail springing, first used on a public coach known as the 'Telegraph'—this supporting a lower body frame than earlier types and being less likely to overturn.

While the mail coach was built to strict government specifications (many being provided by the London firm of Vidler), coachmen and guards were employed by the Post Office, but four-horse teams were hired from inn-keepers and contractors along the route. Stages were between seven and ten miles apart but usually the latter, the guard announcing his approach by sounding calls on his horn or 'yard of tin'. Guards on stage coaches frequently amused the passengers by playing tunes on a key bugle, but this was not allowed on the Royal Mail. The speed of the fastest mail coach, with accurate timing, was an average of 10¼ miles per hour. 'Quick Silver', the only named mail coach on the many routes radiating from London, ran between London and Falmouth, able to cover the leg to Exeter (176 miles) in sixteen hours, allowing for changes and stops for meals. Such vehicles ran until replaced by railway services, during the mid-19th century, although boxlike parcels vans, also known as mail coaches, continued to run in remote country districts until the 1900s.

Ordinary stage coaches continued to run side-by-side with the mail coaches, owned by private businessmen or large companies such as Chaplin and Horne They were slightly cheaper and carried more passengers than the mail coaches, sometimes with fourteen on top, while only four passengers were allowed on the gammonboards of a mail coach. Most stage coaches were painted in bright colours with their names and destinations in large letters, also displaying symbols of speed such as a running fox, crossed whips or horse shoes. Those travelling at night were even cheaper but less reliable than day coaches and were horsed by poorer quality animals. Some of these horses were disfigured by accidents or even blind, a blind pair serving as wheelers and merely following their leaders, although a skilled whip could guide a totally blind team, if need arose. In the outer suburbs or country districts, away from the main routes, there were smaller two-horse coaches acting as feeders to the larger coaching inns. One of the latter is described in *Tom Brown's Schooldays* by Richard Hughes, known to Rugby boys as the regulator or 'Old Pig and Whistle'. Fast coaches running between the larger towns were known by such glamorous names as 'Comet', 'Red Rover', 'Nimrod' and 'Experiment'. Wealthy young men and sprigs of the nobility frequently vied with each other in sitting next to the coachman, bribing him with money or cigars to let them drive a stage or merely hold the ribbons (reins) for a few minutes. Some amateur coachmen were as skilful and perhaps more considerate than the professionals, eventually forming clubs to drive their own coaches and discuss driving matters with those of like mind. The true coaching era lasted only about fifty years, yet during their heyday the coach and its driver (between 1820 and 1840) were objects of veneration to large numbers of people, especially daring youths and right-minded schoolboys, all of whom aspired to drive four-in-hand, either amateur or professional, as soon as they were old enough. The appearance of a coach in a town yard or village street drew crowds from nowhere, as if by strange magic.

Private coaching

Having outlived their usefulness, with the coming of the railways (although stage coaches to Cheltenham and Aberystwyth lasted until 1854), driving such vehicles soon became a popular pastime for those with ample funds. There were also a number of touring coaches run from holiday centres, until the period of the First World War, some of the more popular based on Llandudno and Colwyn Bay in North Wales, for a round trip of 56 miles through the beauties of Snowdonia. Special coaches in this service eventually had more seats on the roof than ordinary road coaches, all facing forwards, although the roof may have been lowered for better balance. Although appearing to have inside seating, some of the later types were known as 'dummies', being too low for inside passengers.

What was known as 'the coaching mania' began during the 1860s and lasted until the 1890s, spreading from Britain to France and later to the United States of America. Early driving clubs, some dating from much earlier in the century, were the Four-in-Hand Club, the Bensington Driving Club and the Four Horse Club. Perhaps the most exclusive of them all, surviving to the present day, was the Coaching Club, founded in July 1871. The sporting Duke of Beaufort renowned as a keen amateur whip and designer of carriages and coaches in his own right, was the first President, there being 125 founder-members.

The aim of Coaching Club members was to drive like a professional

Left *A stage coach converted to a private coach; seen in Dodington Carriage Museum* (K. Bennett).

Right *A model Shillibeer's three-horse omnibus* (Science Museum, Crown copyright).

coachman but to look and behave like a gentleman. It may be noted that several earlier clubs had been banned by the police for furious driving and racing on the public highway, their members acting in a vulgar and quarrelsome manner, ill-befitting persons of breeding. There were two full-dress meets of the club, during the London season, followed by official dinners—later extended to three drives and dinners or receptions. The usual meeting place was outside the Magazine in Hyde Park, on the banks of the Serpentine. Having marshalled themselves into the correct order, with senior members at the head, the procession of coaches moved off, escorted by mounted police, large crowds having assembled to witness their departure. Stages were seven or ten miles ending—by tradition—at Hurlingham, Ranelagh or Roehampton. The average speed was seven miles per hour, but many of the earlier clubs had been in the habit of tearing along at over twice that speed, which was both dangerous and unseemly for heavy coaches in town traffic. On reaching the venue there would be a reception or dinner, guests returning informally later during the evening. It was a rule of the club never to race, challenge or overtake other coaches in either direction.

The private coach or drag appearing at club meetings was sometimes used as a grandstand for other sporting events, such as the Eton and Harrow cricket match and fashionable race meetings. Passengers, as guests of the coach-owner and driver, always rode on the outside and the interior compartment, although kept in smart condition, was never used. Windows and doors were kept firmly closed at all stages of the journey. According to tradition the private coach or drag was never allowed to sound horns or any other type of musical instrument.

Driving a coach, especially in traffic, requires both skill and nerve. Long hours should be spent in learning to control the whip before even touching the reins or mounting the box-seat. An accomplished driver can lift a playing card from the centre of a dining table, shutting his eyes or turning his head, but able to catch the returning whiplash without looking. In this way either a wheeler or leader can be touched without the others noticing. The unskilled or careless driver often caused confusion by striking the wrong horse, cutting his passengers with the loose thong and spattering mud everywhere.

It is claimed that most accidents occur not in travelling but in starting and stopping, often through outside passengers being forgetful or not obeying

instructions. The private drag should have two liveried grooms sitting above the rear boot at the back of the coach. Before the start of the journey these men station themselves at the heads of the leaders, keeping them steady and under control. On arriving, the coachman takes the reins before ascending the box, following a careful examination of his team. He then looks round a second time, now holding the reins, and climbs into his place. The whip is finally taken from its socket and the hand brake released. The given signal is a loud cry of 'sit fast', sufficient warning to both passengers and grooms that the vehicle (18 cwt tare weight) is about to move forward. The normal start is often a quick jerk which might topple an unbraced person over the low side irons, with undignified if not fatal results. After releasing the heads of the leaders both grooms jump well back but run alongside the team for a short distance, making a final check, leaping aboard at the last possible moment. As the coach slows to a halt they jump down again and run to the heads of the wheelers, who in turn help to stop the leaders. Trying to stop the leaders first might cause a pile-up of the team in which the coach slews and overturns. The brake is applied only when a dead stop has been made.

To drive a four-in-hand in the English manner, the driver or whip controls four reins, each split and respectively attached to the off-side and near-side horses. One rein draws the leaders to the left while another draws them to the right, a second pair of reins controlling the wheelers (next to the coach) in a similar manner. The accepted driving position is with the back erect and knees close together but well braced, the legs and lap covered by a rug or apron according to the weather. The driving whip is held in the right hand and the reins gathered in the left, held at a level slightly below the heart, although the exact hand position was formerly a matter of great controversy in driving circles.

Omnibuses

A version of the omnibus, patented by the celebrated mathematician and philosopher Blaise Pascal, first appeared in the streets of Paris during the mid-17th century. It was brought to England during the reign of George IV by George Shillibeer, a former Midshipman in the Royal Navy who left the service at a time when promotion was difficult without money or influence. A coach-

Above *A late type of knifeboard omnibus outside The Horn in Kensington, 1891* (London Transport Executive). **Below** *A 'garden seat' omnibus c 1890* (Science Museum, Crown copyright).

builder and later an undertaker, Shillibeer was above all an entrepreneur and shrewd businessman, always willing to back a new enterprise. He ran his first pair of buses between Paddington and the Bank of England in July 1829, three years after their revival in the streets of Paris. These were single-deckers conveying about twenty inside passengers under the care of polite, well-mannered conductors, each bus having its own free library of standard authors and the latest newspapers. Although a success in financial terms there were, however, objections to any horse-drawn vehicle with more than two horses abreast, Shillibeer at first having three abreast in the French or Russian style. This meant that the first design had to be scrapped, replaced by a fleet of smaller pair-horse buses, conforming to new police regulations. The second versions carried twelve inside passengers, with a single outside passenger next to the driver.

Above *A private bus c 1890* (Science Museum, Crown copyright).

At a slightly later period there were so-called knifeboard omnibuses, with outside passengers perched back-to-back on longitudinal seating of the upper deck, reached by an almost vertical ladder. These caused many accidents and delays and about thirty years later a Captain Molesworth of the Road Car Company, invented the 'garden seat' bus, mounted on elliptical and semi-elliptical leaf springs, and drawn by a pair of horses (although usually mares). The Shillibeer types were much heavier vehicles with solid under-perches, as were the knifeboard types. On the garden seat bus all passengers faced forwards on crosswise seating—at least on the upper deck—this being reached by spiral steps protected by handrails and an outside decency board, the latter to prevent prudish women from exposing too much of their legs and ankles. On the old knifeboard buses it was unusual, if not unknown, for women—with their long and encumbering skirts—to risk an ascent to upper regions. The top deck was open to the elements as were many of the early motor buses, although detachable waterproof aprons were strapped to each seat to serve as a protection in cold or wet weather. Buses of the garden seat type were plastered with signs and advertisements of all kinds, mainly in enamelled iron, for branded goods such as Nestlés Milk, Quaker Oats and Pear's Soap, many of which had their origins during the late Victorian era. Horse buses were retained by many local companies until the First World War, although discarded by the London General Omnibus Company, in favour of mechanical traction, by 1911. Many buses in both London and the provinces were horsed by Thomas Tilling of Peckham, a bus-owner in his own right and, at one time, a jobmaster with the largest number of horses on hire in the world.

Small, single-decker buses were used in many provincial towns, throughout the second half of the 19th century. Some were run privately by country houses, hotels or guest houses and even by the railway companies, both meeting trains and taking people and their luggage to the nearest station. A larger version of the station bus was drawn by two horses, having extra luggage space and room for at least three more passengers at roof level.

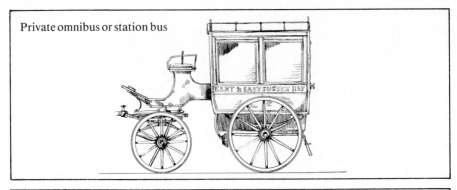

Private omnibus or station bus

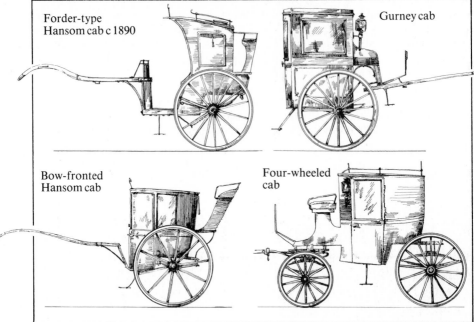

Forder-type
Hansom cab c 1890

Gurney cab

Bow-fronted
Hansom cab

Four-wheeled
cab

Cabs

Apart from hackney coaches of the 17th century, converted from discarded town coaches of wealthy noblemen, the first cab to ply for hire in larger towns was a covered rickshaw-like cart known as a brouette. Like the sedan chair it was designed to seat a single person and drawn by a man between the shafts or handles, being one of the first vehicles to have steel springs. It was first used in the streets of Paris during the 1660s, but later brought to London where it was converted for use with a pony or cob and known as a sedan cart. In its later form the driver led his pony by the bridle, walking in the gutter to avoid other traffic. Sedan carts of the early and mid-18th century could accommodate two passengers side-by-side, facing in the direction of travel.

There was a wide range of both four and two-wheeled cabs during the first half of the 19th century, most of which were driven from the front or side of the vehicle. The coffin cab, so-named as it resembled an open-fronted, up-ended coffin, originated during the 1790s but was mainly popular during the 1800s and 1820s. The driver of this somewhat grisly vehicle was perched on a side seat, directly above the off-side wheel. Later versions seated either one or two passengers at a time and had a falling hood rather than a fixed top.

The American cab of the early 1830s was first used in New York but was also popular, for a brief period, in the centre of London. It had two large wheels and was driven from a roof seat at the front. Four inside passengers were seated on longitudinal side seats, the vehicle entered by means of a rear door and iron steps. The Gurney cab of the same period was very similar, also drawn by a single horse, but considered more comfortable than the American type, by both driver and passengers. The driving seat of the Gurney was fairly low, which improved control and balance. A revived sedan cab or cart came during the 1880s but with room for two passengers on hinged seats, the latter lowered from the side walls of the interior. The tribus was a three-passenger cab of the 1840s entered and driven from the rear. The minibus or Boulnois cab, invented by William Boulnois of London, had longitudinal seats for two passengers facing each other, but was of heavy although narrow construction, resembling a small or minibus, from which the name derives.

The first Hansom cab was named after its inventor Joseph Hansom, the architect of Birmingham Town Hall and several other public buildings. The first version of 1834 was designed with large wheels, above roof level, to prevent it from overturning when cornering or travelling at speed. Its driver sat on the front part of the roof, as with the American cab. Later versions were much lighter and more elegant, especially the type attributed to John Chapman in 1836, this being one of the most popular public transport vehicles of the

A Hansom cab of about 1906 (Science Museum, Crown copyright).

Regent Street, London, in the 1900s. The horse-drawn vehicle still reigned supreme.

century. The Chapman version was driven by a cabbie perched on a high seat at the rear, while the axle was cranked although later changed back to a straight axle, the body mounted on triple springs. Two passengers could be carried, entering at the front by means of a low step and boxed in for safety by folding door-flaps. An even later version, sometimes privately driven and recommended for doctors and other professional men, had a bow-front and side door with drop light, known as a bow-fronted or Brougham-Hansom. A rare three-wheeled Hansom, an example of which is preserved in Hull Transport Museum, has its small front wheel mounted on unique coil springs. The Forder Hansom, constructed by a Wolverhampton firm, with London branches, appeared in 1873. This was light and almost streamlined, with solid rubber tyres, interior looking glasses and silver ashtrays. It weighed only 8 cwt tare. Thousands of Forders eventually operated in the streets of London and other cities, some owned or hired by the main line railway companies. They were faster than earlier types, including the four-wheeled cabs, out-numbering the latter, especially in London, but were less popular in the provinces. Considered fast and dashing in both senses, they were not always thought suitable for an unescorted female of good reputation. Other variants of the Hansom were the rear-door and minibus types, also the hooded cab with a falling or folded hood similar to a cabriolet, which could be driven open in summer. During the 1890s the number of cabs of all types was greatly reduced, mainly due to competition from improved bus services.

Four-wheeled cabs were descended from the Clarence or double-Brougham, most being large enough for at least four adults and two or three small children, with luggage on the roof. They were essentially family vehicles or for staid and elderly persons, while the Hansom appealed to younger folk and the man-about-town. While the driver of the Hansom was often himself smart and young, the four-wheeler tended to be driven by middle-aged or elderly men. Standards varied, but many four-wheelers were decayed and disreputable, the floorboards covered with straw—which soon became very dirty—used to keep passengers' feet warm in cold weather. Old and unfit horses were frequently driven by the poorer owners, used-up as a final stage before passing to the knacker's yard via the open street markets. In later years such cabs were known as 'growlers' because they often creaked or groaned through wear and neglect.

Chapter 4

Commercial, utility, military and agricultural vehicles

Trade vehicles

The fore-runners of most trade and commercial vehicles were clumsy ox-drawn wagons or carts of the Mediaeval period, used in dragging loads from a quay-side to markets or places of storage and dispersal. Later there were special vehicles for carting timber, building stone and coal, with low-slung trucks or drays for barrels, kegs, casks and water containers, adapted to either shafts or pole gear. Their numbers greatly increased during the period of the Industrial Revolution, especially from the mid-19th century. Many comparatively new types, mainly for delivery work, overlapped into the age of the steam locomotive and internal combustion engine, being fairly widespread until a sudden decline during the late 1950s. Although there is now a slow but steady revival of their use, for reasons of fuel-saving and economy, an even larger number are appearing as part of publicity schemes while others may be preserved by job-masters for filming and television purposes. A few of the older and more interesting types have found their way into museums, but not in such large numbers as more elegant coaches and carriages.

Brewers and wine merchants have been among the most loyal supporters of horse transport over the years, especially for heavy horses. With brewers this was a tradition starting during the early 18th century. The firm of Whitbreads, with 18th century origins, keep a replica of a two-wheeled or tandem dray, dating from this period, which often appears in street parades or processions. It

A pair-horse wagon which was still being used by a road haulage contractor in about 1960 (A. Hustwitt).

Above *A brewer's dray of the 1900s* (R.E. Brown). **Below** *A typical London-type coal trolley photographed in 1953* (B.B. Murdock).

is drawn, as the name suggests, by two horses in tandem harness, attended by men wearing 18th century costume. There were numerous types of brewers' drays, carts, vans, floats and trollies throughout the 19th century, including several regional types. These carried barrels in either sideways or tilted positions, while smaller vehicles were designed for wines and spirits or crates of bottled beer. Most had a high-perched driving seat and footboard, while others had slatted bottoms (loading platforms) with either planked or panelled sides (some metal-lined) or removable stakes. Some had combined wood and iron side rails. One of the most outstanding vehicles was the South Wales dray, constructed in a range of sizes from a small or one-horse type to carry six barrels, to a pair-horse dray for ten to twelve barrels. These were well-sprung and iron-stayed, although a number of the earlier versions were dead-axle. The author remembers seeing one of this type in the streets of Cardiff during the mid-1950s, although mounted on pneumatic tyres. The London dray had a lighter and more elegant but less substantial appearance, having what was known as a book box under the driving seat for order books and paper work. Most types were fitted with hand lever or foot pedal brakes and portable loading-skids, the latter carried in a rack under the rear carriage. Covered wagons for both barrels and bottles often had a shorter wheelbase than open

drays, with a lower driving seat. Most types could be used with either shafts or draught pole, according to size and load. The modern brewers' dray or show wagon, perhaps more akin to a type of market wagon than the original working dray, frequently appears in heavy driving classes at horse and agricultural shows. Its driver's seat is mounted on brackets at the front of the bodywork, while the brake is operated by an off-side foot pedal. Some have a nameboard supported on iron standards, like an arch, above the driver's head. The spare man or trouncer, who normally helped with the loading and unloading, traditionally stands in the front part of the vehicle next to the driver, although some share an enlarged box-seat.

Vehicles for delivering domestic coal varied from the elegant London type, correctly termed a trolley or wagon rather than a cart, to the more prosaic lorry, trolley or rulley, versions of which appeared in most parts of Britain until the late 1950s. The London coal wagon with its high, curved front-board and spindle sides, descends from similar vehicles first used during the late 18th century, although modern versions were mounted on semi-elliptical leaf springs. A tailboard let down from behind, while scales and weights were carried on a platform under the rear-carriage. Both earlier and later types had limited lock on account of the large front wheels. Wheels and wooden hubs (similar to those of a farm wagon), were usually painted bright red. The later coal trolley or lorry appeared both with and without a headboard, although a headboard was usual, recording the owner's name and business address on an enamelled iron plate. In London and the Home Counties the trolley had a central partition of vertical and horizontal iron rods, with several bars supporting the frontboard like an iron fence. Although a few were driven from a high-perched seat, the majority were led from house to house but driven back to the yard or stables with the coalman in a standing position behind the frontboard. Trollies used in London had a square or round-topped side board, placed mid-way down each side of the vehicle for chalking up the latest prices. A later trolley of the 1900s, made in various sizes and capacities, had full underlock with both side and cross springs for fore- and hind-carriages. Most carried a dragshoe but very few had brakes.

Domestic milk deliveries were first made with pails, hung from the side chains of a neck yoke, carried by men or women. In later years a variety of three-

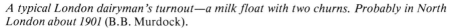

A typical London dairyman's turnout—a milk float with two churns. Probably in North London about 1901 (B.B. Murdock).

wheeled hand cart or barrow was used with straight-sided or conical churns. The two-wheeled float only made an appearance from the late 1890s, adapted from a similar farm vehicle with a low platform and cranked axle. Some types had gimbles to prevent the churns jerking about and turning the milk sour. When milk came to be delivered in bottles, crates and cartons most dairymen, especially the larger firms, changed to a box wagon or van on four wheels, these having full underlock, upward curving shafts and a low driving seat. The hand brake was mounted on a curved rack either in the middle of the footboard or on the off-side of the front platform. Extra crates—mainly for the empties—were carried on the roof, while sides of the box-container or body had sliding doors or curtains of weatherproof materials. Vans of this type were among the first commercial vehicles to have pneumatic tyres, used to deaden the sound of early morning deliveries. Some dairies, including branches of the Co-operative Society, eventually had flat drays or trollies with a canopy top or fixed head and either slatted sides, roller blinds or side curtains. There were a number of low-sprung, step-in types during the 1930s, similar to the American milk wagon, but less popular in Britain than in the land of its origin. After the Second World War there were experiments with several odd and unusual types using balloon tyres, light metal alloys for the bodywork and sometimes having very small front wheels, close enough to give the impression of a three-wheeler. Many of these later wagons were badly designed and, despite the pneumatic tyres, hard to pull, known in the trade as 'horse-killers'.

Bread or bakery vans were adaptations of the normal delivery van of the covered type (with inner racks and trays), which might have flat, straight, arched or curved roofs. The fore-carriage, with most types, was mounted on elliptical leaf springs while the hind-carriage had semi-elliptical springs. Four-wheelers had full underlock. The driver sat on a cross bench or plank, usually opposite a fairly high dashboard, although this was sometimes missing and varied from van-to-van. From the early 1930s there were a few low, step-in types with a well-like front platform, sometimes having cranked rear wheels. A few bakery vans, mainly owned by the smaller concerns, were two-wheeled with canvas covers on hoops above a boxlike carrying compartment.

Below *On the foreshore at Scarborough a fish merchant's cart is seen unloading empty barrels. The date is probably about 1912* (B.B. Murdock). **Above right** *Taken in Scribbans' yard in Birmingham in 1951.* **Below right** *A heavy box van, built by Bonallack and Sons of London. These vans were sepia brown and cream. The date is about 1900. Note the artillery wheels.*

There were large numbers of two-wheeled carts used by retail butchers and fishmongers, driven by delivery boys in striped aprons and either straw hats in summer or flat cloth caps in winter. Those kept by family butchers often resembled a lighter version of the market cart but with an enclosed (slatted) top and sides. The driver was perched fairly high at the front, while the top of the container or bodywork had side rails to support empty baskets. Access to the interior was through double rear doors or by means of a tailboard and letting-down chains. Wet fish was often sold from a flat open cart, the sides only two planks high, the tailboard either let down or kept in a permanently closed position.

Laundry vans were similar to the four-wheeled bakery vans, although a few were also two-wheeled, both types usually having high sides and rear access. Many were of the ledge type with a slight overhang of the upper bodywork.

Delivery vehicles for grocers were either four or two-wheeled of a general type but always covered or headed. The inner parts would be fitted up with ledges and compartments for the various items carried, having scales for weighing-out coffee, flour and sugar, very little of which was sold in packets or tins until after the First World War.

A small general purpose van, its slightly arched roof protected by a water-proofed-canvas or tarpaulin cover, was known as the Coburg. Although used by some bakers and confectioners with small rounds, it was not designed specifically for this trade, but sometimes described as a bread van.

Small delivery vans for hatters and haberdashers were known as tailors' carts,

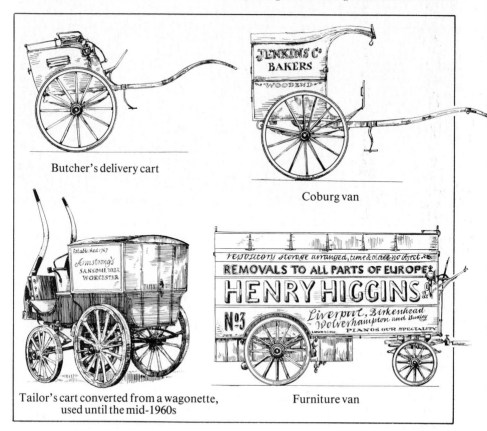

Butcher's delivery cart

Coburg van

Tailor's cart converted from a wagonette,
used until the mid-1960s

Furniture van

although usually four-wheeled. These were sometimes purpose built as the so-called 'omnibus van', but frequently hybrids converted from wagonettes. Scott's, the London hatters, ran a splendid version of the omnibus van in the West End of London until the 1960s, an even larger type of the same vehicle still being used by Rothmans of Pall Mall for the delivery of cigarettes and tobacco to their retail outlets. Rothmans have a magnificent pair of greys, while Scott's van was drawn by a single horse of the hackney type. The Worcester firm of Armstrong's, long renowned in that area of the West Midlands as tailors and haberdashers, ran a small fleet of horse-drawn delivery vehicles, including a hybrid wagonette-type, usually drawn by a black gelding 'Broughton Supreme', a hackney hunter cross at 16 hands 2 ins high and a smart mover, even over the age of twenty. When the horse retired, during the early 1960s, the vehicle was donated to the Worcester County Museum (later the Hereford and Worcester Museum) at Hartlebury Castle, where it is still on show.

Furniture vans usually had cranked rear axles, the wheels fitting into a recess of the bodywork, the rear half of which formed a well for heavier furniture with greater ease of loading. The driver's seat was at roof level, while rounding boards served as an advertisement space and helped to retain smaller items such as lampshades and rolls of carpeting. The length of some furniture vans was between 14 and 16 ft, the larger types drawn by two horses with pole gear. When furniture had to be sent long distances the loaded van was taken to the nearest

Above A large modern van used to supply hotels, etc, with greengrocery during the 1950s.
Below A bakery van by CWS Ltd, Manchester. A fine vehicle owned by Leek &
Moorlands Co-op Society, Staffs, in about 1928 (CWS official photograph).

station and rolled on to a carriage truck, sent to its destination by train and
collected at the other with a hired team. In later years a container system was
devised in which the bodywork could be hoisted or lifted clear of the under-
carriage by crane power.

Fruit and vegetables were delivered on small drays or trollies, some of which
were used for hawking or selling to passers-by, while attracting people from
their houses with street cries, limited to poorer or less snobbish districts. These
may have had permanent or temporary covers but were usually open. The
costermonger's two-wheeled cart was much higher at the back than the front
with curved shafts and the cross seat having a high back rail. In later years some
retail firms and the Co-operative Societies had four-wheeled trollies which

amounted to travelling shops, especially built to serve the new housing estates built on the outskirts of most large towns between the World Wars. This was in the days when only a few people had cars and bus services to the main centres were not as numerous as in later years. There were types for selling grocery, green-grocery, hardware, meat and fish, the latter almost fully enclosed by glass windows and shutters for the sake of insulation and hygiene, having a well-like interior for the salesman. Icecream was sold from small pony carts with elaborate canopy tops and striped awnings, but most of these were replaced by men on tricycles by the mid-1930s.

Delivery of heating oil and lighting or lamp oil was made by a horizontally-mounted tanker or tank wagon, with full-lock of the fore-carriage. The tank rested on a wooden still, or framework of hollow bolsters, having one or more top-fillers. The driving seat was either of the open or box type, or semi-enclosed in the form of a half cab. Some delivered petrol and lubricating oil to garages, in the early days of motoring, when owning a car was a rich man's hobby and there were few commercial motor vehicles for either local deliveries or long distance transport services, at least until after the First World War.

The cartage service of the main line railway companies used many distinctive vehicles from parcels' vans on two or four wheels to low-slung drays and lorries. The most popular railway-owned vehicle was constructed and sold as the 'railway delivery van', although many of the same type were also used by merchants, manufacturers and road haulage firms. They were either covered or open and could be drawn by one, two, three or four horses—sometimes by even larger teams—according to capacity. Sizes ranged from those with a body of 8ft × 4ft to carry 1½ tons to those with an 11ft platform to carry upwards of 5 tons. There were also cranked-axle floats, used for prize cattle and heavy barrels or crates. A few low-loaders, with double shafts, were used for boilers and machinery, these vehicles having solid disc-wheels with broad steel tyres, being in the region of 6 tons tare weight and up to a capacity of 40 tons. The modern railway cart or wagon was often fitted with artillery-type wheels, having iron naves and dust excluders on the hubs, similar but not identical with those used on guncarriages and supply wagons. A type of van for the express parcels delivery service, introduced shortly before the Second World War, appearing at some stations and depots until the late 1950s, had an enclosed or scuttlebox dashboard, pneumatic tyres, electric headlamps and ball-bearing hubs with disc

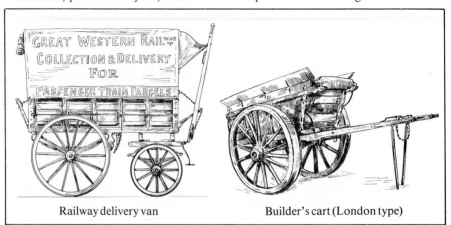

Railway delivery van   Builder's cart (London type)

An oil tanker of about 1900 (The Edgar Bates Collection).

brakes. Without the horse, and with shafts removed, these vehicles were often mistaken for motorvans.

Builders and contractors made considerable use of a two-wheeled builders' cart, similar in many ways to the farm tumbril but with wider raves or side and front boards for overhanging loads. There were also four-wheeled builders' wagons and vans, some made to tip. Stone from the quarry was conveyed to a building site on a type of float slung between cranked axles but having a high front board. A sprung, low-sided timber cart, also sold to farmers, was used for poles, planks and ladders. The so-called contractors' van had a high-perched front seat for the driver and a capacity of 3 tons.

The hay cart used for bringing supplies of fodder from the docks, stations and out-lying farms to large commercial stables and cattle markets, had side and end ladders for balance and support of its load. The two-wheeled London hay cart had a forward extension well above the hind quarters of the horse between its shafts, parallel with the shafts but curving upwards at the front end.

The miller's wagon for sacks of grain and flour was noted for its high loading platform. It resembled the harvest wagon with its carved and chamfered framework, but later types were usually well-sprung and less ornate. This was a frequently headed or hooded type. The corn chandler's van was used either as a covered or open vehicle, being similar to the miller's wagon but with a shorter wheelbase and smaller capacity. Malt wagons were heavy, high-sided types with well-dished wheels, turning in quarter-lock only.

Utility vehicles

These were related to public services, although sometimes in the hands of private enterprise, including street watering carts, fire engines, hearses, carriages for lifeboats, prison vans and many others. Nearly every service and occupation had some form of horse-drawn cart, van, wagon or carriage. A number of the more outstanding types are listed below.

Every large-scale municipal authority, at least from the 1880s, had a department for street cleaning and watering, with appropriate vehicles. Some of the more advanced types had revolving brushes and drain suction pumps, but

Above *One of the fine turnouts from the North Thames Gas Board at the Cart-Horse Parade, Regent's Park, in June 1952* (B.B. Murdock). **Above right** *A pair-horse parcel delivery box van. The photograph is believed to have been taken after the van had been re-decorated in the new LNER livery after Railway grouping in 1923.* **Below right** *A refuse wagon with hand tipping gear, pictured at the Cart-Horse Parade in Regent's Park, 1952.*

the majority of these were late in the day and mainly self-powered by an internal combustion engine. The most widely distributed were square water tanks or carts on two or four wheels, having a rear spread-board or sprinklers, drawn by a single horse or pair, according to size and type. Early types were led through the streets but more advanced models were driven from a high seat at the front end. Capacity was up to 300 gallons but usually 270 gallons. The sanitary or tumbler-slush cart, its horizontal and near-cylindrical carrying box hung on a central pivot between two large carrying wheels, could be emptied by operating a geared windlass on the rear end of the shafts. This was used for emptying the cess pits of houses without piped sewerage, also for transporting liquid lime and mortar on a building site. A four-wheeled tipping wagon or van, lined with metal, for either ashes, street refuse or slush was known as the Margitson and Hek tip wagon, named after its inventors and used by some of the London Boroughs well into the 1950s. This won several gold medals at international exhibitions and was manufactured, under licence, by the Bristol Wagon and Carriage Company, from the 1890s. There were three sizes, the largest of which had a capacity of 2½ cu yds. Such vehicles were drawn at a steady walk by huge shires and Suffolk punches, known as vestry horses, as their work and well-being was decided at so-called vestry meetings of the local council, often held in church vestries before the inception of larger council offices. For road repairs and renewals the old surface was broken up by a four-wheeled road breaker, similar to the hermaphrodite discussed later. The body of the vehicle was filled with heavy weights and tyres of the rear wheels fitted with conical spikes. When main roads had tarred surfaces, from the 1900s, there were horizontally

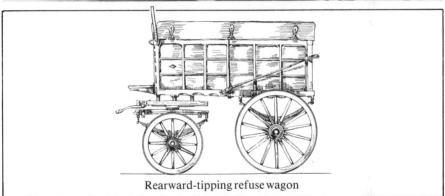

Rearward-tipping refuse wagon

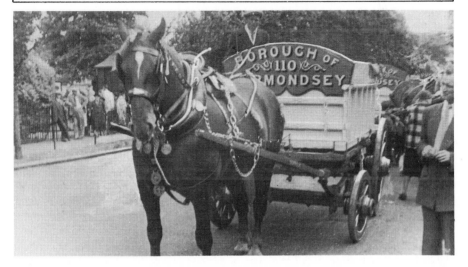

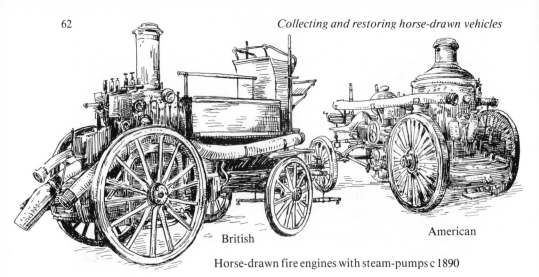

British

American

Horse-drawn fire engines with steam-pumps c 1890

mounted tar-sprayers or tar boilers, on four iron wheels, drawn by a single horse between shafts of tubular iron. A small furnace in the rear under-part of the boiler heated the tar to a liquid condition, having a tall funnel or stovepipe. This was led rather than driven and must have been one of the strangest vehicles ever devised. The fetlocks on the hind legs of the horse were often caked with hot tar.

Fire engines of the type drawn by a single horse and manned by local volunteers were extensively used on large estates and at country houses, from the mid-18th century. They were essentially manual pumps with a supply of leather hose, the more effective types worked by up-and-down levering motions of parallel side bars, needing three men per side as a minimum. Larger types of the same vehicle were eventually used by insurance companies in both towns and cities, a great improvement on the hand-pushed parish pumps with wooden disc-wheels of a century earlier. The first engine with a steam pump was invented jointly by the locomotive and experimental engineers Braithwaite and Ericsson (Ericsson being a former Captain in the Swedish Army, later inventing an ironclad warship). This was on trial from 1829, mainly in the inner London area, and proved a practical and mechanical success but was first used by trained firemen in New York and other foreign cities, before being accepted in Britain. Drawn by two horses harnessed to a coach pole, it was merely a carrying frame for pump and boiler, supported by iron-spoked wheels (of advanced design) with a high-perched box-seat. Exhaust was expelled through a backward-pointing tube in the form of a coiled dragon or serpent. Horse-drawn, steam fire engines with vertical boilers were not used in London on a regular basis until the 1860s, their acceptance depending on the foundation of a full-time Metropolitan Fire Service in 1865. A typical example of this early type was the London Vertical Engine perfected by James Shand and widely used until the 1900s. It was also known as the 350-gallon engine, having double-acting steam cylinders able to pump that amount of water per minute. The driver and officer-in-charge sat on a box-seat at the front, while other firemen rode on longitudinal side benches facing outwards. The boiler and pump, raising steam from cold within a few minutes, was in the care of an engineer-fireman crouching on the tray-like rear platform. There were nine men to an engine and either two or three horses, sometimes harnessed abreast. Three horses as used on the City of Leicester engines, were sometimes unicorn with one horse in front of a pair, the first horse known as a 'cock horse' and ridden by a postillion. It may be noted that a cock horse, usually ridden, was also used on some stage coaches, city buses and commercial drays or wagons, especially in hilly districts. Fire engine horses were often hired from the same Thomas Tilling by whom the garden seat omnibuses were also horsed. They were stabled at the fire stations in pairs and their special, strong but lightweight harness lowered into place, from the ceiling, at the first note of an alarm bell. The main or pump engine was backed-up by other four-wheeled vehicles or tenders with extra hose, spare ladders and a special extending ladder, or escape, on large wheels, the latter carried at the rear of the tender less than a foot above ground level. Large wheels made the escape more stable when dismounted, and easy to man-handle in the fire zone. During the 1890s there were also chemical engines, used for spraying foam, mainly converted from redundant manual types.

The horse-drawn hearse was mainly used from the 1870s to the mid-1930s, being a long, low, glass-sided vehicle in which a coffin was taken to a church-yard or cemetery. Before this period the coffin was either pushed on a hand carriage or taken to the graveside in an ordinary vehicle adapted for the purpose. Farmers and country folk were often taken to their last resting place on a harvest wagon, cart or float. Famous people and naval or military heroes—such as Nelson and Wellington—would have a specially designed funeral car, while others had their coffins borne on open guncarriages. During the second half of the 19th century elaborate funerals became an ideal for families from all classes and social backgrounds, which led to the design of a purpose-built hearse and funeral carriage. The coffin was inserted into the body of the hearse through a small rear door, while wreaths and floral tributes were piled on the roof, the latter protected by elaborate side rails. Most types were decorated with black plumes at the corners. The average hearse was about 12ft

Left *A Shand Mason fire engine of 1898. This has a horse-drawn, three-ram, steam-driven pump* (Museum of Science and Industry, Birmingham). **Right** *A hearse from the collection of the Hereford and Worcester County Museum* (M.H. Brindley).

long and fairly light, easy work for a pair of horses, although some had four horses for show and a lighter, smaller type could be drawn by a single horse. The custom was to walk to the cemetery and trot on the way back, but very few could say that, apart from waiting short periods in cold or exposed places, funeral horses were over-worked or hard done by. Horses were specially imported from Belgium and Holland, usually stallions, and known as the 'black brigade'. They were chosen for their flowing tails and were the only undocked draught horses in London before docking was made illegal. At one time it was thought that an undocked horse might get its tail mixed up with the reins and gain control, causing street accidents.

Ambulances, as special vehicles, also date from the mid-19th century. The earliest types were often converted from a cab or Clarence, usually mounted on solid rubber tyres or even pneumatics. In later years a ledge-sided vehicle was used which closely resembled a station bus. Some of the more advanced types were of military origin, either on two or four wheels, adapted for civilian use. These latter could accommodate up to four stretcher cases at a time, having rear doors and either hooded or open driving seats of the box-type, drawn by a pair or team of horses. Ambulance carts, drawn by a single horse or pony, were specially designed for narrow tracks in mountainous areas. Before the coming of ambulances sick or injured people were often carried in ordinary vehicles or on make-shift stretchers such as a shutter or hurdle.

Horse ambulances were used to recover sick and injured animals, mainly horses, military and civilian types being very similar. They were high-sided, two-wheeled carts, drawn by two or more horses, but sometimes by a single horse. They were usually entered from the rear, although some had both front and rear entrances to save the difficulties of backing-out. The high tailboard was let down to serve as a slatted ramp, the whole bodywork being fairly low on cranked axles. During transit the injured horse was supported by a body sling, hung from an arched iron above the open top of the vehicle. Some early types were roofed over, while others might have a temporary hood of canvas drawn over hoops. The driver sat on a small seat above the near-side wheel, although some military types (with two or more horses) were in the charge of a mounted driver or postillion. Horse ambulances were much in evidence at racecourses

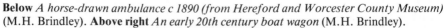

Below *A horse-drawn ambulance c 1890 (from Hereford and Worcester County Museum)* (M.H. Brindley). **Above right** *An early 20th century boat wagon* (M.H. Brindley).

and frequently used by the railway companies. Some of the latter were four-wheeled and may have been adapted from a low-slung, four-wheeled float used to convey prize cattle to the railhead.

The dead horse cart, of which there is an excellent scale model in the Science Museum, South Kensington (Land Transport Gallery), was used by the horse butcher or knacker, to collect a dead or badly injured horse either from its stable or the scene of a street accident. Horses which were badly injured or had broken legs were pole-axed or knackered in the street. This was an open-ended vehicle, the dead body winched on to a loading platform over a lowered rearward flap or ramp. Such vehicles were low-sided, on two wheels, drawn by a single black horse.

The prison van or Black Maria was introduced during the early Victorian era and painted jet black but usually having the royal cypher of Queen Victoria (known to the Cockneys as M'ria or 'Ria) displayed on the side panels of the main bodywork. It was used to take prisoners to or from jails and police courts, also for quelling street riots, some of the earlier types having external side bars to which police might cling like strap-hangers, when riding to the scene of a disturbance. The Black Maria was usually driven to a pair of horses. It was entered from the rear at street level, by means of a low step. The fore-wheels could turn in full-lock, while the driver's seat was perched fairly high. Small windows were barred, but on some types they were confined to upper lights of a clerestory at roof level. Hand brakes were often of the screw-down type.

The lifeboat carriage was a form of carrying frame or cradle for a lifeboat of the coastal rescue service, mounted on large wheels of the artillery type, having dust excluders and draught washers on the hubs, the latter used with towing ropes for man-handling. The fore-wheels were slightly smaller than the rear wheels, well dished but able to turn in half-lock. Crew would enter the boat on the carriage which would then be towed out to sea by a team of heavy horses, hired for the purpose, floated into the surge at appropriate tide levels. Horses, grazing in meadows along the cliff tops, would hear the warning signal or maroon, fired when a wreck had been sited, and gallop to the lifeboat station of their own accord.

Bathing machines were first used by George III and his family at Weymouth, during the second half of the 18th century. At that period it was claimed that sea water had healing properties and most people who bathed did so for health reasons on medical advice. They undressed in a van-like machine and were drawn some distance out to sea then ducked by the specially trained nurse or bathing woman in charge of the machine. There would be steps and doors at either end of the machine, the wheels being usually well-dished with iron naves. Being large and cumbersome they were seldom turned, the horse—often ridden by a small boy—changed from one end to the other for a return trip. Farmers and other horse owners sometimes sent their heavy horses afflicted with troubles of the legs and feet to work for a season in the bathing machines, by way of a cure. During the second half of the 19th century when seaside holidays became widely popular for all who could afford them, whatever their state of health, the machines were treated more as bathing huts, often confined to the foreshore.

Military vehicles

Early military vehicles were based on the dead-axle Flanders wagon, often in the care of hired civilian drivers. In later years there was a Royal Corps of Waggoners and in more recent times the Royal Army Service Corps of soldier-drivers. After disasters in the Crimean War of the early 1850s, during which the allies lost far more casualties through disease, exposure and neglect than on the field of battle, there were numerous reforms, especially in the supply and medical services. New transport vehicles were high on the list of priorities, with a special carriage and wagon department opened at Woolwich Arsenal, and boards of serving officers to design and test a series of both two and four-wheeled types, suitable for the most rigorous field conditions.

The most enduring military vehicles of the 1860s, were versions of the GS or General Service wagon, which could be hauled by two or more horses and either driven from a sprung box-seat over the fore-carriage or by a mounted driver. The first mark was introduced in 1862 while the final marks (ten and eleven) both came in 1905. While average types were about 9ft long some, used in the Boer War (drawn by large teams of mules), were 13ft in length. Experiments

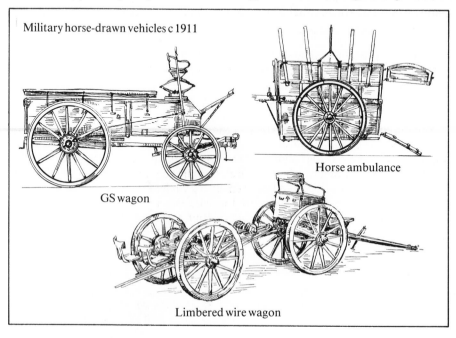

Military horse-drawn vehicles c 1911

Horse ambulance

GS wagon

Limbered wire wagon

Military limbered wagons c 1910.

were made with both underlock and springing (of the bodywork) but the most effective type for both field and garrison work was found to be a wagon with limited underlock and a strong perch. Spring wagons with smaller front wheels and full underlock had to be loaded with greater care than dead-axle types, while high-sided wagons with underlock were likely to overturn on rough tracks in the battle area. The GS wagon was mainly used for food supplies and general stores, although there were eventually large numbers of specialised vehicles including ambulances, water carts, forge carts, wire wagons, travelling cookers, mobile pigeon lofts and tool carts (for the Royal Engineers).

During the early part of the 20th century many transport vehicles supplying the highly mobile units of cavalry and artillery were in the form of a limbered or articulated wagon, having almost identical fore and hind bodies, drawn by teams of two or four horses. This was basically the Limbered GS Wagon Mk 1 of 1906. It was used at military bases and camps for general cartage purposes—mainly to save petrol and fuel oil—until the end of the Second World War.

Two-wheeled carts were less frequently used than wagons as they needed greater skill in both driving and loading, also carrying less per vehicle in proportion, and lengthening the line of march. Some, however, were needed in rough, mountainous terrain and for light work in or near barracks. These were usually Maltese carts drawn by a small horse or pony—also by mules—but sometimes converted into hand carts. They had slatted floors and low sides but could be boarded-up for coal, coke or builders' materials.

A unique type of military vehicle was the limbered wire wagon for laying land lines and cables at ground level, as opposed to the heavy and lumbering air line wagon. This was first used by the Royal Engineers but later by their off-shoot, the Royal Corps of Signals. It comprised two limbered bodies, the hind section carrying spools of wire operated by men sitting on low seats and followed by an outrider with a ringed staff to guide the wire out and prevent it from being snagged on obstacles. Drawn by a team of four or six horses this worked at the gallop over rough and undulating terrain, laying wire much quicker and more efficiently than its mechanised successors, which were either half-tracks or six-wheeled lorries.

The bridging equipment which the Royal Engineers used for pontoons, was carried on low-slung wagons drawn by teams of six horses controlled by mounted drivers. These were similar to lifeboat carriages, an incongruous note appearing—from the military view point—in the form of spare anchors hanging from the rear of each wagon which helped to moor the pontoons in swiftly flowing rivers. General Glubb Pasha, later of the Arab Legion, served with this section of the REs as a junior officer, during the First World War, writing an interesting and informative account of these vehicles in his memoirs published as *Into Battle*.

Farm vehicles

Farm or agricultural vehicles, as they might be recognised in modern times, are of mediaeval origins but improved or modified during the 18th and 19th centuries. They may be divided between two-wheeled carts and four-wheeled wagons, with the addition of open horse lorries, drays and shallow boat wagons towards the close of the Victorian era. Many later vehicles were interchangeable for commercial and agricultural purposes. Few of the older types now survive, unless preserved in museums or by enthusiasts. Many were destroyed towards the end of the Second World War as the result of exposure, neglect and vandalism, frequently rotting away on roadside verges. They had been called out for military purposes, wheeled into positions where they could be utilised as road blocks and strong points in the event of an invasion, but few were reclaimed after the war as they were often beyond repair and largely replaced by tractor-drawn trailers or modern carts with pneumatic tyres.

In hilly districts low carts with open ends were frequently used, known in the Cotswolds and the west of England as wains, but in Wales and the border

Below *A typical Sussex wagon with panelled sides and single shafts. Note the ladders for overhanging load which are positioned front and rear and that the fore-carriage allows only quarter-lock* (Science Museum, Crown copyright).

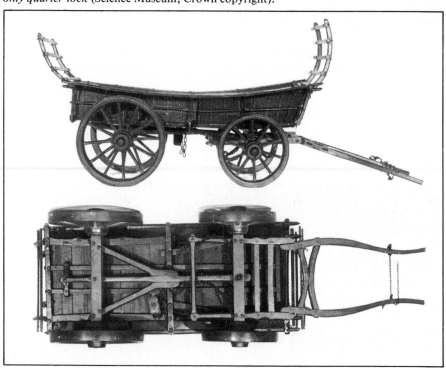

Above *A miller's wagon.* **Below** *A typical country spring cart pictured in about 1900.*

counties as gambos. In some parts they even had wickerwork sides in the mediaeval tradition. Most were drawn by a single horse, ranging from the heavy shire-type to the Welsh cob. The early two-wheeled dung cart or small tip cart was normally fitted with lengthwise rather than crosswise floorboards—for easier unloading or scraping out—as the wooden structure tended to warp under damp loads and exposure, cross planks soon forming awkward ridges. Later types were known as Scotch carts, first imported to East Anglia at a time of agricultural depression when local farmers were selling out to thriftier men from the Lowlands of Scotland who could still farm at a profit where others failed. From the mid-19th century many similar carts, strongly but economically made, were also being constructed in English workshops and factories. They were sturdy and up-dated versions of the tumbril, which had been used in most parts of Western Europe for several centuries, also being the prison and execution cart of the French Revolution.

The hermaphrodite, once popular on small holdings as an economy vehicle, had the rear body of a cart with an extension supported by a detachable fore-carriage. It could be used as an ordinary tip cart for most of the year, although converted into a hay or harvest wagon in late summer. It could be bought for about £20, during the late Victorian era, which was less than half the price of a normal four-wheeled wagon.

Above *A farming scene from about 1900. The vehicle is a typical farm tumbril cart or 'tup'* (B.B. Murdock). **Above right** *The old hay wagon at Dodington Park Adventure Playground* (Keith Bennett).

Wagons in the flatter eastern counties were known as box types, while those in the more undulating western counties and the West Midlands were bow wagons. They were often drawn by singles, pairs or teams of heavy draught horses, sometimes as tandems but in the eastern counties by pairs with double shafts. The box wagons of East Anglia, the south-east and East Midlands had much higher, straighter sides than bow wagons. They had a heavy framework and side planks, chamfered for decorative purposes and to reduce weight, this being done with a spokeshave. Most had a small declivity or notch near the front, into which the fore-wheels turned, rather than the fully waisted effect of other wagons. They could carry up to 8 tons and were well over a ton in tare weight. The length was 12ft 1in to 13ft 4ins and width 5ft to 6ft 7ins. The fore-wheels were between 43 and 49ins and rear wheels 62 to 69ins. The most popular colour for the bodywork was blue, although in some areas it was orange or buff. Wagons of East Yorkshire (the East Riding) were frequently drawn by a pair of horses harnessed to pole gear.

The most typical bow wagons were found in Oxfordshire, widely distributed throughout the South Midlands, with minor variations. They were painted in

Bow wagon   Box wagon

characteristic colours of yellow and red. The main structural characteristic lay in the shallow bodywork, appearing above the rear wheels as a rounded or pronounced bow-shape. The side planks were fixed behind narrow spindles rather than a massive oak framework, the platform narrowed down or waisted just behind the fore-carriage to improve the turning circle. Such wagons were usually drawn by a single horse in shafts, although often assisted by a chain horse in tandem. The length was about 14ft with widths of 5ft 3ins to 6ft 6ins. The fore-wheels were 48 to 51ins wide and rear wheels 58 to 62ins. The undergear of most wagons was in two main parts, connected by means of a coupling pole or under-perch, being without springs or suspension of any type.

Towards the end of the 19th century local craftsmanship declined in favour of cheaper, factory-made products, using deal side planks and imported timber. Shallow, so-called boat or barge wagons, some with full underlock and able to tip, were introduced at the turn of the century.

The Kentish hop wagon had shallow sides but tall, almost vertical end ladders. It was used from the late 18th century for carrying both sacks of garnered hops and hop poles, according to season. A similar type of vehicle was also found in the hop gardens of Worcestershire and Herefordshire on the opposite side of the country.

Water carts similar to those appearing in city streets were also used for spraying liquid manure on the land, at least from the 1870s. They brought water to remote cottages, in time of drought, when most of the local wells had dried-up, also to steam engines used for ploughing and other purposes in fields well away from the farm buildings.

The shallow-sided, two-wheeled timber cart previously mentioned was ideal for odd jobs about the farm, carrying short lengths of wood, fence stakes, ladders and other tools or spare parts. It was usually mounted on cross springs.

Logs, tree trunks and larger pieces of timber were either slung from two wheels, supported by chains under an arched framework, known as a bob, neb or pair of wheels, according to the part of the country in which they were found. These were often very useful in country timber yards and at village saw-mills. For long distance transport of logs a four-wheeled carriage was used, having bolsters at either end, joined at fore and rear ends by a coupling pole.

Romany encampment

Caravans

There were several types of caravan, vardo or living van, used by gypsies, show-men and other travelling people. Those preferred by most gypsy or Romany folk from the mid-19th century (before which they lived under canvas, often in tents mounted on two-wheeled carts), were known as 'bow tops', having small wheels and a roof supported by a bow-shaped framework. The ends, however, were panelled, with deal planks based on an oak framework. A cheaper, less formal type was known as the 'open lot', of which a few are still being made, having reduced end panelling supplemented by canvas curtains. The ledge-type caravan was a larger and more substantial affair with large rear wheels, overhung by the upper half of the bodywork. The Reading vans, first made in the town of that name, were the largest and most elaborate type, although sometimes appearing as miniature versions. They were frequently owned by wealthy horse dealers and wintered out of season in a market place or inn yard on a semi-permanent site. Most types were furnished with fitted bunks, folding tables and a patent stove, the latter known as 'the policeman in the corner', being heavy, dark and upright. Entrance was through a front door, over steps which were let down between the shafts when the caravan drew to a halt. Most types were hung about with carrying boxes and containers, including a built-on hen coop. A comparatively rare type, near extinction for many years, was the brush wagon, often hung with external racks for brooms and brushes, the latter made and sold by the owners in the fenlands of East Anglia. The brush wagon, unlike any other type, had a rear door, always facing away from the direction of travel. Caravans in the hilly districts of the north and west were usually lighter and smaller than those found on the better roads of the south and east.

The original caravan of travelling showmen was known as a Burton van, first constructed in the Burton-on-Trent area of Staffordshire. It was drawn, like most Romany caravans, by a single horse, although a second horse was some-times attached by means of an out-rigger, not always to help pull the vehicle but as a means of breaking and training to harness work. In later years some Burton vans were drawn by traction engines, forming part of a showman's road train. Like many vehicles during the transitional period it could be fitted with either shafts or a triangular drawbar (draught connector). There was a certain amount

Saloon-type van

of carving and gilding of the framework as with the Romany caravan, also a clerestory (mollicroft) roof. The wheels were fairly small, fitting more under the bodywork of the vehicle than at the sides. The better type of gypsy van had larger wheels or at least broader gauge of the track between them, able to travel down rutted lanes or over heathland without overturning, while the narrower based showman's van kept mainly to well-surfaced streets and roads.

During the late 1890s wealthier showmen, with circuses and travelling funfairs, commissioned much larger and longer living vans, known as saloon types. They had side doors rather than front or rear doors and were slung fairly near to road level, although having cupboards or compartments under the floor known as belly-boxes. The interiors were partitioned-off into living room and bedroom, sometimes with a kitchen annex. A real fireplace often replaced the iron stove, sometimes with an elaborate marble surround and overmantle. Most of the furniture was free-standing including sideboards, china cabinets, dining tables and elegant bedsteads with brass knobs. They represented the height of luxury for their type and, in later years, were often mounted on pneumatic tyres, pulled by a lorry or tractor unit. They were almost too heavy for a single draught horse and sometimes appeared behind a pair or team of four. Many were hauled to and from the show-ground by horses but loaded on to flat trucks at the nearest railway station, travelling most of the journey by goods train.

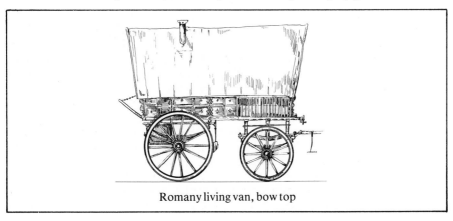

Romany living van, bow top

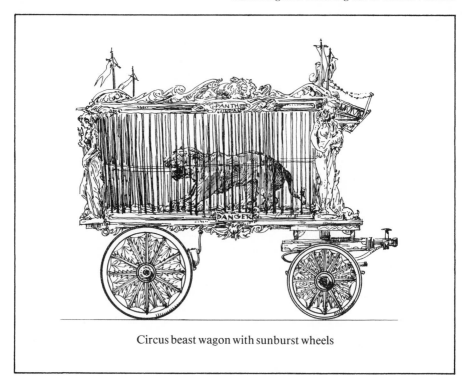

Circus beast wagon with sunburst wheels

Showmen's special vehicles

All types of carts, trucks and wagons were used by travelling showmen, some in the form of mobile cages for wild beasts such as bears, wolves and tigers, while others contained props, poles, rounding boards and baskets of costumes. Those used to contain the galloping horses of the steam roundabouts were known as horse trucks. Others carried mechanical organs, generating sets for electric lighting schemes and centre engines for the larger rides. Most were equirotal with covered tops and small but sturdy wheels with extra spokes for heavy loads, often decorated with in-filling material known as a 'sunburst effect'. Large numbers of these vehicles were made by the firm of Savage of King's Lynn.

With circuses a number of vehicles were used for the grand parade only, this being a street procession before the first performance which served as a welcome publicity gimmick. These types included the band wagon with painted surfaces and glittering mirrors, also the tableau truck or float. The latter was either a small, flat truck with gilded statues representing a theme from history or popular literature, or a much larger vehicle with human figures and sometimes trained animals, posing for patriotic subjects such as 'Brittania and the British Lion' surrounded by typical human races and animal life of the colonial empire. A so-called 'Twin Lion Tableau Wagon', formerly appearing with Sir Robert Fossett's Circus and Menagerie, is now in the Circus World Museum, Baraboo, Wisconsin (USA). It is 17ft 6ins high with three telescopic platforms, surrounded by carved human figures (larger than life) and surmounted by two gilded lions.

Chapter 5

Foreign types

The following are discussed in alphabetical rather than chronological or regional order for greater convenience of reference.

Araba: A Turkish family carriage of the 18th and 19th centuries. A four-wheeled vehicle drawn by a pair of horses, but sometimes by oxen or camels. Low-sided and entered from either front or rear. Sometimes driven from a low seat at the front but more frequently led on foot by one or more servants in charge of the draught animals.

Australian road wagon: A strongly-built phaeton used both in Australian cities and over the rougher roads of the outback. Usually drawn by a single horse. Mounted on two crosswise, elliptical springs at front and back. The shafts curved downwards and were attached to axletrees at the rear end. The foot pedal brakes acted on the rear wheels. The dashboard tended to curve forward at the top.

Canadian caleche: A two-wheeled vehicle, used either as a private or public carriage. Widely used in the French Canadian provinces, throughout the 19th century. There was seating for two passengers in the main bodywork while the driver perched above the front-end on what amounted to a ledge rather than a driving seat.

Cape cart: A two-wheeled pleasure cart, usually hooded and mounted on thoroughbraces, with polegear for a pair of swift horses. It was first used in the

An Australian road wagon of c 1900 (Science Museum, Crown copyright).

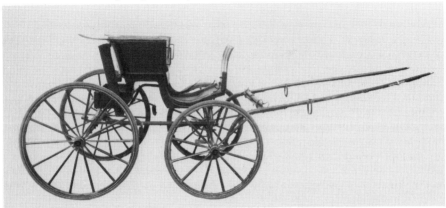

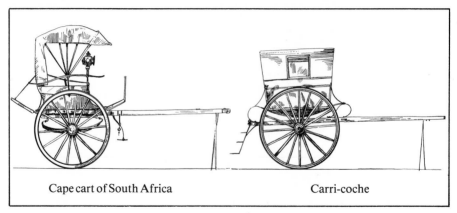

Cape cart of South Africa   Carri-coche

Cape Colony of South Africa but later in Australia and New Zealand. Its strong, heavy design made it ideal for military service and large numbers were frequently owned and driven by British officers during the Boer War. There were both front and rear seats with room for three passengers and a driver.

Caretta: An ancient Italian cart also widely used in Sicily. It is now regarded as the ancestor of many later two-wheeled types. Usually a country vehicle, found in districts south of Naples until the 1950s. Noted for richly painted side panels in a decorative style which dates from the Middle Ages.

Carette: A type of public carriage or small omnibus used in the suburbs of Australian towns, during the second half of the 19th century. Divided into smoking and non-smoking compartments, having both side and rear doors with steps to street level. The bodywork was fairly low, for better riding and easy access. The driver's seat was slightly raised and covered by an extension of the canopy-roof.

Cariole: A mainly unsprung version of the cabriolet used on the mountain roads of Scandinavia, especially in Norway. Its long shafts provided a certain amount of spring or resilience, although a few later types had under-springs or thoroughbraces. Of narrow construction, to suit the narrow, winding roads of this area, it normally seated a single person, this being the owner-driver.

Carri-coche: A so-called 'cart-coach' of Brazil used as an omnibus, from the mid-19th century. Drawn by two horses in the care of a postillion. Mounted on untanned ox-hide thoroughbraces and entered through a rear door. It seated six persons, three aside, on longitudinal benches.

Carramata: Light, two-wheeled cab or private cart of the Philippines, drawn by a single pony. The driver and two passengers were all seated under an extension of the canopy roof, supported by corner pillars.

Corbillard: A type of French hearse used throughout the 19th century. It descended from an even earlier country coach of the 17th century. The modern version was mounted on elliptical under-springs, having a forward passenger compartment similar to a Brougham, to the rear of which was attached a glass-sided compartment for the coffin. The high-perched driver's seat was at roof level. Drawn by a pair of horses.

Coucou: French two-wheeled cab with two crosswise benches for passengers. The driver sat on a seat or ledge above a metal or wooden apron-shield. Similar to the Canadian caleche, from which the latter may have derived. It was widely used from the mid-18th century onwards.

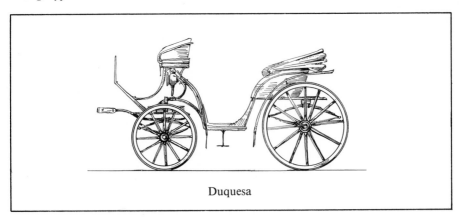

Duquesa

Dak: A primitive four-wheeled carriage of India, used for carrying mail and passengers. The driver sat on a high seat at roof level. Interior seating was in the form of crosswise benches. The name applies almost as much to the service as to the vehicle as there were also dak ferries and river boats.

Diligence: The name of this vehicle derives from the French word for promptness, relating to an early stage coach which ran between Paris and Lyons during the 18th century. Widely used, at a later period, to carry passengers and mails in both France and Switzerland, with similar vehicles in Germany, Austria and other parts of Eastern-Central Europe. The driver of the later types sat on a roof seat at the front, which he often shared with several passengers. There was also a cross seat at the rear of the main bodywork, under a falling hood, known as the banquette. Known in Switzerland as a post coach. Three, four and five horses were all fairly common, one sometimes ridden by a postillion.

Duquesa: A type of open carriage, seating two passengers on rear seats and two on the driving seat, widely used in Spain until the 1920s. It was drawn by two horses. A smaller, single-horse version was known as the duquesita.

Ekka: A two-wheeled cart of India, drawn by a single pony. The original, or native, version, later improved for the use of British officers and civil servants, was large enough for one person only. Most were driven by the owner but others were led through the streets by a servant. The draught gear was in the form of a pole above the back and hind quarters of the draught animal, secured by means of a breast strap.

Fiacre: French name for a light carriage, widely used as a hackney cab from the 1650s until the mid-20th century. They varied in size and shape but the original version carried six passengers or three aside, on longitudinal benches. A similar but much smaller vehicle was used as a station cab in English country districts. The Fiacre was named after a Celtic saint by whom a crude ambulance service was first established, also hospitals and almshouses. The first public cab rank in Paris was outside an inn named after St Fiacre.

Fresian sjees: A form of light gig with curved and richly ornamented bodywork, used mainly by Dutch farmers and country folk in a northern province of Holland. It was carried on thoroughbraces with a low dashboard, the latter also carved and hand-painted. The Fresian sjees was drawn by a distinctive light draught horse bred in the same area, usually black with thick mane, tail and fetlocks. Some types have been adapted for pair driving with a pole and belly bugle, the latter being a padded metal girth attached to the pole. This vehicle was introduced during the second half of the 18th century but decorated in the even earlier rococo style. It is now used for show purposes and a competitive game of ring spearing, in which a passenger seated next to the driver aims at suspended rings with a lance or spear.

Gharry: In Calcutta, Bombay and other cities of India this is a type of open cab or public carriage, similar to the Victoria. It is drawn by a single horse and further known as a Fitton gharry. A similar type is also found in North Africa towns and other parts of the Near and Middle East.

In many country districts of India the gharry is more likely to be a crude form of omnibus, perhaps a smaller version of the dak carriage. It is square or oblong in shape, entered through sliding doors at the sides and fairly high above road level. The windows are slatted and there is often a double roof for improved insulation.

Guaga: A public carriage of Cuba. It had a long, low body on small, cart-like wheels and resembled a tram or horse car.

Harmamaxa: The four-wheeled harem carriage of the Ancient Persians, large enough for two women reclining on couches or hammocks. Usually with fringed curtains and awnings supported on several pillars or uprights. Either led or driven.

Hecca: A low-slung gig or country cart of India, simillar to the Ekka. Usually a dead-axle vehicle, its shafts meeting at a point above the withers of the single horse or pony. The driver crouched in a cross-legged position on a ledge at the front of the passenger compartment. There was only one passenger, veiled from public gaze by deeply fringed curtains.

Jaunting car: An open passenger car with sideways or back-to-back seating, also known as a side car. Widely used in the streets of Dublin and the south of Ireland from the mid-19th century until the 1930s. A few are still preserved for use as tourist attractions. Said to have descended from the trottle car of Northern Ireland, invented about 1815. There were six passengers, three per side, their feet resting on angled footboards. The driver or jarvey sat on a slightly higher seat in a central position.

An Irish jaunting car of about 1906 (Science Museum, Crown copyright).

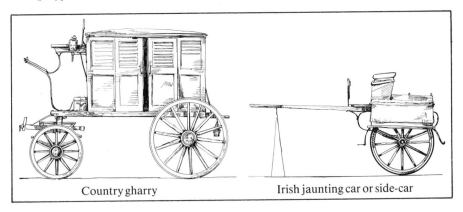

Country gharry   Irish jaunting car or side-car

Kibitka: A primitive Russian post coach used for over two centuries. It was a four-wheeled vehicle without any form of springing or suspension of the bodywork. In later versions of the mid-19th century, passengers sat on cushions stuffed with hay above rope hammocks. The top was a canvas cover on bow-shaped hoops.

Lineika: Privately-owned carriage of 19th century Russia, seating four passengers facing each other, as two per side. Drawn by a 'troika' or three horses abreast. A larger and up-dated version of the droshky.

Oboze: A large Russian stage wagon, used in country districts west of the Urals. Usually a dead-axle type.

Savanilla phaeton: A light pony-style phaeton, widely used as a public carriage in Bangkok, Siam (known as Thailand since 1949), from the mid-19th century onwards.

Sérge: A two-wheeled car or carriage drawn by two horses, found in Portugal and the Azores. Similar to the sedan cart of the 18th century, with leather curtains rather than glass windows. The horses are controlled by a postillion.

Stolkjaerre: A Norwegian two-wheeled carriage or cab, driven from a low-slung rear seat. Large enough to carry two passengers in the style of a Hansom cab. It was usually harnessed to a sturdy Norwegian pony of the fjord type.

Talika: A four-wheeled cab or public carriage of Constantinople (Istanbul). It was similar to the English growler but had slatted window blinds.

Tarantass: A Russian travelling carriage, the bodywork of which resembles a punt or pontoon, suspended on longitudinal (parallel) poles, with axles at either end. It was a crude form of the Berlin and was drawn by a troika or larger team.

Telega: A larger version of the tarantass, used as a public coach.

Tonga: A two-wheeled carriage of India, drawn by a pair of horses or ponies harnessed to a backward-inclined centre pole by means of cross bars, similar to curricle gear. The passengers sat back-to-back on a broad centre seat, under a canopy roof. It was widely favoured as a transport vehicle and form of draught gear by the British Army in India, this being a style of harness with which large numbers of Indians would be acquainted when employed as native drivers.

Trottle car: A two-wheeled car of Ulster or Northern Ireland, introduced during the early part of the 19th century. The shafts were thick beams at an angle of about 25 degrees, fitting between a bodywork of narrow planks and small, low-slung wheels. A version with sideways seating was an ancestor of the jaunting car.

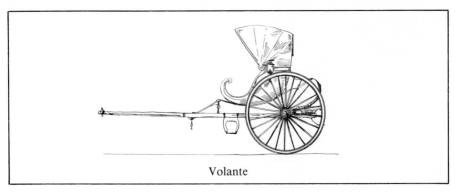

Volante

Vettura: A hired carriage of Italy and Sicily, seating four people. Introduced during the late 18th century.

Volante: A two-wheeled Spanish vehicle also used in countries of South America and the West Indies. The seating arrangement was well in advance of the wheels and sometimes below the level of the axle. It was drawn by two or three horses in the care of a postillion. Many of the later types, used in Cuba until the 1920s, were constructed in Britain or the United States.

Wurst wagon: A German hunting wagon on four wheels, long and narrow like a *wurst* or German sausage. Ridden astride by huntsmen or members of a shooting party, their feet supported by a common footboard on either side. Later used by light infantry troops and considered a military vehicle, from about 1750.

Since the Second World War a number of European countries, in which many of the above vehicles have developed, now have their own driving clubs, similar to those in Britain and the United States, some actively encouraged by the British Driving Society. Members greatly contribute towards the upkeep and preservation of local types, which may be given an airing at festivals and horse shows. West Germany alone has several hundred clubs devoted to equestrian sports, including both riding and driving. France has many clubs supporting local horse shows while there are further important groups in Denmark, Holland, Sweden and the Republic of Ireland, to name but a few. Behind the Iron Curtain driving flourishes in several countries, especially Hungary and Poland, mainly under state patronage but fielding teams which are always near the head of the table at international events, especially cross-country driving.

Chapter 6

The American scene

Americans have depended on the horse for opening up a continent and the development of their civilisation far more than people from any other part of the Western world. This held equally true from the prairies and forests of Canada to the mountainous borders of Latin America. European settlers were, at least from the mid-18th century, drivers rather than riders of horses. They needed vehicles for rough tracks and trackless wastes, some of which were first drawn by oxen or mules but mainly by teams of horses, the latter preferred for their greater speed and quickness in adapting themselves to the ways of men.

Among the many 18th century vehicles preserved at the colonial centre of Williamsburg, Virginia, several farm carts and wagons, even two-wheeled tumbrils, have a centre pole for a yoke of oxen. There are wains, gigs, carriages and coaches to be drawn by horses, but perhaps the most characteristic vehicle is the Conestoga wagon. This was first used for general haulage and farm work in the eastern states but later by settlers and pioneers further west, especially for overland treks. It has been wrongly termed the 'prairie schooner' on account of its high canvas top, which resembled a spread of sail, although experts claim this to have been the name used for a smaller and later wagon of the Gold Rush period. Conestogas appear to have originated in the farming community of the Conestoga Valley, Lancaster County, Pennsylvania, about 1755. While owing something of its design to the English farm wagon, it was essentially for pole draught with a large team and noted for high, panelled sides with bow-shaped hoops, the latter averaging ten in number, supporting an extensive cover. Such vehicles were strongly made but usually dead-axle, without brakes or springs,

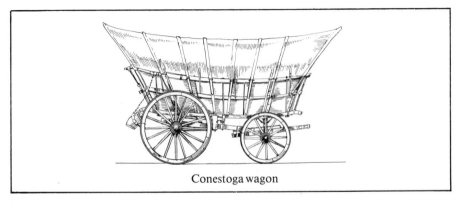

Conestoga wagon

This Concord coach, looking as though it might be attacked by red indians at any minute, is in fact a modern reconstruction built for show purposes. Constructed and driven by Monsieur Gerard Naprous (Mrs Anna Jones).

although in later years a few seem to have had hand-lever brakes acting on the rear wheels, in addition to the slipper or dragshoe. They were able to cope with the worst possible terrain from rock-strewn valleys to mountain ranges and broad rivers. They were usually drawn by six horses and less frequently by even larger numbers of mules or spans of oxen. They belonged more to settlers of English, German or Dutch origins before the 1840s, and although some reached the far west the majority were confined to an area east of the Rocky Mountains or between the Alleghenies and the Mississippi. The later type of covered wagon or true prairie schooner, was a less attractive but much lighter vehicle, with square, flat sides but also having hoops and canvas covers. The Conestoga, like the English farm wagon, was limited to quarter-lock. The large fore-wheels had twelve spokes while the rear wheels were even larger with from sixteen to eighteen spokes. It may be noted that the later covered wagons appealed to a far different type of settler than the earlier wagon, being made for greater speed but smaller loads or family groups.

Another large but characteristic vehicle of Northern America was the Concord coach, many also finding their way to British colonial and Commonwealth territories such as South Africa and Australia. This was the American stage coach, drawn by either six or four horses, and originating in the east but found highly serviceable (with six-horse teams) on the central plains and in the foothills of the Rocky Mountains. It carried passengers and mail from the early part of the 19th century until superseded by railroads, many being constructed in the New Hampshire town of Concord, from which the name derives. Those in the western states were first controlled by the Holladay Company but later by Wells Fargo, there being very few on the former trunk routes after the 1870s, although some coaches survived in remote areas until about 1907. The strongest and most reliable types were made by the well-known firm of Abbot-Downing, being even sturdier when ordered for the far west than for the better road conditions of the eastern seaboard. They descended from an earlier and much lighter coach without doors or windows, known as the open or mud wagon. The prototype bore a slight resemblance to the English-style stage coach, with which it may have shared the roads of some colonial states for a limited period at its inception. It carried nine inside passengers with three on folding or jump seats. Up to seven were allowed on top, at the discretion of the guard or messenger. The bodywork might be described as oval or egg-shaped with ample curves and strong but finely constructed joinery. Windows were protected by roll-down leather blinds. Upper works rested on longitudinal thoroughbraces of toughened leather strips, hung from iron standards or uprights. Brakes acting on the rear wheels were applied by a foot pedal on the off-side of the box-seat. A rearward-sloping luggage boot above the rear axle had a reinforced leather cover, held in place by three straps per side. There was also a smaller mail and luggage compartment under the driver's seat, above which the messenger rode 'shotgun'. The tare weight was in the region of 2,500 lb for the larger types. The fore-wheels had twelve spokes and the rear wheels had fourteen spokes. With a team of six an extra but detached pole, swing or swinger was used between the second pair. A fair number of this type are to be seen in historical and carriage museums, also in private collections, not forgetting the Circus World Museum, Baraboo, Wisconsin, which claims to have the original Deadwood Stage of the Buffalo Bill Wild West Show.

Single horse, four-wheeled buggies were the most popular vehicles in the United States for over a hundred years, having many different types and derivations. They were medium-sized, all-purpose run-abouts, useful in both town and country, surviving in rural backwaters until after the Second World War, although a special version is still in use among people of the Menonite and Amish sects. They claimed descent from a shallow or tray-bodied vehicle of German origin, having little in common with the two-wheeled, round-backed English gig of this name. The wheels of the American buggy were equirotal or nearly so, rarely showing much contrast between front and rear wheels. They could be headed or covered but were frequently open, while many had falling hoods of leather or canvas. Later types had crosswise leaf springs in the same style as the Model T Ford. Buggies, unlike some other types of vehicle, were rarely seen outside the land of their origin, not having the universal appeal of European carriages, perhaps for snobbish reasons. Oddly enough a few were imported to Britain by wealthy people, to drive as a hobby, during the second half of the 19th century. These latter sometimes appeared at local and national horse shows up to and during the Second World War. Buggies had straight rather than strongly dished wheels, with limited lock, except in the case of the cut-under buggy. A few of the better known types are described as follows.

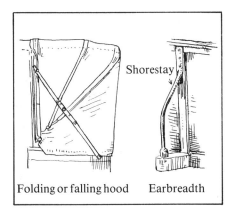

Folding or falling hood   Earbreadth

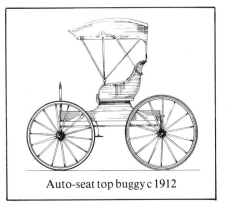

Auto-seat top buggy c 1912

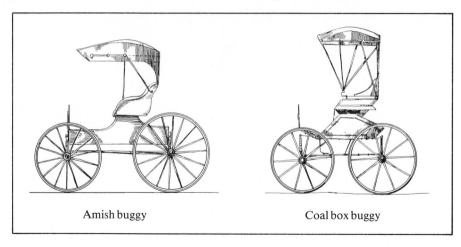

Amish buggy   Coal box buggy

Amish buggy: This is one of the few buggies still in production on a fairly large scale, apart from those made to order. It is used by members of the Amish religious sect, flourishing as a farming community in Pennsylvania, Ohio and Indiana. Their beliefs compel them to dress and behave in the same manner as when their ancestors first came to America, using the same transport and agricultural methods.

The Amish buggy is one of the most characteristic of its type, the basic tray-shape mounted on large but light wheels, having transverse or crosswise springing, front and rear. There is a shallow inner foot or frontboard, an upright leather or leather-covered dashboard and two candle lamps. The high-backed driving seat is upholstered with either a quilted or button-back effect, having arm rests made from curved irons, there being room for a driver and single passenger. Some later types were hooded with what became known as an auto-top or folding top, this being almost identical with the folding roof of early touring cars or convertibles (automobiles). An even larger version, having a square boxed-in appearance, may be enclosed on three sides for all-weather protection. Such vehicles, in common with many other buggies and road wagons, were easy to manufacture, light to handle and convenient to store.

Cut-under buggy: This was slightly larger than the average buggy or small wagon, having a high-backed driving seat above an arch of the bodywork. The arch or cut-under allowed full-lock, which made it easier, if not always safer, for driving in traffic or turning in narrow streets. It was usually hooded and regarded as a town vehicle.

Coal box buggy: A small and light vehicle, with front and back wheels very near together as a short wheelbase. The bodywork was contained within a space between the axles. The rear part sloped backwards and resembled, in profile, a coal box or scuttle, from which its name derived. The body interior was 30ins wide and wheels 48ins and 58ins. It may be noted that in this and other descriptions of American vehicles the first figure represents the fore-wheels. There were ten spokes per wheel. Painted a daring red colour with gold striping or lining out.

Jenny Lind: An early type named after and driven by the Swedish opera and concert singer of that name, during her successful tour of the United States. Slightly more elegant than the average buggy, with a canopy top. Noted for its elaborate style of decoration, fitting and lining-out. Leather curtains could be rolled down on either side in adverse weather conditions. The dashboard often had a convex or outward curve. The bodywork was 30ins wide, while the wheels were 47ins and 50ins.

Business buggy: A type favoured by the small businessman and commercial traveller. It had fairly high, well-upholstered seating and a folding or falling leather hood. The sides were protected by rattan canework which looked smart but needed less attention than equal areas of paint and varnish. There was a rear compartment of the tray body for samples and overnight luggage. The body was 28ins wide, with wheels of 36ins and 48ins.

During the second half of the century there were a number of slightly larger and heavier vehicles (compared to buggies), known as wagons. Some were very similar to buggies, from which they may have derived, while others were quite different, having extra seating.

Doctor's wagon: A first cousin to the business buggy mentioned above and sometimes termed a buggy in its own right. It was introduced during the 1860s and still used by older medical men, or in country districts, until the early 1920s. From the mid-1890s the upper part of the body was painted jet black with green lining out and inner trim, while the lower part was covered with decorative canework. The falling hood frequently had silver mountings. A compartment at the rear, although smaller than on the business buggy, was ideal for the medical bag and small hand luggage. Wheels were 36ins and 48ins, usually with ten spokes at the front and twelve spokes at the rear.

Jump-seat wagon: This was a fairly light vehicle for its type, although having a fixed top and both front and back seats. It could be converted into a single-seater by folding or pushing and 'jumping' the rear seat into a forward position. The body was 40ins wide and wheels 46ins and 49ins/50ins.

Three-seat platform wagon: A large semi-open vehicle used in country districts by families and small parties. There were three rows of seats, all facing forward, under a fixed top which in summer, might be fringed like the Surrey. The length was 10ft 6 ins. The wheels were 40ins and 48ins with a gauge of 5ft and upwards. The fore-carriage had flattish longitudinal springs, while the hind-carriage had transverse springs (platform springs). The colour was jet black, lined or unlined, with bright red wheels and under-works.

Rockaway: Also known as the Depot Wagon, frequently used to meet incoming trains at the nearest station or railroad depot. In England this would have been known as a station wagon. A smaller version of the three-seater platform wagon, with two rows of crosswise seats and roll-down leather curtains at the sides. About 36ins across the bottom of the floor space, although its bodywork sloped outwards becoming much wider at the top. The gauge or track was 5ft.

Curtain-quarter rockaway: A more substantial yet elegant version of the rockaway, dating from the mid-1880s. The rear could be enclosed as a separate passenger compartment, partly protected by either slats or glazing, in front, although apertures on either side of the rear seats would have roll down curtains. Usually coloured green with black or white lining-out. The body was upwards of 47ins wide.

Bike wagon: A light exercise or runabout wagon, very similar to a buggy but having even more substantial construction and a high-backed driving seat. Its unique features were cranked or so-called bike wheels and axles, with wire-

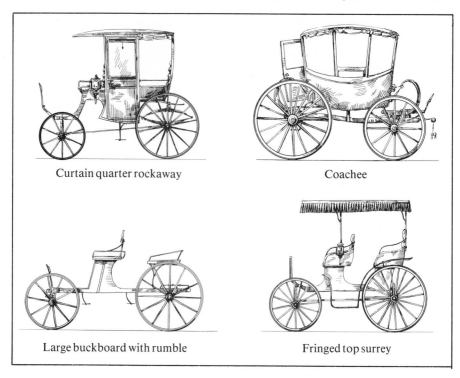

Curtain quarter rockaway   Coachee

Large buckboard with rumble   Fringed top surrey

spoked wheels. Often carpeted and upholstered in velvet. The body length was
56ins with an outside width of 23ins.

Slat-bottom road wagon: Similar to the business buggy but having a highly
resilient floor of arched slats, plus a unique form of springing. The latter was a
near-flat coil suspension, above both axles. The fixed hood had a neat rear
window of oval shape. The body width was 27ins to 28ins. The slatted floor,
slightly raised towards the centre, made it a lightweight structure, comparatively
easy to clean, harbouring less dust and dirt than vehicles with solid floors.

Other characteristic vehicles of North America were mainly developed from
the above types, especially those for passenger or pleasure purposes. A few
other examples, although not perhaps in lineal descent, are described below.

Coachee: Apart from the Conestoga wagon this is the earliest vehicle yet
mentioned, dating from colonial times. Outwardly it appeared like a small
family coach but having sideways seats rather than cross-seating. The body was
entered through the back by means of a single iron step. Although headed there
were rarely any glazed windows, the only passenger protection being leather
curtains or blinds of the roll-down type.

The coachee could be either privately or publicly owned, proving very
popular in Philadelphia, Boston and other eastern cities from the 1770s to the
1820s. It was taxed as a pleasure vehicle. During the 1780s there were 157
coachees in Philadelphia set against 33 ordinary coaches, 35 travelling coaches
and 22 owner-driven phaetons. Most types had large C springs and were drawn
by two horses harnessed to a centre pole. The driver's seat was part of the
forward structure of the bodywork, between the front springs. The wheels were
well-dished.

Buckboard: A light yet strong four-wheeled vehicle. Similar to certain types of buggy but having a single, flat underboard rather than a tray-body. This was well-braced, especially under the seat at the fore-end, to avoid jarring on badly-made country roads. Although first used in New England, it was very popular on ranches and settlements in the far west, where even cart tracks were a luxury. The single cross-seat was low-slung in relation to the wheels, being only slightly higher than the tops of the rear wheels. The high dashboard had a pronounced outward curve. Because of its firm bracing, with iron stays, it could take great punishment and was frequently driven across country at speed without falling apart.

A later version, dating from the 1880s, sometimes had a slatted floor and a rear seat, or rumble. Where two seats were used the bottom board appears to have been about 87ins long and 29ins wide, although a single-seater was much shorter. A small number of both types were exported to Britain and other parts of Europe, exhibited at horse shows by driving enthusiasts. Wheels were 40ins and 45ins with 56ins gauge or track.

Jogging cart: A light, two-wheeled vehicle for a single horse between shafts, usually without a falling or fixed hood. This was used in the country to exercise harness-racing and trotting horses. It later developed into a racing vehicle in its own right and became the fore-runner of many types in this sphere. The twelve-spoked wheels were higher than the solitary driving seat, which was directly above the axle, with a low dashboard and slatted floor. Later versions were sometimes designed for two persons.

Surrey: There were several popular versions of this vehicle, which was made in both horse and pony sizes. The small or pony size was usually drawn by a pair harnessed to a pole, but sometimes by a single pony in shafts. The body width was 30ins and wheels 30ins and 38ins. There were both front and back seats for three passengers and a driver. Usually an open vehicle with arm rests of iron scrollwork. The crosswise, elliptical springs were similar to those of the buggy and road wagon.

The fringe top Surrey was a vehicle suitable for larger horses, semi-open and used mainly for summer driving. It had high sweeping fenders or mudguards over front and rear wheels. The interior was upholstered with blue cloth and there was usually a dashboard of patent leather. While the bodywork was painted in lined or unlined black, the wheels were either bright red or Brewster green. The fixed canopy roof was mounted on four steel uprights, having swag-like fringes at least a foot deep. The solid floor had velvet fitted rugs, while the side lamps (oil or candle) were of the square type normally associated with travelling carriages. Exterior fittings were of solid silver. Wheels were 39ins/40ins and 44ins with a gauge or track of 56ins.

A cheaper type of vehicle known as the poor man's Surrey, or spring wagon, had a removable rear seat, which could be utilised for parcel or luggage space. This was normally an open type without hood or canopy top, drawn by a single horse. Later on more refined versions had a folding hood and light mudguards, known from the early 1900s as the auto-top Surrey. A few of the latter type are still made and used in rural areas.

Trap: In Europe this usually means a light two-wheeled vehicle such as a governess car or tubcart. 'Trap' is a term avoided by purists as either slang or an inexact description. In America in the 1890s it was a four-wheeled vehicle with both front and back seats, fairly high and well-upholstered. Access to the rear

One-horse chaise c 1810

part was by dividing or turning aside the front seats. The rear seats could be folded down to make room for luggage. It appeared both with and without a falling hood. With some models only the front seats were hooded. The sides and arm rests were protected by wooden struts or fenders.

A later version of the mid-1880s had back-to-back seating in the style of a European dogcart, the rear seats mounted by means of a step iron. When used for sight-seeing, the rear seats could be made to face in either direction, at whim. The body width was between 33ins and 37ins. The wheels were 41ins and 45ins/48ins. The gauge or track was 56ins.

Road cart: A two-wheeled open vehicle introduced during the 1880s and mainly used in the eastern states. Almost European in character and appearance, with a well-upholstered cross seat for two, the body mounted on sideways elliptical springs of exceptional length. It usually had high mudguards or splashers and curved rather than straight shafts. It was ideal for a pony, cob or small horse. A version of the same type was a mere skeleton for harness racing and exercise purposes.

Chaise: This was the 'One Hoss Chaise', celebrated in history and literature. Similar to an English gig or buggy of the early 19th century, immortalised in the poem by Oliver Wendell Holmes, quoted in his *The Autocrat at the Breakfast Table*. The chaise was remarkable for its high, falling hood, usually in a raised position, and unique form of suspension. The latter consisted of thorough-braces from the ends of the shafts near the dashboard to much higher points at the rear of the bodywork, forming diagonals about 5ft in length. Mounted from a step iron fixed near the rear end of the shafts.

The Wonderful One Hoss Chaise is well worth reading as, apart from its humour, it offers an interesting account of the methods of construction and materials used.

Sight-seeing wagon: A large, four-wheeled, semi-open vehicle, drawn by a team of four horses. Widely used in parks, show-places and holiday resorts, during the 1870s. It seated twenty people and a driver on both upper and lower decks—the upper parts being reached by a ladder. The seats in the lower-centre part faced outwards on the knifeboard plan, while those at the rear faced backwards. Four sets of double seats on the upper deck faced either backwards or forwards, with four passengers facing in either direction. The upper-centre seats were back-to-back. The small front wheels had cut-under, able to turn in

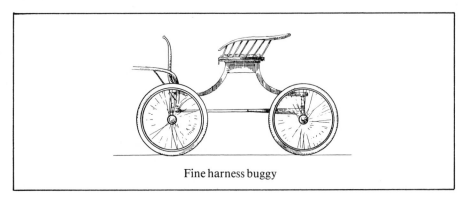

Fine harness buggy

full-lock, which tended to make it unstable and dangerous for overall weight, unless driven with great care and skill. Regarded, even in its own day, as something 'weird and wonderful', few survived for more than ten years.

Skeleton wagon: A four-wheeled version of the skeleton road cart, used as a one-man harness racing or exercise vehicle. The driving seat was much lower than either front or rear wheels. The bodywork was a mere frame to support shafts, seat and wheels, being very light—even by racing standards. Wheels were 47ins and 49ins, with a gauge or track of 52ins. There were ten spokes to each wheel, each spoke being less than half an inch in thickness.

Sulky: An up-dated American version of an earlier European exercise cart. The modern version was developed during the 1900s and is still manufactured for harness racing and showing. The term 'sulky' was often used in connection with horse-drawn vehicles or farm machines having a single driving seat, lacking room for passengers or other operatives, and considered anti-social. Wire-spoked wheels were fitted with pneumatic tyres and resemble those of a pedal cycle or baby carriage. The driving seat was at least 27ins above ground level, on a tubular steel framework. The long, outward curving shafts, in the form of a horse-shoe, have an extreme length of 87ins. The wheels vary between 26ins and 29ins. It was usually coloured dark green with gold striping or lining-out.

Harness buggy: Also known as a 'fine harness buggy', used in showing and exercising trotting horses, especially in 'fine harness classes' at shows and fairs. These are still manufactured in respectable numbers and may be described as up-dated versions of the original buggy, with wire-spoked wheels, bike axles and rubber tyres. The bodywork is 52ins long and 16ins wide. The wheels are 26ins diameter (equirotal). Adapted for European showing, usually in hackney classes, as the Mill's wagons.

An alternative version had slightly larger wheels with an arched or solid cut-under framework, in place of the tray body. Both types are fitted with fairly high dashboards, often lined with patent leather.

Carts and farm wagons

There were numerous carts and large wagons used for agricultural and commercial purposes from the earliest colonial period, but the majority developed during the second half of the 19th century. Farm wagons although sturdy and appearing in various sizes were mainly developed from the straight-sided design, based on a shallow tray, from which buggies also derived. They were aesthetically less pleasing than traditional British types and often produced

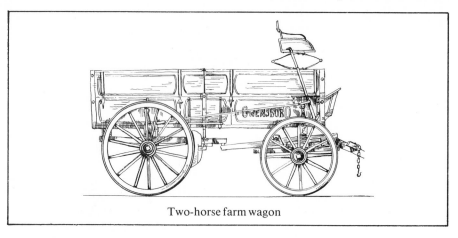

Two-horse farm wagon

with the needs of large scale production and quick delivery in mind. Many were noted for having the name of the firm or craftsman-builder printed or transferred on a lower side panel of the bodywork, near the fore-end. Types ranged from single to pair-horse wagons and those for larger teams. There were both dead-axle and fully sprung types, the latter mounted on elliptical leaf springs. Most had well-sprung driving seats above the fore-carriage and could be adapted for either shafts or draught poles. Most vehicles were of limited lock, while others had full under-lock, with or without an arched cut-under section. Some of the finest American farm wagons were constructed by the Studebaker Company of South Bend, Indiana. The first Studebaker was a country blacksmith also constructing farm carts to order. His two sons joined him in the family business and helped to found a commercial empire which manufactured agricultural and military wagons, ambulances, coaches and eventually automobiles. Their farm wagons, produced in thousands, were sent to all parts of the world. A display or show wagon was kept for exhibition purposes, being inlaid with gold medals awarded by various government bodies and agricultural societies in North America and Europe.

Another important manufacturer of farm and commercial vehicles was Alexis Coquillard, the descendant of an old French-Canadian family of trappers and fur-traders. Many of his wagons were sold to pioneers trekking to the west and had to be built to the highest possible standards of strength and endurance. A large number of his vehicles had the patent Sarven wheels, with metal hubs or naves and sixteen spokes each, similar to the artillery wheel. It was the Coquillard firm which broke the world record for selling and delivering the most commercial vehicles—of any one type—on a single order (1906), needing shipment in a special train of twenty freight cars.

Other wagon makers of note were Fish, Parry, Marietta, Auburn and Owensborough. Perhaps the most outstanding of the buggy and light carriage makers was the Columbus Buggy Company of Columbus, Ohio, while rival firms of Cunningham and Brewster specialised in better class carriages and four-in-hand road coaches or drags, the latter widely favoured during the late 19th century—by wealthier customers—as in Britain and France. The finest Concord coaches, as previously mentioned, were built by Abbot-Downing of New Hampshire. Some of the finest axles, long considered the work of specialists, were manufactured by the Dalzell Company of South Egremont, Massachusetts. At one period Elkheart, Indiana, was considered an important centre for wagon, cart and carriage building, from which arose the expression, 'I don't care who made it, it's from Elkheart'.

Notable types of farm wagon and commercial vehicles are described below.

One-horse farm wagon: The earliest versions of this type were fairly light, but large and strong, general-purpose vehicles. They had heavy wooden hubs or naves and under-perch, also a driving seat with solid wooden sides mounted above the front end on double (transverse) elliptical springs. Later versions of the 1900s had iron naves and a seat mounted on sideways springs. Neither had brakes and seldom carried drag-shoes. The earliest type had wheels of 40ins and 44ins with a gauge or track of 60ins. The tare weight would be 825 lb. Later wagons were often much smaller with a tare weight of only 500 lb. Most were constructed with two-plank sides, or one plank fitted above the other on each side.

The spring wagon: A shallow tray-bodied wagon, the under-carriage mounted on elliptical springs (platform springs), crossways at the front and sideways at the back. There would be a plain wooden dashboard, slightly higher than seat level. The wagon was mounted by means of a single step-iron, near the off-side fore-wheel. The body was 90ins long and 40ins wide. The wheels were 38ins and 42ins. It was drawn by a single horse in shafts. A slightly smaller version had a cut-under and full-lock.

Cotton frame and seedbed wagon: A vehicle popular in the deep south and south-western states, widely used for cotton harvesting and cultivation. The inner part of the bodywork had a top plating of iron with spurs or inner-struts to hold cotton bales steady while travelling over roughly-made plantation roads. Deep side panels above the lower bodywork could be up to 20ins/22ins high. The early type, mainly for pole draught, was limited to quarter-lock and without a driving seat. Later types had both fully-sprung driving seats and full under-lock. They were mainly drawn by a pair of mules or larger teams of mules or horses. Those used in the almost tropical conditions of Texas were soaked in hot linseed oil before painting, which helped to prevent them from cracking and peeling.

Mountain wagon: This type was used on rough, mountainous tracks, especially in the far west. Noted for its reinforced build, sturdy ironwork and extra-large brake blocks. The latter were to hold back a load on stiff gradients. It was driven from a fairly high but well-sprung seat, the average type bearing loads of up to 6,500 lb. The wheels were 42ins and 44ins. A large tool box was fitted at the front of each wagon, also serving as a footboard. Pole draught was for two or more horses.

The largest type of mountain wagon, mainly appearing on the Pacific seaboard, had a body known as the Californian rack or rackbed. Its tare weight was about 1,500 lb but it could load to over three times that amount.

Timber wagon, carriage or lumber buggy: These were variations of the European timber carriage or tug, used for identical purposes. They were usually articulated in two sections, joined together by a coupling, or reach pole. The latter was often cut from a forest tree, with the bark left intact. Large, transverse bolsters at both ends supported the main weight of the log or tree trunk, between upright staples or stanchions. Some timber wagons had rear wheel braking, applied at the fore-end of the hind-carriage by means of a bow-shaped brake lever. The reach pole at the fore-end was supported by a rearward extension of the draught or centre pole. The largest wagons of this type could bear a weight of up to 6 tons. A specially reinforced carriage, with four wheels to each end or limber, could carry up to 10 tons but these were very rare.

Two-wheeled carts: Mainly used in the eastern states, on farms and plantations, or in country towns. A typical coal cart with steel axles but wooden naves had a distinctly European or British appearance. It could be constructed in both tipping and non-tipping versions, able to carry up to a ton of coal, bagged or loose. Unlike many of the smaller farm carts it had propsticks under the shafts, to support the load or vehicle while at rest. Its single horse between shafts was led rather than driven. The wheels were 5ft in diameter.

Various so-called dump or tip carts were used for plantation work and by builders and contractors. These were either framed and panelled types or used with plain sides and box-containers. Most versions tipped automatically when unhooked at the front end. Later and larger types, however, had a more sophisticated form of gearing, hand-wound by means of a handle above the shafts.

Many two-wheeled carts, especially in colonial days, were drawn by mules or a yoke of oxen on either side of a draught pole.

Red River cart: This was one of the most successful but least attractive vehicles ever used. It mainly appeared in Western Canada, especially Manitoba, although some also crossed into the United States. During the Red River Rising of Indian Half-breeds it was often the only means of transport and communication, as railways were sabotaged and out of use for long periods, at least beyond the built-up areas.

Red River carts were often driven until they fell to pieces and were seldom given much care or attention by their owners. They made a terrible creaking sound, both while travelling and while being loaded or unloaded, often seeming on the point of collapse but enduring for many years. They were pulled by horses or oxen, sometimes by a horse and ox (or even a cow) yoked together. Like the Conestoga they were able to tackle almost any type of terrain and could even be made into a raft for floating across rivers and lakes. The wheels were of large dimensions with a variable number of spokes. There were neither wedges, blocks, nails, plates, bolts nor metal parts of any description. The only means of support and connection were strips of rawhide. It was said that a Red River cart could be made by any moderately intelligent person with a few tools, such as axe and drawknife, thus being easy to repair and replace. Large numbers were made by the settlers themselves and frequently outlasted both factory and craftsman made vehicles from the east.

Trade and delivery vehicles

Many of these were introduced during the second half of the 19th century, especially in an era of great business and territorial expansion during the 1880s. There was perhaps an even greater variety of these types in North America than would be seen in Britain or other European countries at the same period.

Ice wagons: These were widely used in most towns and cities before the days of cheap electric refrigerators. Some, however, were still to be seen in slums and mature suburbs until the Second World War. There were two main types, both high-sided, but one having a projecting or canopy top which extended over both

Ice wagon

driving seat and rear entrance. The latter was slightly larger than its alternative and drawn by a pair of horses hitched to a centre pole. It had a built-in box seat appearing as a form of cab, and side windows protected by roll-down blinds or slats. There was a shallow step for interior access and a spring weighing machine, both protected by the rearward part of the canopy. This could normally handle 2½ tons of ice. The smaller version with high sides and a flat top, would carry half a ton less, usually constructed with a heavy under-perch and limited lock of the fore-wheels. A high box-seat had a footboard but rarely any type of dashboard.

Milk wagon: The milk round or dairy wagon, for supplies of bottled milk, was a familiar sight in most towns and cities until the late 1950s. It was fairly low and easy to mount, with a cut-under of the fore-carriage and a well-like driving position, near the centre, in which the driver stood rather than sat. There were sliding doors on both sides, with either solid wood or slatted and glazed panels of the upper bodywork. Reins controlling the single horse or pony passed through apertures in the windscreen. Being difficult to drive, the horse was frequently led, especially in heavy traffic, the low centre platform admirable for loading and unloading but allowing poor visibility ahead. The capacity of the largest type, introduced during the 1900s, was about a ton. The most widely distributed version was the Parson's wagon, named after its designer and manufacturer. The inner height was just under 6ft, at the driving position. The length was 109ins by 42ins. Rubber shod wheels were 40ins and 42ins/43ins.

Bread van: Similar to the milk wagon but with a better look-out and driving position, while having fewer glazed and slatted side panels. There were, however, two drop lights for the cab and opposite sliding doors. It was entered from road level by means of a single iron step. An interior foot pedal controlled brakes acting on the rear wheels. It was mounted on both crosswise and lengthwise (platform) springs. The average length was about 8ft, with an outside width of 40ins. The wheels were 38ins and 43ins.

Butcher's van: A solidly constructed wagon, 8ft and more in length. It was used as a travelling shop for the door-to-door sale of meat products, especially in the outer suburbs. Drawn by a pair of horses or a single horse in shafts. The interior was fitted-up with meathooks on rails or side racks, having steak boxes for smaller cuts, a chopping block and even a small refrigerator. Usually lined with white cotton duck and having a removable slatted floor. A projecting rear

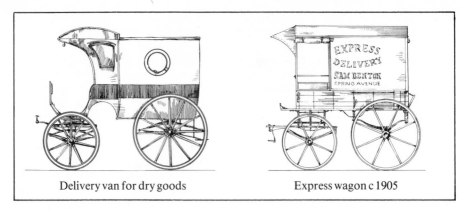

Delivery van for dry goods   Express wagon c 1905

canopy formed a shelter under which customers could wait to be served. There were opposite sliding doors at the front of the cab or driving position.

Oil wagon: A tank wagon, in most respects identical with the European or British type, previously described. This may well have been of American origins, dating from the 1890s. American types were less likely to have an enclosed cab than those seen in Britain.

Delivery wagons or vans: Those used by grocers and other retailers or merchants were of several different sizes and styles. Perhaps the most impressive was the wholesale grocers' wagon, which supplied shops, hospitals, hotels and canteens rather than families. The upper half of the interior bodywork, and sometimes the exterior, was frequently covered with white or cream cotton duck for better insulation. Mounted on both elliptical and semi-elliptical springs, with a forward projecting front canopy and medium-sized footboard. About 10ft long with an average width of 48ins. The wheels had twelve spokes at the front and fourteen at the back, with either wooden or iron naves, usually the former.

The ordinary or general street delivery van, popular from about 1882, was lighter and shorter than the wholesale grocers' van or wagon. The wheels were 38ins and 48ins with ten spokes at the front and twelve at the back. The sides of the rear body were curved outwards while the front canopy of the roof bent slightly downwards, although others could be straight, arched or flat. Most had square, round or oval windows (glazed) on both sides of the driving seat, with elaborate, brass-mounted, carriage-type lamps. A so-called 'cab-fronted' delivery van used in the dry-goods trade, had a very smart appearance with cut-under for full-lock, a raised and curved canopy above the crosswise driving seat and upward curving shafts. This was more elegant than some pleasure carriages, especially if painted and lined-out in the correct style and not too gaudy. The inward curving sides of the bodywork were 6ft long and 39ins wide, at floor level. A similar vehicle was eventually used in Britain.

The express wagon for delivering small parcels and valuables, often in connection with other transport services and the railroad companies, had a short wheelbase and was usually drawn at a smart trot by a single horse. The body length was 86ins with a floor width of between 45ins and 46ins. The often removable canopy top was at least 58ins from the floor of the loading platform. The driver sat well back in the forebody, having only a small toeboard and seldom a dashboard. Sides were either canvas or thin wooden panels, while the lower bodywork (deal planks) was only a foot high on each side with an even narrower tailboard. The wheels were 39ins and 52ins.

Lightweight (four-wheeled) delivery vehicles were often used for market work, also appearing at railroad depots and in the streets of country towns. The seat at the fore-end was often well-cushioned or padded, having a low backrest. There were both sprung and dead-axle types in this category. Raves, or outwardly projecting flaired-boards, protected the wheels from overhanging loads. These types were drawn by either one or two horses. The length of the body was about 90ins.

Fruit rack wagons were used in market areas or on fruit farms for the carriage and delivery of fruit or vegetables, especially berry fruits at harvest time. They were similar to the open, lightweight wagon mentioned above but with removable side stakes and racks above the upper bodywork. They were drawn by a single horse or mule. The dimensions were about 87ins long by 40ins wide.

Furniture dray: A spring-mounted open wagon, used not so much for removal work but in conveying items of furniture from shop or warehouse to home or office. It was well-sprung and supported, especially at the fore-end, with side rails and roping points along both sides. In wet weather the load was protected by tarpaulins or waterproofed sheets.

Stake or stake-sided dray: Either a sprung or dead-axle wagon, sometimes bearing a load of up to 7 tons. They were mostly painted bright red, especially in New York City, where they would be hauled by picked teams of Normandy stallions which were controlled from a high-perched seat mounted on elliptical springs. The side stakes or strakes, secured by top chains, were removable. A popular version of this type was the beer wagon or Budweiser, for either casks and barrels or bottles in crates. These were drawn by eight-horse teams frequently matching (imported) Clydesdales, which served as a useful advertisement for brand names and brews. With the increase in modern traffic such teams were relegated to shows and street parades, at least from the 1930s.

Transfer dray: A flat wagon or dray, often with side stakes or bolsters, used for conveying long pipes, poles, girders or rolls of newsprint. Some were also used to convey props and scenery for stage and travelling shows. Drawn by two or more horses, hitched to a wagon pole slung fairly low. Up to 14ft in length with full under-lock and a high-perched driving seat. The wheels were 34ins and 36ins.

Coal wagon: Either a high or low-sided vehicle, lined internally with sheet iron. Both were hauled by either one or two horses, the latter essential for steep gradients. The high-sided type had a well-sprung driving seat and footboard above the fore-end. Both types had full under-lock, necessary for turning in narrow streets and busy coalyards. The low-sided type was led rather than driven, unless returning empty.

Although some of the above vehicles are still in limited daily use, there are

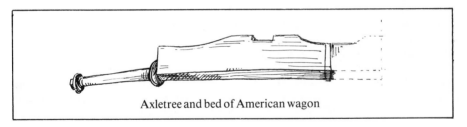

Axletree and bed of American wagon

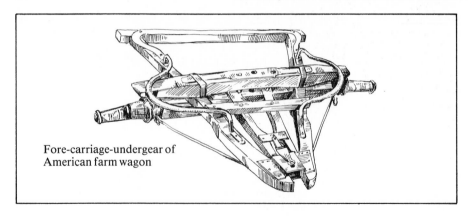

Fore-carriage-undergear of
American farm wagon

also fair numbers to be seen in museums and preserved by individual enthusiasts, given the chance of display at shows or in street parades. It may be stated, by way of summary, that most American horse-drawn vehicles have the following characteristics: (a) Four- rather than two-wheeled. (b) Strongly made to withstand extremes of weather or climate and difficult terrain. (c) More types are designed for teams or pairs than for the single horse. (d) Wheels are either much larger or much smaller in proportion to size and length of a vehicle than with European types. The smaller wheels usually have more spokes than the British types. (e) There is a greater use of patent wheels than in other countries. (f) By a strange paradox many vehicles have either much longer or shorter wheelbases than in most other parts of the world, but usually the former, especially for freight or farm work.

Finally, it should be noted that less use of the whip appears to be made than in Europe, except for formal driving.

General developments in America

Early American horse-drawn vehicles made up in strength and utility what they at first lacked in elegance and aesthetic charm, although even the latter was acquired—especially by more expensive types—towards the end of the 19th century. During the Civil War, imported vehicles from Europe were banned as a needless luxury, for which shipping space could not be spared. This proved a long-needed incentive to local designers, craftsmen and manufacturers, especially with the opening-up of the west, during the post-war period. While pioneers and settlers needed farm wagons and overland transport, a general increase in prosperity, with the founding of new fortunes and an actual lowering of prices, brought a demand for luxury vehicles and pleasure driving which could not have been met by the most enterprising importers, unaided. In the fullness of time American firms were exporting their vehicles to all parts of the civilised world, but mainly agricultural, utility and commercial types.

During the 1870s and until the 1900s driving single horses, teams and tandems became even more popular than in Britain and France. The upper classes of American society constantly vied with each other in the elegance, smartness and variety of their turn-outs. Sons and daughters of even moderately wealthy families were trained to drive four-in-hand as a social accomplishment—at least from the 1880s—which became as important to them as music, dancing, fencing and deportment might have been to their European cousins. While in London and Paris pleasure driving was a socially acceptable pastime and the resort of many amateurs, it was not to everyone's taste at any social level. In America, for over twenty years, it appears to have been an obligation bordering a mania, treated with a seriousness only the leisured and wealthy could appreciate. For a well-to-do American of that period not to drive would be even worse than his great grand children confessing total ignorance of the internal combustion engine. The National Horse Show held in New York City, with its glittering gold cups and many events from which professional drivers, dealers and horse-owners were barred, was a climax of the social season. This was reflected in many lesser but still important shows throughout the eastern states at such places as Lenox and Harrisburg, some of which are still active and well-patronised.

American women were always well to the fore in leisure driving and are known to have managed large teams, with professional skill, even in colonial days. Visitors from Europe marvelled at the daring of women and girls on the box-seat, an art which appears to have greatly over-shadowed riding side-saddle from the 1850s. A lead may have been given by the wife of President Cleveland (22nd President of the United States), who exhibited an almost passionate fondness for driving and collecting carriages. During her husband's term of office she filled the stables of the White House with large numbers of horses and fashionable vehicles, frequently being seen in the parks and avenues of the capital accompanied by a gentleman friend or admirer on her left, with a negro groom or tiger in the rear seat. Being a lady of great beauty and natural vanity she always arranged to drive from a seat of high cushions so that her escort was at a lower level and forced to look up at her as though in adoration, which she may well have deserved.

In New York and Boston fashionable women drove high-stepping pairs on the roads and avenues of the public parks, especially in Central Park, New York. Some of the former carriage drives were termed speedways, even in those early days, and skill with the whip was often allied with a need for excitement and the thrill of speed. There were numerous driving schools and academies, many of which specialised in the tooling, or driving and presentation of fours-in-hand. From the year 1896, when the enthusiasm for driving was at its height, large numbers of both sexes went abroad to study advanced driving in London, Paris and other centres, while some of the greatest European whips—including the French-born Morris E. Howlett—came to teach in America.

A number of American amateurs, both owners and drivers of coaches, spent long periods in England. The first of these was the celebrated whip W.G. Tiffany, followed by Colonel Delancey Kane and the popular A.G. Vanderbilt, the latter eventually renowned for his well-appointed coaching stables at Red Hill, then a picturesque suburb of South London on the Surrey side of the Thames. Popular with all classes of people, especially horse fanciers and driving enthusiasts, Vanderbilt was better known to the public as 'Vandy', treated with the affection and respect due to royalty. Elected to the exclusive Coaching Club during the 1900s, he was responsible for putting a coach back on the main London to Brighton Road, aided by his wife—also a keen amateur driver—and subsidised from his private fortune. Coaching naturally declined in Britain after the outbreak of the First World War and Vandy returned to New York, but was later lost at sea when his ship (the ill-fated *Lusitania*) was sunk by enemy action. In recent years the mantle of Vanderbilt has fallen on the shoulders of the equally talented and successful American John M. Seabrook, acclaimed on both sides of the Atlantic and, like Vandy, invited to join the English Coaching Club.

In recent years there has been a great revival of driving and the ownership of horse-drawn vehicles, throughout the United States and Canada. There are numerous clubs and societies interested in both the use and preservation of carriages and the horses which draw them. Perhaps the foremost amongst these is the Carriage Society of America Inc, which has branches in most states of the Union and subscribers in all parts of the western world. One of the great advantages of membership is to receive the quarterly publication of the *Carriage Journal*, early numbers of which may soon become collectors' items in their own right. Annual meetings or conferences are held by the society, usually at a place of interest to the so-called carriage 'buffs' making up the rank and file of membership, a popular venue being the Colonial Museum at Williamsburg. There are also many branch and regional events such as driving courses and clinics with social meetings to discuss mutual points of interest. Films and slides are shown while, at the end of the meetings, there may be a sale of surplus carriages and equipment, a percentage of the money raised being ear-marked for local or central funds. The society and its journal are noted for their professional advice to both novice and veteran, while all members and associates may be supplied with an up-to-date directory of services and equipment.

In America there are many groups and individuals with unusual or deeply specialised interests, not only concerned with vehicles in general but with particular types of stage coach, carriage or farm wagon. In the south-western states, especially Arizona, there are groups known as Wagon Train Associations, their special concern being the preservation of old vehicles used by the pioneers.

The American Driving Society is another vigorous body but of a more general character, holding numerous weekend and vacation courses, with tuition for beginners, in such delightful rural settings as Topsfield in Upper New York State. This group, with its distinctive badge of crossed whip and post horn imposed on a harness collar, is open to subscribers of all ages, with half price subscriptions for those under eighteen, for whom there is a special warmth of welcome. The American Driving Society circulates a news journal known as *The Whip* with full details of competitions and driving events for which their members may be eligible. The Draught Horse and Heavy Breeds fraternity is catered for by their own societies and a journal known as *The Evener*, a term relating to the spreaders and connections used in heavy draught work. Those interested in hackney driving and showing may subscribe to the bi-monthly *Hackney Journal*, published at Peekskill Towers, Peekskill, New York State, an important centre for light harness activities. It would be almost impossible to find a serious interest in the world of driving and horsemanship which does not have its following, with societies and literature. Even the English Shire and the Shetland are not forgotten, although the shire and other heavy types now tend to be eclipsed by the colourful Belgian draught breed, as a matter of fashion.

Combined driving activities with dressage, marathon, cross-country and scurry or obstacle courses are as popular in America as in Europe and, from most accounts, even more hair-raising. Shows and auctions are still popular, highlights being the great Amish Horse Sale, held for the past hundred years at New Holland as an annual event, the Devon Horse Show in Pennsylvania and the Royal Winter Show in Toronto (Canada), during November, this latter marking the end of the North American season. Other events are listed in a later part of this book.

There is still a wide range of carriage and equipment produced for the American driving enthusiast, also agencies and auctioneers prepared to deal with such items, most of which are advertised in trade, professional and society magazines. Some agencies also specialise in the insurance of horses, vehicles and their drivers. Prices at carriage auctions are healthy and encouraging, one of the last Concord coaches to have run in the State of Kentucky being auctioned in that state (1978) for $38,750.

Some American museums and collections

The United States has always been well-provided with museums, galleries and large scale collections, both public and private, covering almost every aspect of national life. Among the most outstanding are those organised, founded or supported by the great manufacturing concerns such as Fords of Detroit, the Studebaker Company of South Bend Indiana and El du Pont de Nemours of Wilmington, Delaware. An off-shoot of the du Pont Corporation is the Elentherian Mills Library and collection, with a whole range of information relating to horses and horse-drawn vehicles, from learned tomes to trade catalogues, periodicals and plans or sketches by makers and inventors. This is a closed and not a lending library, but may be visited on application and the contents studied under ideal conditions, with the chance to photograph, record and photo-copy.

Among other great national exhibition, record and reference centres is the Smithsonian Institution of Washington, which apart from having a number of interesting vehicles, produces many useful guides and pamphlets. It has recently published a unique book on *Carriage Terminology* compiled by Don H. Berkebile, a member of the Institution, drawing widely on their collection of old documents, pictures, prints and back numbers of former coach builder's journals such as *The Hub* and *The New York Coach Maker's Magazine.*

The Henry Ford collection at Dearborn, Michigan, is part of the Edison Institute, named after one of America's greatest inventors, to enshrine the history of the American people and their way of life. Many of the items on show were acquired by the Ford Company or donated by Mr and Mrs Henry Ford, collected long before the First World War, although the museum was not opened until 1929. Horse-drawn vehicles are well displayed in a section of the Transportation Gallery. All exhibits were either made or used in America and include a coachee of 1812, a three-wheeled pony phaeton used by General Lafayette while recovering from an illness, a rare American gypsy wagon or living van (more like a baker's van than the European type), a tiny Brougham drawn by a Shetland pony used by General Tom Thumb the circus midget and performer and a fourteen-seater band wagon of the type formerly used in carnival processions and circus parades.

The Studebaker collection of historical vehicles has been recently rehoused in the Discovery Hall at the Century Centre, South Bend, Indiana. The bulk of the exhibits are typical examples of the cars (automobiles), wagons, coaches and carriages produced by the Studebakers over the years, donated to the local authorities when the company ceased making and repairing road vehicles in 1966. Outstanding items include the carriage in which President Lincoln drove to Ford's Theatre on the night of his assassination, also the state carriage presented to Lafayette when he was made an honorary citizen of the United States, in recognition of his help and friendship during the War of Independence. There is also General Grant's travelling carriage of the Civil War period and several other vehicles associated with past Presidents and leading American citizens, from early colonial days to the present century.

The World Circus Museum at Baraboo, Wisconsin, is a useful source of information and pleasure for those interested in travelling shows and their vehicles which—before the era of mechanisation—were almost totally dependent on the horse. Their collection includes band wagons, beast wagons and a wide range of carriages and coaches used in the circus parade, as much a show as the later performance in the sawdust rings. There is also a Ringling Circus Museum with many fine show vehicles, at Sarasota, Florida, this being in the grounds of a colonial-style mansion owned by one of the Ringling Brothers, successors to Barnum and Bailey.

Perhaps the most important centre for equestrian interests in North America is the $35 million Kentucky Horse Park, site of the World Three-Day Event in the Autumn of 1978. This is situated near Lexington in the heart of America's (horse-breeding) blue grass country. It is still under construction, at the time of writing, but will eventually include barns and stables with representative types of carriage and breeds of horse, plus collections of hand-carved models with restaurants, cinemas, information centres and even a camp site for the tents and trailers of long distance visitors. Further attractions will include rides in coaches and carriages driven by museum staff in period costumes or liveries, with demonstrations, parades, lectures, film shows and conducted tours of the outer paddocks. An important central feature is the International Museum of the Horse, tracing the history and development of every known breed.

Chapter 7

Components

Wheels, tyres and axles

The axle of a horse-drawn vehicle is either a form of bar or a centre beam (with tapering arms at each end), both of which are known as axletrees. The arms point slightly downwards and, in some cases, slightly forward to prevent the wheel wearing too much against the linch pins or securing pins. Wheels with hollow hubs or centres (naves) are fitted to either end of the axle arms, the hollow being known as the axle box or pipe box. In Britain few vehicles have been fitted with wooden axle arms, apart from certain farm wagons, for a number of years. The so-called short arms or stubs fitted to either end of the axletree or bed, used mainly on heavy wagons, were either bare wood or shod with iron wearing plates, but were later made entirely from iron or steel. The straight-through, or rod-type, axle is mainly used for carriages and lighter vehicles, also known as a continuous axle, although sometimes supported by a wooden casing. At one time it was embedded in the woodwork but is now held in place by metal clips on the underside.

There are two main types of continuous axle, which may be termed simple and patent. The simple, or common, type although of straight-forward construction is mainly used on cheaper vehicles and requires considerable attention, especially greasing.

Patent axles have been introduced at various intervals since the early 18th century, but those surviving the test of time are the collinge and the mail coach. The former type, once known as the Patent Axle in its own right, was invented by an Englishman named Collinge towards the end of the 18th century. Manufactured by Collinge and Company under patents, it first attracted attention when fitted to the newly introduced cabriolet during the 1800s. It was,

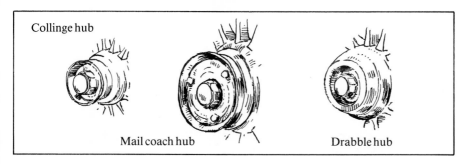

Collinge hub

Mail coach hub   Drabble hub

however, found satisfactory for a wide range of vehicles, especially the lighter and more elegant type. Exploited and imitated for over a century and a half, the invention became common property and a common noun, soon dropping the capital letter, although ignorant people often termed it a 'Collins axle' or merely a 'Collins'. Main features of the original type include: (a) A large axle-collar on the inside of the wheel, in and against which the axle box turns. (b) A straight or parallel arm. (c) A loose outer collar or collet, prevented from turning by a flattened area on the arm. (d) Both left and right-hand threaded nuts, having the inner nut bearing against the collet. (e) A linch pin passing in front of the outer nut. (f) An oil cap turning with the wheel and screwed into the hub.

A half patent axle was a modification of the above, popular in the United States of America from 1835. It had a single end-nut, while the collar was covered by an outer box.

The mail axle was first used on the English mail coach and stage coach during the second half of the 18th century. An axle box was fitted to the hub by means of three long screw-bolts, through the hub and through a back plate, the latter forming part of the flange on the axle-arm. This stood up to terrific punishment and—at a later period—was the main form of axle used for fire engines and ambulances. In the event of an accident it was thought almost impossible that all three bolts would snap or give way at once. This made it one of the safest but also one of the most expensive axles ever designed.

The Mather Thousand Mile Axle was patented in America in 1898, its makers claiming that it would run for at least a thousand miles without relubricating or other attention. This made use of inner, spiral grooves into which oil was fed at a mid-way point. The turning grooves passed the oil continuously from one end of the axle box to the other, with each revolution of the wheels, taking an exceptionally long period to dry-out.

The cranked or dropped axle, as used on the float and governess car, also on the rear end of the larger type of furniture van (with a well floor), had a bend near the extremity of the arm (at right angles) for low carriage of the bodywork, an advantage in easy loading.

Drabble axles were of the type often used on farm vehicles and the living vans of Romany folk or showmen. They were made, like the majority of axles, by specialist firms or craftsmen. The main distinctions were between London drabble and Yorkshire or North Country drabble. With the London type a square bar or section of iron connected the outer extremities. Each arm fitted in this manner had two counter-threaded nuts. Yorkshire drabble had a separate axle for each wheel, the fixings being through linch pin and washer.

The artillery-type wheel had an all-metal hub or nave into which the spokes were bolted, similar to various American types such as the Sarven wheel and the Archibald wheel. British artillery wheels, as used on guncarriages and supply wagons, usually had external dust excluders (caps) and loops or drag-washers, the latter used when a gun or wagon had to be man-handled in a small space by means of drag ropes.

Wheels may be defined as either discs (solid wheels) or a framework of curved/circular outer members, both turning on a central axis. With spoked wheels, the spokes radiated from a central hub, sometimes known as 'the spider', forming connection between the centre and rims of felloes—the latter word pronounced 'fellies' as it was formerly spelt. There are two main types of felloe, one being sawn and the other bent. While the bent version is often termed

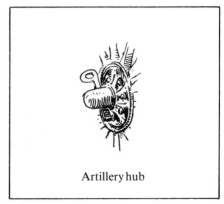

Artillery hub

Left *A wooden hub for a farm wagon of the late 19th century* (Museum of English Rural Life, Reading).

a rim the alternative is a 'sawed' felloe. Each felloe contains apertures for two spokes. Wheels are said to be either straight or dished, although this is a matter of comparisons, all wheels being slightly dished. Extravagant dishing in which, if the wheel is placed horizontally, the spokes would appear as a deep cone, was introduced during the late 16th century. This was thought better than straighter wheels for bearing loads above the average, especially over uneven surfaces. The bearing or plumb spoke, directly under the hub, whatever the angle of dish, was always at right angles to ground level, accepting the greatest stress in the strongest position. The spokes were trimmed or shaved (spoke-shaved) to form the correct contours, fitting into apertures of the hubs and felloes by means of wedge-shaped tongues or tangs, while felloes were fitted together with dowel-like pegs. It is not widely recognised, in considering the structure of wheels, that all spokes of a wooden wheel are rectangular, where they fit into the hubs, the lower ends known as feet. A third of the way up each spoke, and for the remaining two thirds of its length, the shape tends to flatten out becoming oval or pear-like, seldom if ever flat or circular in section. A few round spokes have been fitted to certain prototypes—which also sometimes appear on badly-made models—but these are rare and certainly not typical. The inner face of the felloe is slightly convex rather than flat, while its sole (under part of the tyre) widens outwards and downwards to its lower side or belly, into which the 'points' of the spokes are fitted.

Ring or band tyres, replacing the strips or strakes of earlier days, are of iron or steel screwed, riveted, nailed or bolted into place. The method of application by shrinking the white hot metal band on to the wooden rim, was introduced by a man named Hunt in 1767. Steel tyres came much later but are said to wear more evenly than iron tyres, being less likely to either crack or flake.

Rubber tyres were mainly adopted during the second half of the 19th century, some kept for town and summer driving only. They were aids both to riding comfort and the over-all preservation of the vehicle, through cushioning the load and aiding suspension. The first pneumatic tyres were introduced by an Englishman named Thompson, who also made suggestions for a solid rubber tyre—about the same period—during the 1830s. Both designs seem to have been premature or badly publicised and either little used or ignored. Large pneumatic tyres certainly lacked elegance and although re-introduced at a later period their use or mis-use on horse-drawn vehicles is still a matter for heated controversy. Solid rubber tyres, also a form of cushion tyre with inner air spaces (not inflatable), were first used on cab wheels, especially Hansom cabs. One of the pioneers in this department was the Earl of Shrewsbury and Talbot, by whom investigations had been made into the properties of rubber while a student at Berlin University during the 1870s. In later years the Earl became the Chairman of a limited company owning a large fleet of London cabs. The main objection to an early use of solid rubber tyres was the fact that they often slipped and worked loose, also that they wore down rapidly on hard surfaces. This was remedied by the introduction of hardened, or vulcanised, rubber and the invention of a tyre held together by stout wires passing through the centre of the rubber. The base of the tyre was fixed in a channel of steel placed round the circumference of the wheel, its flaired sides preventing strain and loss of resilience under weight and stress. By 1901 the rubber tyre was held even more firmly in its channel by small side wires which proved cheaper and easier as a form of application, less harmful to the rubber than piercing its centre. Some tyres, however, were merely clinched or clamped into the channels under an inward turn of the rim.

Pneumatic tyres, during their early days, at least from the 1880s, when they were re-introduced by an Irish vet named John Boyd Dunlop, were mainly used on light exercise carts and harness racing vehicles, especially the road wagons of America. They were also used on a wide range of commercial and farm wagons during the 1930s, although often as a fad or fashion, looking modern and up-to-date even when not always practical. Pneumatic tyres were later used on certain railway drays or horse lorries, during the Second World War, to replace springs, enabling the makers to turn out a cheap, light and efficient vehicle as quickly as possible, while lowering production costs, in keeping with national (war-time), campaigns for greater utility.

Springs

The leaf springs used on most forms of horse-drawn vehicle are flexible, graduated lengths of steel (originally iron) bolted together and rarely more than $\frac{5}{8}$ in thick. They vary in number according to needs, especially regarding their position and type of vehicle used.

Before iron or steel leaf springs were introduced, the coach builder had to rely on what were known as thoroughbraces or toughened leather slings, also on whips or strips of tough but flexible wood, later replaced by iron. Early metal leaf springs were known as whip springs, used in conjunction with leather straps and heavy, longitudinal under-perches joining rear and fore-carriages. The C, or cee spring, also known as the scroll spring, with adjustable braces, came towards the end of the 18th century, as previously mentioned. The combined use of under-perch and C springs made a vehicle more stable when its team was controlled by mounted drivers or postillions, eliminating a tendency to lateral sway.

Grasshopper, or shallow, semi-elliptical springs and later fully elliptical springs came during the 1790s and 1800s. These helped to revolutionise the design of smaller carriages, which eventually became independent of the under-perch. There are numerous variations of both lengthwise and cross-springing, joined together by D links and known in certain combinations as platform

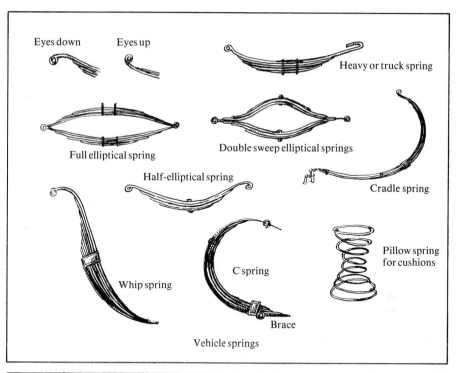

Eyes down   Eyes up

Heavy or truck spring

Full elliptical spring

Double sweep elliptical springs

Half-elliptical spring

Cradle spring

Whip spring

C spring

Pillow spring for cushions

Brace

Vehicle springs

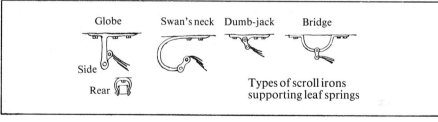

Globe   Swan's neck   Dumb-jack   Bridge

Side

Rear

Types of scroll irons supporting leaf springs

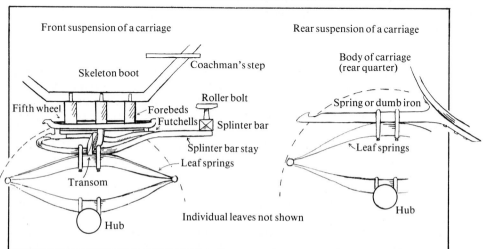

Front suspension of a carriage

Rear suspension of a carriage

Skeleton boot

Coachman's step

Body of carriage (rear quarter)

Fifth wheel

Forebeds

Roller bolt

Spring or dumb iron

Futchells

Splinter bar

Splinter bar stay

Leaf springs

Leaf springs

Transom

Hub

Individual leaves not shown

Hub

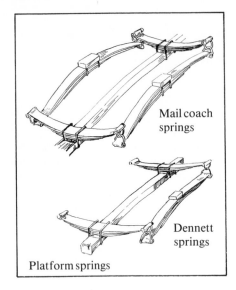

Mail coach springs

Dennett springs

Platform springs

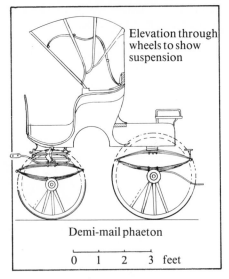

Elevation through wheels to show suspension

Demi-mail phaeton

0   1   2   3   feet

springs. These latter improved suspension by a better distribution of body weight, raising springs nearer to the under-body. Complex systems of coil springing, as with the fore-carriage of the three-wheeled Hansom cab, were introduced at various stages throughout the 19th century but few survived being intricate and costly, difficult for anyone but experts to adjust and maintain.

With some vehicles, especially military types and American farm wagons, the driver's seat was sprung while the body was unsprung and dead-axle. The early stage coaches were not allowed to have sprung seats as it was thought that drivers on long journeys might be too comfortable and fall asleep, with disastrous results.

The loop or eye through which the leaf springs were hung or secured to the bodywork—at each end—were known either as 'eyes down' or 'eyes up' types, eyes positioned above or below the outer leaf.

Undergear and bodywork

The under-carriage of primitive carts and wagons was based on either A or H frames of rough timbers. A considerable advance was made by the introduction of the under-perch or coupling pole, uniting fore and hind parts for greater strength and stability. Perches were used on many larger coaches and carriages even after the introduction of elliptical leaf springs, but were gradually phased out for smaller and lighter vehicles from the second decade of the 19th century.

Both fore and hind-carriages of the traditional four-wheeled vehicle were at first built up on a system of cross beams or bolsters, the ends of which—and the undersides—supported the axletrees. Futchells, known to wagon builders as hounds, formed a group of longitudinal members under the fore-carriage for extra support, necessary in retaining the sway bar which steadied the front gearing. The sway bar bore against the underside of the perch or pole and assisted in pivoting the fore-wheels in underlock. The main axis for pivoting was a short front or through pin.

A horizontal or fifth wheel eventually allowed a complete turning circle, this latter fixed between the body and fore-axle, held in position by a through or king bolt. It was often two wheels of iron or steel, the upper wheel sometimes fixed to wooden segments. There were also lighter versions known as half circle or half-elliptical wheels, which are self-explanatory.

Rearward projecting dumb or spring irons were frequently used for hanging elliptical and three-quarter elliptical springs, while those at the fore-end were supported by stay bars also supporting a crosswise splinterbar. Connection between springs and framework on the average coach or carriage was by means of horizontal jack bolts. On some vehicles half-elliptical springs were attached to loops or scroll irons which have several different names and types.

Bodywork of a coach is based on a panelled framework, divided into sections or quarters, with a felt-lined roof and outward opening doors, on opposite sides. There is usually a folding step or steps under each door in corresponding positions. Fixed iron steps or step irons are used for mounting the driving and other outside seats, fixed to the shafts of a two-wheeled vehicle but otherwise attached near the lower end of the footboard or wherever appropriate. The heavier type of passenger vehicle, such as the mail or stage coach, had the under-part of the body supported by sturdy wooden members (called 'rockers').

The driving seat, often known as the box or box-seat, on a coach or carriage, is mounted above a hollow structure with curved side panels, in later years termed a skeleton boot. This rests on crosswise forebeds or members (three in number) in turn supported by the framing of the fifth wheel and a crosswise transom, in contact with the forward projecting stay of the splinterbar and the upper half of an elliptical spring, on either side. In early days the box was a chest or container for either repair tools or valuables. A footboard in front of the driving seat is supported by under brackets at an angle of about 35 degrees. Some lower and lighter vehicles have a vertical dashboard or dash (splashboard) along the top of the footboard. Single or double arm and back rests surround the top of the driver's seat, also known as seat or side irons. On some older types of carriage the box-seat is isolated from the main bodywork, above a rounded or turtle-backed boot.

At the lower front end of a coach or carriage, beneath the footboard, is a crosswise splinterbar with upright roller bolts for the attachment of traces or swingletrees, according to draught requirements. Shafts, where these are used, may be secured by prong-like futchells or attached by loops and eyes. The pole for coach or carriage is inserted through a central aperture below the splinterbar, continuing towards the fore-axle.

Glass windows are also known as lights, while the types that may be raised and lowered with straps, in a well of the sash, are droplights.

Vehicles such as the landau, with a folding hood or head, have their flexible covers suspended on hoopsticks, raised by means of a pivoting rod or hood-counterbalance—for each side or quarter. At one period all hoods were made of harness leather, treated with various polishes and dressings which created an unpleasant odour and increased the stuffiness of interiors, especially in humid weather. The sides of a vehicle with a fixed head often had scroll-like false irons, purely for decoration. The upper surface of many fixed heads was patent leather.

The typical English coach or carriage, throughout history, tended to be—like her warships—straight or wall-sided. This also applied to certain types of mail and stage coach, the straight rather than curved sides of which may have looked more elegant than other vehicles but were a restriction on inner space and comfort. In general terms the outward curves and bulges of a passenger vehicle, appeared more pronounced in Eastern rather than in Western Europe.

With commercial wagons, vans and carts the carrying box or body has a platform or loading platform to bear the load, also known as the main side or bottom side. The vertical front end is known as the front board while the side panels are of lengthwise boarding and the rear end (often made to fall open) is the tailboard, endboard or tailgate. Tailboards are supported on either side by wedge-like tailpegs of conical shape, pressed through loops and secured by small chains. A diagonal metal stay frequently supports the rearward side panels or planks, known as a shorestay. The latter is mounted on a wooden side projection known as an earbreadth. A raised driving seat or bench at the fore-end is supported by curved irons, straight irons or double wooden uprights known as fore pillars, corresponding with similar end or hind pillars at the rear of the vehicle.

Beading is used on all types of vehicle to conceal joints or external apertures, especially between panels.

Draught gear

This is in the form of shafts or poles, according to the type of vehicle and number of horses used. Shafts, originally known as thills, are straight or curved bars level with the flanks of the horse between them, although at a slight angle, by means of which it is attached to the vehicle. They are usually of laminated wood, especially for lighter draught, but also shaped from solid wood. There are metal fittings and ferrules also leather bindings, according to type and style. At one time light shafts were lined with whalebone but this declined as the commodity became scarce and expensive. Single shafts are by far the most popular although, for more than three centuries, double shafts were used on East Anglian farm wagons and later for some of the brewers' drays of London and the Home Counties. These would be for a pair of horses working side-by-

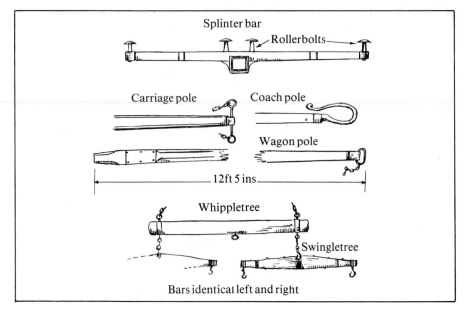

side although, in most cases—where an extra wagon horse was needed—it would be hitched to the front of the shaft horse, in tandem. In military transport units an outrigger was sometimes used, especially for two-wheeled carts and horse ambulances, this being a form of sideways extension bar similar to the spreader attachment of gypsy living vans. Shafts conformed to the shape and size of the horse between them, being wider and deeper at the rear or beeching end than at the front, also turning slightly outwards towards the top or front. Shaft couplings were usually lugs or loops on part of the fore-carriage (axles, futchells, etc), connected by means of eyes to the actual shafts. In later years the connection was protected by a block of moulded rubber known as a shaft rubber or anti-rattler.

The draught or centre pole separates a pair of horses (wheelers) next to a vehicle, to which they were attached at the fore-end. The pole of a wagon usually had an enclosed metal loop at the head, while a carriage pole had two small rings, and a coach pole a large hook looped back on itself. Traces from the harness are attached to roller bolts on the splinterbar or to horizontal members hooked on to the splinterbar, known as swingletrees, whippletrees, whiffletrees or draught bars. In some harness arrangements the swingletrees were joined together by a doublebar or spreader. With other types of double harness horses or mules were attached to the poles by padded metal bands round the girths known as bugles or belly bugles, popular in Holland and South Africa for heavy draught work, also with a pair of horses harnessed to a Fresian sjees or country gig. Curricle harness, also the draught arrangements of Indian native carts such as the tonga, depended on a set of horizontal bars or rollers, extending from a centre pole and resting on pad saddles of each horse, main draught, however, being from side traces and swingletrees.

Traces for horses in tandem lead back to the shafts or a tandem bar ahead of the shaft horse, while the leaders of a four-in-hand or six-horse team, have swingletrees attached to a doubletree at the head of the pole or to harness of the pair immediately behind them. Vehicles drawn by large, swiftly moving teams such as the Concord coach of North America, often had an extra or detached pole between the second pair, known as a swing pole or swinger.

Brakes

These are based on a retaining mechanism locking the wheels of a vehicle by friction or pressure to retard motion. They are only effective in the permanent and practical sense on four-wheeled vehicles. The first type of brake was the dragshoe, slipper or slide, known in country districts as the drugbat, forming a hollow wedge under the near-side rear wheel, fitted before descending a hill. This prevented the vehicle from over-running its team. A drop chain locking round a spoke and felloe of a wagon served much the same purpose. To prevent a vehicle running backwards while ascending a slope there was a pointed and forked dogstick or dragstick/stave under the rear axle. Some vehicles, especially military wagons, had a roller or roller scotch chained under the back near-side wheel to serve as a revolving wedge.

The later and more conventional brake consists of a shoe or slipper in direct contact with the tyre, having a beam or block supporting the shoe, while a rod (later a strong wire) transmitted motion from lever-arm or handle to shoe and beam. Brakes, as we now recognise them, were mainly developed during the late 18th and early 19th centuries, operated by hand lever or foot pedal. A hand

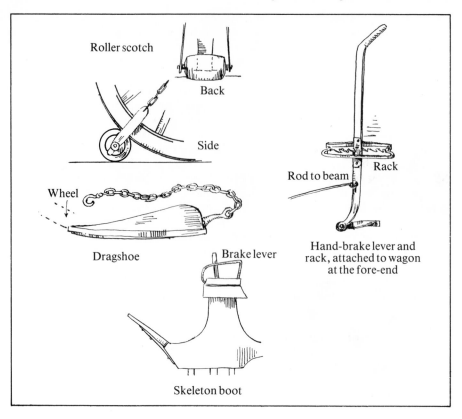

wound screw-down brake, meant to lock a stationary vehicle by turning a hand wheel, was also carried on certain vehicles, especially commercial wagons and drays, being a special feature of the so-called dealer's trolley—a vehicle about 10ft long and carrying loads of up to 30 cwt.

Making hand brakes was highly skilled work, usually the domain of independent and specialist craftsmen. It was soon discovered that a rubber-lined brake shoe acted much better on metal tyres, while metal was preferred for solid rubber. With later, more elegant carriages the long connecting bar of the break lever was replaced by a so-called Bowden wire, hidden within the bodywork of the vehicle. Lever brakes were usually pushed on and pulled off, rather than the reverse.

Some delivery vans of the late 1930s, especially those of the railway cartage services, eventually used hub or disc brakes.

Lamps

These were considered to be essential for a vehicle used in the early morning, late afternoon or evening. They were either candle or oil lamps, although in later years electric battery lamps were introduced, especially for internal lighting. Candle lamps were considered more reliable and certainly more elegant than other types, their odour being less offensive than oil. They were also easier to clean and maintain, in general terms. Wax candles of superior quality beeswax were used, contained or mounted in long tinplate tubes. Coiled springs within the tubes forced them gradually upwards as they burned down. A new candle would always have its wick singed directly after insertion. Most lamps were brass or brass mounted, although some were of white metal throughout.

Town or dress coaches had round lamps, while those for long distance travel frequently had square shapes. State coaches sometimes had four lamps, one on each corner of the bodywork, but most were used as a pair at the fore-end only. The mail coach had a three-aspect lamp mounted in the centre of the footboard and four side lamps, or two per side. Spare lamps were carried on coaches in leather-lined cases.

Cart lamps, sometimes used on vans, wagons and heavier types of commercial vehicle, were mainly square but rounded at the top, with protective bars across the lens. They frequently had a cross-handle or loop at the top and were secured to the vehicle by means of a loop passing over the bracket. On some types the loop would be secured by a small brass padlock.

Coach and carriage lamps make ideal ornaments for both interiors and exteriors of private dwellings. They look remarkably effective in a glass-fronted porch, flanking the side pillars of a Georgian doorway or in the angle of a staircase. Very few of those used for furnishing and decorative purposes, however, are now genuine, in the sense that they ever adorned a wheeled vehicle, although excellent replicas have become available during the past few years.

Trim

The inner trim or upholstery of coaches and carriages was produced from a variety of materials, depending on fashion and availability. Perhaps the earliest traditional covers were made from leather or skins, as were the original weather-proof curtains which guarded windows and apertures, before the introduction of glass. Leather was certainly hard wearing and suitable for most climates and weather conditions. Many early coaches were lined both internally and externally with tooled, embossed and often scented leather.

From the mid-18th century there was a preference for hard-wearing satins and figured tabaret in a wide range of colours. Tabaret was a silk stuff of French origin, with alternating satin and watered surfaces, the watered or wavy effect produced by calendering or passing under heated rollers. It was a material greatly favoured by upholsterers of the 1760s and '70s, especially coach-

Evacuating the Royal Family from Buckingham Palace to Windsor at the start of the Second World War. Note the fine lamps on these vehicles (B.B. Murdock).

trimmers. Damask, velvet, ducape and coteline were other popular textiles in this era. Padding materials were horse-hair (from the tail rather than mane or fetlock), also wool flock, doe hair and shredded whalebone. Extensive use would later be made of waisted or pillow springs (coil springs) under the restraint of webbing, while the quilted and button-back effect was popular from the second half of the 18th century.

Leather upholstery revived in popularity during the mid-19th century, being highly fashionable from the 1870s, morocco leather or kidskin often being used.

Side curtains, in the days of glass windows, were frequently lutestring, some-times known as lustring or lustrine, dating from the late 18th century. This was a corded silk with glossy face, noted for both smart appearance and long wear.

Floor coverings for coaches were usually fitted Brussels carpets or velvet pile rugs, often above a layer of oilcloth.

Accessories and various decorative inlays would be made from a variety of metals, alloys, ivory and mother-of-pearl.

Carriage clocks

These sometimes have to be carried or displayed in both closed and open vehicles for certain show-events, but are also excellent time-keepers and ornaments in almost any surroundings. Interest in them has greatly revived since the late 1960s and there are now many serious collectors.

The first were used as travelling clocks in private coaches and chariots, towards the end of the 18th century, greatly in demand by Englishmen and women making the Grand Tour of European capitals which was said to complete their formal education. A French invention, but later made in Switzerland and England, they were first carried—like spare lamps—in padded leather cases. The first types were made possible only after the invention of lever escapement and great technical improvements which allowed less than five minutes deviation in twenty four hours, making them more reliable than any other small clocks up to that period. An important feature was a strong, rectangular casing, usually brass, with toughened but clear glasswork (bevelled at the edges), necessary for jolting and rough usage during travel. They also had a top loop for hanging on brackets and were sometimes known as bracket clocks.

One of the first important makers was Abraham-Louis Breguet of French-Swiss descent but working for the greater part of his career in the royal and imperial town of Versailles near Paris. Surviving the Revolution as a distinguished master craftsman he undertook many orders for the French Government, both under the Republic and during the reign of Napoleon I. By 1796 he had perfected his famous *pendule de voyage* which was considered a great improvement on any of its predecessors.

Breguet clocks were long regarded as in a class by themselves and exported to all parts of the world, and widely copied in other countries of Europe and America. Other clocks were made on both sides of the Swiss frontier in the Jura and at places as far apart as Lyons and Saint-Nicholas-à-Aliermont near Dieppe. They were not made in England until the 1850s, although large numbers had been smuggled into the country even during the Napoleonic Wars. By this time there was less need for travelling clocks, with the advent of railways and cheap pocket watches, and many of the English types were for mantlepieces in studies and smokerooms.

Later centres for Swiss carriage clocks were Geneva and Neuchâtel. Although not as beautiful as French clocks they eventually became even more reliable and perhaps the finest time-keepers in Europe. This was because, at that time, fewer Swiss clocks were actually made, each receiving greater care and individual attention, becoming masterpieces of accuracy and later of external design.

Famous makers were Breuet, Henri Jacot, M. Drocorot, P. Garnier, M. Soldano and M. Bareux. Their products were made either to special order or distributed through retailers and agents. Names appearing on the dials are usually those of the retailers rather than the maker or craftsman.

The repeater type from which the modern alarm clock stemmed, was introduced shortly before 1850. This was operated or set by means of a small knob at the top of the clock. Later types not only struck on the hour but also the previous numbers of the hours and chimed for quarter hours.

Some of the finest modern versions of this timepiece were now made by the Matthew Norman organisation of London and Bale (sic), under the trade mark of an elegant Brougham. These are usually eight-day clocks, examples being both square and rectangular and the less familiar oval type, with variations of the cross or top handle.

Materials

A wide range of basic materials was used in coach, carriage and wagon building, the chief being wood and metal, with leather appearing in a secondary role. While wood was mainly for wheel spokes, felloes, body and upper works, metal featured in the construction of under-works, springs, brakes, hand-rails and many accessories.

The most popular and highly valued timbers were ash and oak, of native growth but from hedgerows and isolated trees rather than copse and woodland. Hedgerow timber was found to be hardier and more reliable than forest trees. Ash was used for framework and bracing, being of tough, fibrous texture lacking elasticity but taking much longer than other woods to warp and twist. Although very strong it was much lighter than oak.

Oak was used for spokes, body frames and underframing, especially on agricultural wagons and carts, being of fairly young growth, for preference, but not too young. Unfortunately oak contains acids tending to rust and corrode metal surfaces with which it is in contact. It is also unsuitable for vehicles exported to much warmer climates or used on foreign service. In conditions of great heat there is a tendency to develop longitudinal cracks or heartshakes.

Elm is a tough, cross-grained wood, unlikely to crack, split or splinter, except under severe pressure. It was used for hubs, axlebeds or cases, floor-boards, rollers and side planks. Exposed to water and damp weather conditions it became even more durable and thus ideal for the bottom-boards of certain canal craft. It also stood up well to excessive boring of holes, screwing, hammering and the driving of nails and sprigs. Unfortunately its wavy, strongly marked grain made it difficult to paint or varnish.

Of the many foreign and imported timbers pine, often known as deal, was the most frequently used. This was shipped from the Baltic countries and North America in planks, baulks and battens. There were several varieties but the best known was yellow pine. This was a soft wood, fairly light but firm and durable, used for the side boards and planks of many carts and commercial vehicles but unsuitable for heavier work or long periods of stress and strain. In coach and carriage building it was used as a cheaper substitute for mahogany, in which case it was limited to interiors and lined with leather and cloth. White deal, or ordinary pine, lacked firmness even by the standards of soft wood, and was used (to a limited extent) for temporary or inferior work.

Teak, from Burma and the East Indies is a firm and highly durable wood used for footboards and in military wagons designed for tropical service. Its inner oils help to preserve metalwork from rust and corrosion, also to repel infestations by wood-damaging insects.

Sabicu is a rare tropical wood, firm and durable. Related to the acacia, it grows mainly in the West Indies and Central America. It was mainly used for felloes on large wheels but limited by its cost and small import quota.

African oak is a dark, strong, closely-grained timber, related to the wood of the orange tree. It was used for wheel spokes and parts of military vehicles selected for tropical and overseas service, especially in Africa and Northern India. It stood up to extremes of heat better than English oak, being less prone to shakes, although not as enduring in European climates.

Mahogany is a firm, durable wood, imported—at its best—from Cuba and Honduras, although the former was of superior quality. It was used for superior panelling, both interior and exterior, with coaches, carriages and delivery vans. Its smooth surface and the attractive colour of its grain made it excellent for polishing, also ideal for the way it responded to paint, glue and varnish.

Pedowk is a durable hardwood of the East Indies, flexible but inclined to warp after a certain period. Used to a limited extent for making wheel spokes.

Greenheart is an exceptionally hard wood of the laurel family, distributed throughout South America. Used for wheel spokes and sometimes for felloes.

Rock-elm, hickory and various lancewoods of North America and the West Indies were sometimes used for straight shafts. Although straight-grained and flexible they were also liable to warp and twist. Lancewood would also crack and splinter on sudden impact.

The chief metal for horse-drawn vehicles was always iron, appearing in axles, bars, stays, hoops, hinges, bolts, nails, tyres and plates. Steel often replaced iron in later years and was mainly for tyres, leaf springs, suspension bars and tubular fittings, also, in the course of time, for axles. Copper could be used for sheathing and beading while buckles, wheel hoops, oil caps, rings and plates were often made from brass. Axle nuts or axletree nuts of the finest quality were made from gun metal, which was an alloy of copper, tin and/or zinc. Other metals and alloys were for accessories and decorative work. Leather was necessary for straps, inner trim or upholstery and wheel washers.

There was a limited use for ivory in the form of studs, buttons and rollers, mainly for inner trim. Pearl shell or mother-of-pearl was sometimes used for inlaid work of coach and carriage interiors.

Just as there were wide selections of materials there was also a diverse number of highly trained craftsmen, especially for finer workmanship on coaches and carriages, from the second half of the 18th century. These are listed by W. Bridges Adams in his book on *English Pleasure Carriages* as follows: body-makers, carriage-makers (working on under-carriages or gear), carvers, smiths, trimmers, painters, heraldic painters and designers, draughtsmen, axletree makers, spring-makers, formers, trunk-makers, joiners, turners, curriers, japanners, ivory workers, lace-makers (for trimming blinds and curtains), platers, chasers and embroiderers.

Chapter 8

Repairs, restoration and renovation

Most of the work under this heading was formerly undertaken by the local wheelwright or any firm of coach and carriage builders, which might have been centred either on a large city or small market town. A few of these have managed to stay open throughout the universal recession of their trade, although many closed for good, especially before and shortly after the Second World War. It may be noted that the war-time period provided a short stay of execution, during which a number of horse-drawn vehicles were still needed to save petrol and imported fuel. Since the revival of interest in driving and preserving old vehicles during the early 1970s, a number of new concerns have launched themselves into a small but rapidly expanding area of combined crafts-manship and industry. These may be the inspiration of younger people although frequently relying on the expertise of older hands, some of whom may have deferred well-earned retirement to impart their skills to a rising generation. The following description relates to a visit paid to Richard Brereton in the foothills of the Black Mountains near Painscastle, Powys, in 1978.

A gig of about 1910 (The Edgar Bates Collection).

A typical newspaper delivery cart owned by The Suffragette *newspaper. Photographed in August 1913* (B.B. Murdock).

Richard uses a complex of barns and outhouses on his parents' farm of Wern Newydd, which he has fitted-up with workshop tools and several handy gadgets of his own invention. He entered the business, which developed, like many enthusiasms, from a hobby to serious and demanding work, about ten years ago. He began with the restoration of a long-neglected dogcart and graduated to repairs on vehicles owned by personal friends and local people. Warming to his subject, as he acquired skill and confidence, he was soon employing craftsmen from a nearby village and set about enlarging his workshops. Discovering a steady demand he began to search out and buy old vehicles, restoring them to as near perfect condition as possible. The accent was on sound workmanship and respect for the traditions of his craft, bringing a new lease of life to carriages and other vehicles which might otherwise have rotted away on junk heaps.

A keynote may be termed versatility of approach, as Richard is now able to undertake almost any work connected with horse-drawn vehicles, apart from inner trim and upholstery, although this can be arranged through business contacts. There is also a limited amount of work connected with old motor vehicles of the vintage type, some of which are very near the description of horseless carriages.

The crafts involved in this work demand a high standard of skill and finish. Most customers being enthusiasts, take a serious interest in their orders or commissions, and would be knowledgeable enough to spot the smallest error or incongruity. One of the hardest tasks is finding enough timber of the right type and quality, especially well-seasoned ash, which seems to be a nation-wide problem with most wood workers.

As with other carriage restorers, distance presents no obvious difficulties. Vehicles to be repaired are collected and returned at the earliest possible times by Land Rover and low-loading trailer. Richard has worked for many individuals, groups and authorities, yet one of his most rewarding commissions was the restoration of a private drag, once the property of Lord Leconfield, made by Herbert Whitlock of London, for its new French owner.

At Wern Newydd the workshops are approached through an area of covered storage space, formerly a large barn. This contains lengths of wood and other raw materials on one side, with a selection of vehicles awaiting attention in the opposite bay. Passing through double doors into the work area there are shops on both right and left with gigs, dogcarts and carriages in every stage of stripping down and rebuilding. To the right are paintshops where some of the vehicles, mounted on temporary wheels, were drying-out. Along the left-hand wall of the wood shop, to the left, was a series of jigs and clamps on a work-bench in which laminated shafts may be moulded, under pressure, to the correct contours. Opposite was a retyring machine for the replacement of solid rubber tyres in their channel grooves. Electric power or band saws have replaced the old-fashioned saw pit but, while time-saving methods and materials have helped to increase production, with most of the work it is both impossible and unthinkable to skimp or take short cuts.

Mr Brereton was kind enough to co-operate in answering the following questions, which may be of some interest to owners and enthusiasts.

Q: 'What are the most common repairs you have to make?'
A: 'Replacing felloes, and making new shafts after accidents.'
Q: 'Do you find there is a greater need for general restoration or for a few minor and specific repairs?'
A: 'There is a greater need for general restorations rather than for part restorations and minor repairs.'
Q: 'To what extent—if at all—do you use non-traditional materials, such as plywood and plastics.'
A: 'We rely completely on traditional materials except for the floor panels of vehicles, for which we use plywood.'
Q: 'Do you think a carriage should have a general overhaul and examination, and at what intervals?'
A: 'A carriage which is fairly well used should have (ideally) an examination at the end of each season (once every twelve months).'
Q: 'What are the proportions of home and overseas clients, needing your services for repair work and restoration?'
A: 'About forty per cent of our work is for overseas clients.'
Q: 'Would you say more younger or older people were interested in this hobby?'
A: 'I would say that driving (and an interest in the vehicles driven), is now divided almost equally between young and old people.'
Q: 'Is more work done for showing and eventing or for people who merely collect vehicles or drive without showing?'
A: 'Fifty per cent of our work is for clients who show and compete in events. Twenty per cent who drive for pleasure. Thirty per cent for museums and private collections.'
Q: 'What materials do you find the most difficult to obtain?'
A: 'Good quality seasoned ash and oak.'
Q: 'If presented with a run-down vehicle, in need of general repairs and overhaul, what parts would you consider the worst affected?'

A: 'The parts worst affected are the items which incur the most stress, ie, shafts and wheels.'

Q: 'Would you start restoration with the wheels of the vehicle or the body-work, or have different people working on different parts at the same time?'

A: 'When we start work on a vehicle it goes through the wood shop first, where we generally start with the wheels, and build up from there. It is then stripped down again and all the iron work shot-blasted (to get rid of rust), before being taken into the paintshops, where it will be finally assembled after completion of the paintwork.'

Q: 'Do you encounter more dished or straight wheels?'

A: 'I think you will find that nearly all wheels are dished. Even though some look straight, they are more likely to be dished by a few degrees. If there is no apparent dish it is possible—due to drying out of the timber—that they have lost their dish.'

Q: 'Do you have more two-wheeled or four-wheeled vehicles through your workshops?'

A: 'We have an equal number of two and four-wheeled vehicles.'

Q: 'Are more repairs and renewals needed for accidents and breakages than for wear and tear?'

A: 'Thirty per cent of our work is for accident repairs and seventy per cent for general restorations and building new vehicles to order.'

Q: 'What is the average age of most horse-drawn vehicles brought to you for restoration and repairs?'

A: 'The average age is between sixty and eighty years.'

It would appear from further conversation with Mr Brereton that the most popular vehicles were gigs, dogcarts (both two and four-wheeled types), ralli cars and governess cars, with phaetons for cross-country events.

While the use of traditional materials and methods should be applauded, it is interesting to note that some manufacturers of modern vehicles for competitive driving, now use all-steel wheels with welded spokes and shock-absorbers (coil springs) for the bodywork. The hubs of this type being flat or of low profile, the wheel, and consequently the vehicle, sacrifices something of both dignity and aesthetic charm. Yet such vehicles fill a gap and are here to stay, being of proven worth for three-day events, especially in marathons and cross-country trials. The most outstanding of the firms working almost entirely on modern lines is the Harewood Carriage Company, founded in 1971 by Stanley Johnson of the Holdsworthy Industrial Estate, Devonshire. The order books of this concern are usually filled for at least eight months ahead, with many of the carriages going overseas. Johnson rarely if ever produces replica vehicles or authentic restorations and relies very much on steel, extra-strong marine plywood and wheel-hubs of cast epoxy resin. Regarding the use of plywood, many restorers object to this material or use it—like Mr Brereton—in a strictly limited fashion. Although a matter of taste and personal experience, the use of laminated wood was first developed in connection with building horse-drawn vehicles, but not always accepted by more conservative elements. Museum workshops have been known to use plywood for small-scale renovations, over a number of years, and it may be safe to compromise by saying that much depends on the strength of the wood and the permanence expected of the finished work. The experience and record of the Harewood Company, in this respect, is fully reliable and above reproach. Like many of the traditional carriage makers of former days they work very much to special order, even taking into account the dimensions of the horses used for pulling the vehicles. A number of ready-made vehicles, especially the cheaper types, have always been produced in Britain, but not nearly so many as in America, which is why exact or standard dimensions of British vehicles, even within a few inches are unrealistic.

It may be noted that the trend is now to keep the more valuable or antique type of vehicle as a show-piece, although even if this were not the case there would be far too few of the older vehicles to serve general requirements. It is obvious that metallic structures withstand shock and accident better than wooden bodies, while the shallow hub is far better for negotiating obstacles. Retirement of old vehicles, however, should not mean that they are permanently locked away, although not subjected to rigours of work for which they are no longer suitable and perhaps were never intended.

Do-it-yourself

It was often said that the Red River cart, widely used in opening up the north-western parts of Canada and the United States, could be made by anyone with a few simple hand-tools and sufficient timber. Such vehicles, often made by the settlers themselves, frequently outlasted factory or even craftsman made importations from the east. Given will-power and enough time for trial-and-error, it should be well within the range of possibilities for an enthusiast to repair and construct any type of vehicle, although in the world of today time may be even more valuable than money, while producing craftwork to the highest standards needs long hours and perhaps years of practice.

There are, however, certain adjustments and precautions which should be made by all people having the care and responsibility of horse-drawn vehicles, either for active use or display. It is not widely recognised that items in museums and private collections, especially those displayed out-of-doors, deteriorate even quicker than those in regular service. As with the human and animal body, regular exercise—drawing the line at over-work and abuse—is of greater benefit than a state of perpetual ease and inactivity.

A newly acquired vehicle should be placed under cover as soon as possible and have chocks put under its wheels. Those which are intended for display but in need of repair and restoration, should be kept well away from other exhibits, roped-off and inaccessible to probing fingers.

Maintenance

Vehicles left in stationary positions for long periods should have their wheels turned at regular intervals. It is also advisable to provide hard standing of planks or flat stones to prevent the worst effects of rising damp. Store and/or display in a place which is well-ventilated, also with reasonable access both for the vehicles and those examining them or serving their needs. There should be no connection between coach house and stable, where horses are still kept, and the coach should be well beyond the range of manure heaps as ammonia from them tends to damage the upper surface of paint and varnish. When a vehicle is not on display or in use it should be kept under a light dust sheet or cotton cover, which must never be allowed to get damp.

Some think that only the harsh conditions of winter are harmful to vehicles left in the open, forgetting or seeming unaware that an even worse enemy is strong sunlight, especially when it is on an exposed site for days or weeks on end. The warmth of summer, also exposure near plate glass windows (for indoor exhibits), blisters or cracks paint, sometimes shrinking the underlying woodwork in the same process. One local authority (which shall be nameless) wasted considerable time and money having paid for the restoration of a stage coach and exhibiting it in a barn, with added picture windows, through which it could be viewed from the outer courtyard and gardens. Almost needless to say the effect on the new paintwork alone was disastrous, leaving a pattern of cracks and crazes after only a few hours of strong sunshine, which became an abstract work of art in its own right. Some form of external—if only partial—screening, in such cases, is essential to prevent the worst effects of direct light and heat taking their toll. The ideal coach house should not be dark and cold but only moderately light, especially if intended as a place of prolonged storage.

Always make sure that gutterings are kept clear of foreign matter and well-scrubbed out. This further applies to any other nooks and corners which are not too obvious, or to parts out of regular use.

Great care should be taken to keep the shafts clear of the ground or floor, either in a raised position or supported by a form of light stand or trestle. Do not drop them suddenly or even lower them without extreme care. These are the most vulnerable parts of a vehicle, other than the wheels, easy to fracture and loosen the ferrules or other metal attachments. With a working vehicle it is a good idea to place a waterproof cover over the upper framing, especially after a long session of road work, as hauling tends to strain wooden members, opening cracks which rain, damp and harmful insects may penetrate.

If a vehicle is to be left out of doors for any length of time make sure that it is well away from overhanging trees. Drips from the branches of trees and shrubs may be more persistent and harmful than squalls of rain encountered on the highway. Tarpaulins, weighted or well-roped down, would seem to be the obvious solution in such cases.

Closed or headed vehicles often need an examination and renewal of the underfelt, also a regular airing of the interiors. Doors and windows should be opened and shut as often as the wheels are turned, at least once a week when the vehicle is on show. Drop lights should be lowered and raised and the windows kept well-polished, the latter if only for the sake of self-respect and pride in appearance. Always use a good quality window cleaning solution, supplied in bottles or cans, which should be applied sparingly, rubbed over thoroughly and polished immediately. With the better type of solution there is no need to wait for drying-out before polishing. Opening doors and windows is also good for working parts, especially handles, catches and hinges. This further applies to locks, clips, levers and other gadgets or items which must be kept well oiled and used as intended.

A folding head or hood is better kept for long periods in the raised position rather than lowered and folded. Leather aprons and blinds which are normally kept rolled back should be unrolled at regular intervals. Ring the changes by raising that which is normally lowered and straightening the rolled and folded. If the vehicle is indoors for long, wheel it out for occasional airings.

Exposed brass and copper work needs fairly constant attention, with a routine of polishing at least twice a week, if the vehicle is on regular display or in daily use. If this is not possible or the vehicle is placed in temporary storage, metal surfaces require a thin layer or coating of grease. This may be wiped off with a spare rag, in a few minutes, when the vehicle is needed for use or display. Very few of the patent lacquers sold to protect and preserve brass in these conditions are of any value for more than a short period, while the application of grease may be much quicker and cheaper. Make sure that grease and lacquer are not allowed to contact textile, leather or rubber surfaces, which may soon fade or perish in consequence. There are several excellent metal polishes on the market but according to the articles in many old journals and magazines the best cleaning aids for silver, brass or copper are hard work and elbow grease. In the case of copper all harmful acids and scouring grits or powders should be avoided without reserve.

Vehicles which have been on the road need extra care and cleaning, it being a sensible rule that a carriage should never be stored or put away without cleaning and examination. Dust attracted in summer is always harmful to paintwork and external surfaces, while the slush and mud of winter both harbour damp and turn to dust when drying out. Avoid cleaning and washing down a carriage in strong sunlight. Hosing down is the first stage of cleaning, this being done in a large enough open space, although shaded rather than too exposed. It is certainly better to hose than to fling buckets of water about in a random, uncontrolled manner. Wheels often need special treatment with careful cleaning of the spokes. Wheel-brushes of a conical type are sold for this purpose, but they should not be rubbed into the spokes and felloes too hard as they spoil the varnish. Hand methods are preferable as grit and mud combined with pressure from bristles tend to leave scratch marks and scourings. For thorough cleaning the wheels should be jacked-up in turn. Follow the hosing with a good sponging over, using a large sea sponge saturated in water and working from the top to the bottom. Clean, cold water is essential and should not be stinted, but do not saturate the vehicle so that excess moisture penetrates its lining or inner-work. After the sponging, rub down with a leather before polishing, and dry out as

At the entrance to Tower Bridge, London, on the south side, a group of horse-drawn vehicles await the opening of the bridge. The year is 1901 (B.B. Murdock).

much and as quickly as possible. When paintwork is allowed to dry of its own accord the result is an unsound, stained and streaky appearance.

A vehicle which is much exposed or kept out-of-doors for long periods needs a thorough rather than a casual inspection and washing down, at least every few weeks. Every twelve months this should be followed by an overall varnishing, using a proper oval varnish brush with a waisted handle. It cannot be over-stressed that the right tools always provide the best service.

It may be worth noting that horse buses of the Victorian and Edwardian eras were thoroughly washed down and examined every night, after coming off duty. A week-long overhaul took place each year, timed to a day, in which almost every part was dismantled and either renewed or refurbished. Not a spring or bolt failed to undergo rigorous tests for what were then the hardest-worked passenger vehicles of any age, type or country.

Always see that the interiors of coaches and carriages are given the right care and treatment. With leather upholstery make sure that outer surfaces are kept supple and well-cleaned, not subject to undue weight or stress. If it is necessary to place luggage or any other solid object on seating or against side squabs and panelling, the area should be first protected with a rug or light matting. Interiors in use soon become dusty and should be cleaned at least once a week with a damp sponge or chamois leather. Avoid the use of both dry dusting or too much water, the former tending to scratch with unseen but gritty particles (especially enamelled or treated leather surfaces), while the latter allows damp to penetrate the inner lining. Take additional care in wiping out seats or backrests with pleats and seams, where extra dust may lie concealed. To revive dull leatherwork, often a type suffering from over-long neglect, wash down with water which is clean and warm but not too hot. Use sparingly with a small amount of good quality curd soap, clearing up with an almost dry sponge or chamois leather. There are several brands of leather reviver on the market but satisfactory results may be obtained with an application of olive oil or neat's foot oil in small quantities, although an excess should be wiped-off afterwards. Stains may be removed with soap and water or the use of a small amount of linseed oil on a soft rag. Do not use petrol or paraffin, both of which are destructive to leather, especially when having a treated or enamelled surface. Untreated leather and soft hides have a fine nap and should be cleaned with a medium soft brush. Stains may be removed from this type of surface with a similar piece of leather, through rubbing or buffing, also with fine quality glass-paper. Morocco is dyed leather or kidskin and needs to be cleaned without wetting, using a soft brush and duster, unless the dye is known to be fast.

Cloth or textile upholstery needs to be well brushed down. If there is a definite nap on roof, cushion and seat linings this should be brushed forward in one direction, while side trimmings should be brushed downwards. Avoid using damp cloths or too much moisture of any kind as this may penetrate interior wadding with disastrous results.

Carpets and floor coverings should be removed periodically and well brushed in the direction of the grain. Stains and dirt on carpets may be removed with an application of rectified benzine. A generally shabby carpet or rug should be washed in warm water and scrubbed with carpet soap. It is the normal practice for the carpet to be rubbed with quantities of soapy water then sprinkled with borax powder, which is worked in with a scrubbing brush, then rinsed-off and allowed to dry. Fibre mats require heavy beating. Oil cloth must be removed

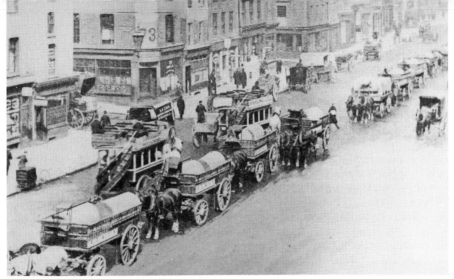

Somewhere in London—en route from the Bricklayer's Arms Station to a Fleet Street newspaper office—South Eastern and Chatham Railway wagons. The date is 1901 (B.B. Murdock).

when the coach or carriage is out of use as any air-tight floor coverings, causing sweating, may lead to rot and decay of the floor boards.

Leather heads or hoods need an occasional application of neat's foot oil, especially in the folds.

Rubber used for solid tyres or anti-rattlers, should be lightly sponged over from time-to-time, but wiped dry and kept well clear of grease or oil and out of direct or intense heat. With a working vehicle inspect the tyres after each run and extract any deeply embedded grit or slivers of metal, etc, which might otherwise cause splits. Parts near the rims of tyre channels may show rust marks which may be wiped clean and treated, as a precautionary measure, with graphite, the latter available either as paint or in blocks. Tyres not required for immediate use or display may be lightly brushed over with French chalk, which is one of the best preservatives on a short term basis, but needs infrequent if regular renewal. The working vehicle may be patched-up, when tyres are worn down, with sections from old lorry tyres, but these are unsuitable for exhibition or display purposes. For ordinary black rubber a good quality boot polish has been suggested as an all-purpose preservative although others prefer a non-oily varnish. It is possible but expensive to revulcanise rubber but, once it has begun to perish, it is usually better to invest in a complete renewal. Test for perishing with the pointed blade of a penknife, the inner surface of a tyre seeming to crumble beneath a hard and almost inflexible outer surface.

Oiling and greasing

While this is desirable for small working parts it is essential for axles, hubs and the larger movable-components. This further applies to the semi-protected bearings and screw-parts of brakes and pivots or under-lock of the fore-carriage. Leaf springs also benefit from regular oiling, which prevents rust and aids the free-sliding and necessary expansion of the individual leaves. Parts which appear corroded or clogged, especially the holding parts or jackbolts and shackles of springs, may first be treated with penetrating oil.

A commercial vehicle, or one in regular use, needs the axles greased at least once a month. The more sophisticated types have oil boxes or grease caps on the ends of the hubs, according to type and design, which should be kept well filled or packed as appropriate. As a general rule the less sound the axle the more necessary the lubrication, to prevent undue wear on the inner hub or nave, leading to a dangerous inner play of the bearings. In replacing a wheel which may have been removed in connection with greasing, or merely for examination, make sure that it is refitted properly without crossing the threads of the axle nuts, also that it is well-balanced. Check for balance by spinning a jacked-up wheel with a firm touch of the hand, waiting for it to stop or break-back. If properly balanced it should turn a half revolution in the opposite direction immediately after free-spinning.

Castor oil is the best medium for lubrication, sweet oils tending to become sticky and likely to defeat their own purpose by gumming up the parts which should be free and open.

Renovation

While restoration is often deemed the work of experts, sometimes on a long-term basis, renovation concerns anything from stop-gap repairs to making a vehicle road-worthy for the immediate future. Renovation may be the normal work of owners and amateurs but rarely involves high standards of expert knowledge, crafts techniques or historical research. Sometimes, however, it may be desirable or necessary to fall back on expert opinions, especially those of a wheelwright or blacksmith.

Stopping holes or cracks in woodwork may be done, especially before a thorough cleaning, painting or re-varnishing, by filling and levelling with knifing putty or resin fillers. Woodwork which shows signs of cracking or rotting should be treated with an application of dry rot fluid which at least limits or retards the rotting process. Make sure, with such applications, that the surface area is well cleaned and cleared of dust, dirt and flakes of old paint, also thoroughly dried out. This is because layers of moisture may be sealed within hollows of the woodwork by subsequent outer coatings, causing further, and highly dangerous, inner rot.

Wood rot is always a bugbear, but less frequently found in the framing and partially protected underworks, which are also of harder wood than the side panelling, less prone to softening and deterioration. Wheels rot and decay with greater rapidity than other parts, also being more likely to suffer from accidents and external breakages. Perhaps the worst parts to suffer are the points or outer extremities of the spokes, where they fit into the felloes. Hot weather and over-work in such conditions leads to a shrinkage and general loosening of spokes and felloes, remedied by standing the wheels in water which causes them to expand and regain their former shape. Romany folk often drove their vans and carts through fords and running water for this purpose, while in the diary of the Rev Francis Kilvert there is an entry to describe how a vehicle in which he travelled during a tour of Cornwall, was driven into deep ponds to cool the feet of the horses and ease the wheels.

When iron and steel tyres become loose through accident, heat-shrinkage or over-work they must be removed and shortened, then reshrunk over the rim of the felloes in a process known as cuttings and shrinking. This needs to be done on a proper tyring platform at ground level and is usually the work of several men. The wheel is first laid horizontally on the circular platform of stone and

Above *Fitting an iron tyre on a wooden wheel* (Museum of English Rural Life, Reading).
Below *W. Hesbrook, horse-breaker of Newport in Shropshire c 1900. The pony is harnessed to a panel cart. Note the coach just visible in the shed* (B.B. Murdock).

metal—held in place by a turnkey inserted through the hub into a hollow of the platform and adjusted by a screw-rod. Sometimes a furnace or oven is used for heating the tyre but this is often done in a large bonfire of wood faggots made-up in a convenient open space, not too far from the platform. The necessary strip of metal is cut to the right length and placed well into the centre of the fire, then passed between rollers and reheated. It is taken from the fire by two men using tongues or dogs and finally placed over the circumference of the wheel as quickly and carefully as possible. The circumference of the tyre is 1½ ins less than the size of the wheel, but expands with heating (although difficult for an unskilled person to adjust at any temperature). The rim of the tyre is banged down by means of hammering, while others stand by with watering cans to assist in the 'quenching' or cooling-down process. As the tyre cools it also contracts, driving the spokes and felloes more firmly together than mere hammering or external pressure.

Springs need almost as much care as wheels, and should be watched for the least signs of rust and wear. No vehicle of the sprung type will run safely or smoothly on rusty springs, which should be dismantled by unscrewing the clips and centre bolts. Each leaf should be scrubbed with a wire brush and shot- or grit-blasted, this done—in the latter case—by means of compressed air in a sealed chamber. When thoroughly cleaned and overhauled the leaves should be smeared with grease, but not to excess. Make sure that any unwanted grease or oil used in lubrication is wiped clear, especially before cleaning the paint or bodywork of the vehicle. Thick, dirty grease or clogging oil are traps for still more dirt which forms a hard layer known to old carters and waggoners as 'coom'. When wheels and springs were long neglected and covered with this substance, which made them dry and stiff, they were described as being 'all coomed up'. When springs fracture, this is often due to the centre bolts being insecure and not sufficiently solid in a part where play is undesirable. Breakages are more likely to occur in the front springs as these are usually less sturdy than rear springs, with greater weight of draught exerted on the fore-carriage. Rust inhibitors should be applied to all ironwork, especially in exposed places. This may be old-fashioned red lead plus zinc chromate, applied with a stiffish brush.

Leather-work straps should be treated with saddle soap, which is excellent for keeping them pliable and in sound condition. A valuable preservative may be further mixed from an old recipe in which a small amount of glycerine is added to equal amounts of melted beeswax and neat's foot oil.

When an infestation of moths is suspected in the upholstery of a closed carriage, this may be cleared by vapour from a mixture of camphor and turpentine, placed in a saucer or open container on the carriage floor. All windows and doors should be firmly closed during this operation.

Restoration

Complex work in this area needs research techniques and a certain amount of study, especially if it is intended not only to make a vehicle road-worthy but as it appeared in its original form. If it is a family coach or carriage this involves some acquaintance with heraldry and the traditional colours or crests with which door panels and lower quarters may have been painted. These were also the colours of liveries worn by coachmen, grooms and footmen attending the vehicles.

For making a thorough restoration it is always useful to produce a number of sketches and plans, showing the vehicle in 'before' and 'after' sequences. The ability to draught ideas and make visual notes was always stressed to apprentices in this line of business, which may also have applied to the majority of crafts. According to an article in *The Blacksmith* for January 1901, on the craft of carriage making, 'Nothing so cultivates the eye and trains the hand to accuracy as freehand drawing'.

The first step is always to make a survey and detailed examination of the vehicle. Produce as many sketches or take as many photographs as possible, following up with measured drawings and a simple plan or outline chart for colour work. To get an idea of the original colours it may be possible to remove part of the leather lining of shafts or probe under fittings of a hood. There is usually some small place or part where the paint has been protected from the effects of strong light, showing brighter or paler, like patches of wall-paper under picture frames. Wherever possible try to make comparisons with other similar vehicles.

For extensive repairs and renewals it may be necessary to block-up the body and remove the undergear, wheels and footboard. A socket or adjustable spanner may be found necessary for all wheels and their removal. Ideally there should be a special wrench and set of tools for each vehicle in use, formerly carried on most larger types in a kit known as a budget. A list of essential tools for restoration and repair should always include a range of hammers, an adjustable wheel spanner for axle nuts and a reliable jack. Linch-pins may be removed by levering with any suitable wedge-shaped instrument, especially a cold chisel.

If in doubt make sure that wheels, at least, are examined by a qualified wheel-wright. New axleboxes and axle stubs may be the work of a blacksmith but always under the direction of a knowledgeable person, which is one of the occasions when sketches and measured drawings may be found useful. Most of the earlier or traditional vehicles were divided between owner-driven two-wheeled vehicles with sixteen spokes per wheel and the larger, four-wheeled vehicles with generally twelve spokes at the front and fourteen at the back. The former type along with a few smaller four-wheeled vehicles were made by a carriage-maker while the majority of coachman-driven four-wheelers were the concern of coach-builders. There were, however, notable exceptions, some commercial vehicles having even more spokes for both two and four-wheelers.

When passenger vehicles have been neglected for some time the seat cushions of the upholstery are either in poor condition, through damp and mildew, or entirely missing. It was an old trick to remove seating from a vehicle, often for domestic re-use, when it was to be sold, scrapped or pensioned-off. Provided the external appearance is traditional there is no reason why the internal padding should not be foam rubber or something equally modern and comfortable, especially if the vehicle is for regular use. Some museums and collectors with open vehicles on display sometimes protect the seating with a layer of transparent plastic, but where this is used always allow for the circulation of air and a certain number of vent holes.

A button-back effect for upholstery always looks smart, especially for interior backrests of the larger vehicles. The following are simple instructions for buttoning through foam-rubber (latex) or plastic substitutes. First the positions of the buttons are clearly marked out on the foam block and holes punched through the marks. Holes are then marked on the corresponding cover, making a slight allowance for compression. Pull through and secure with a reef knot, making sure that a cloth patch or tuft is inserted between the knot and underside of the cushion.

If it is decided to get rid of badly worn upholstery, which may be frayed or moth-eaten, make sure that a few samples are preserved for matching and future reference. Always keep such items in a wallet or drawer, away from strong sunlight.

Parts of woodwork suspected of woodworm infestation should be cut out and dipped in a solution of Cuprinol, or other reliable chemicals. Any renewal of woodwork may be undertaken by a person reasonably competent in the techniques of cabinet-making, which are several stages more advanced than plain carpentry. Keep as much as possible to the original wood and resist the temptation to patch up with off-cuts of anything available. While controversy still surrounds the extensive use of plywood, this is certainly good enough as flooring material.

Dealing with cracked side panels, especially on convex or outward curves, is a particular hazard in restoring the older type of coach or carriage. It may be remedied by filling the apertures with a small section of soft wood in strips, these being slightly thicker than the original panel, securing the edges with glue and trimming flush when thoroughly dry.

Colour schemes and striping or lining-out, when not in family or heraldic colours, were subject to whims of fashion and these must be well understood for authentic restoration. Lighter and brighter colours were usually associated with the late 18th century or Regency period, while darker, sombre colours are much safer for the Victorian era. When in doubt paint black, which always looks smart and effective. The harsh and gaudy colouring appearing on some pleasure vehicles at modern resorts, should be avoided at all costs. Shocking pink, pea-green and magenta have no place in any coach or carriage house.

The above are merely basic considerations as whole volumes could be written on metalwork, woodcraft and upholstery, to name but three of many crafts involved. As previously stressed, much depends on time and space available, with a high premium on craft experience.

In the early days when vehicles were comparatively simple and unsophisticated, wheelwrights, wagon- and coach-builders were often masters of several crafts. Most of their ideas were carried in their heads and very little committed to paper. Yet as styles became more complex, also the work more involved, there was greater specialisation and the use of plans or blueprints essential, needing the services of trained draughtsmen and designers. Sometimes scale models were made for demonstration purposes, all finding near parallels in the work of early boat-, barge- and ship-builders.

Towards the end of the 19th century the larger commercial plants were using a variety of machines to aid them in the more tedious and time-consuming operations. These had a particular bearing on wheels both in manufacture and repair. Wooden naves were eventually turned out by a special cutting machine, its blades or cutters set at various heights and depths, producing a finished nave or hub in one quick operation, almost untouched by hand. Felloes were made on a so-called radial machine, while iron tyres were fitted on a tyring table in which the assembled woodwork emerged from a well at the bottom of the table (under-side) to receive the glowing metal, which sank—on making contact—beneath a level of cold water.

A vehicle undergoing restoration and fitted with temporary wheels (M. Williams).

Traditional hand tools

The original hand tools for shaping spokes and other components are obviously cheaper than mechanical or power-driven equipment, but increasingly hard to find. A feeling for their proper use may be acquired through practice, mastery of technique often proving its own reward. In the early stages timber was roughly hewn with an adze or hollow axe, being a tool of prehistoric and almost universal origins. The frame saw was widely used in reducing smaller lengths of wood, while holes were bored with a long-shanked twist auger. The spokeshave, drawknife and heavy-cased jack plane, along with the hollow plane or jarvis, were smoothing and shaping tools, almost self-explanatory. The circular or wheel-like traveller and spoke set-gauge were measuring instruments, while the buzz was a form of handy V chisel, used for making points of the wheel spokes. A more complex tool for boring, known as a boxing engine, was used for making holes through wooden hubs, needing great accuracy to contain and support the smoothly fitting axlebox of cast iron or even stub arms partly covered by wearing plates. This latter gadget had a screw-down centre part which entered an auger hole, while a grip in the form of three side prongs, at top and bottom, held the hub steady. Felloes were drawn together and united by a samson, which was in the form of two parallel rods with screw-threads at one end, tightening two oblong clamps against the wheel. Spoke dogs or levers drew spokes on the spider nearer together so that they would fit into apertures of the felloes.

Many of the tools mentioned above may be seen and examined at several folk museums, especially the Museum of English Rural Life, Reading University, and St Albans City Museum, which latter has one of the largest collections of craft tools in Britain.

Painting

This is part of the finishing process which requires special attention as it contributes not only to outward appearance but to long service and durability. In the old days numerous coats of lead paint were laid, alternating between dead white and yellow ochre, often with great speed of application. After these had hardened in the space of a week or two, they were rubbed down with pummice stone and water, all external marks being eliminated and the surface made as smooth as possible. Two coats of white lead were then applied and rubbed down with sandpaper. The final colours came next, applied in up to three coats and treated with six coats of copal varnish. Two qualities of varnish were used, the hardest and most enduring being for the wheels and underframe. Before polishing all metalwork was japanned. Between eighteen and twenty coats were needed for a satisfactory paint job and even today a number of coach and carriage restorers still think in these terms. After several months of use and road work the gloss of the body would be revived by special hand polishing using combined oil and rottenstone, the latter being a silicous form of decayed limestone, deprived of its chalky matter. This was ideal for most parts of the vehicle, including both wood and metalwork. Wooden underparts were often allowed to remain unpainted as a breathing space or surface. Some coach painters refused to paint under upholstered parts for the same reason, but this is now done according to discretion and the wishes of the customer.

At one time a newly-painted coach or carriage would rest under cover for at least several weeks before going on the roads.

Modern painting

Although some people resort to spray painting techniques these are far from being to the highest standards, producing what has been termed a pitted or orange peel effect. Unfortunately paints of the quality needed for better class coachwork are increasingly harder to acquire than in former days. Some colours, especially reds, now greatly lack in richness and depth. For reasons of economy, less time is spent in preparation and rubbing down, often meaning that surfaces are less smooth than they should be, at least by pre-war standards. Yet whatever the approach it is always advisable to buy the best materials possible, especially brushes. In the long run this proves a sound economy as a good brush, well looked after, outlasts several inferior specimens. When brushes are not in use they should be thoroughly cleaned and suspended, bristles downwards, by a hole through the handle and a wire loop, in a container of turpentine. Varnish brushes should be reserved for this purpose alone. All brushes must be treated with care and both tested and perhaps broken-in, on trial surfaces, before use.

While craftsmen of only a few decades ago mixed and ground their own paints, it is now fairly common practice to use ready-mixed colours, purchased by the tin or drum according to the quantities needed.

After preparation of the tools and ground, through cleaning and scrubbing, it may be necessary to strip-off old paint to the bare surfaces. This is mainly done using chemical paint remover. The blow torch and scraper or knife are now less frequently used than in former days and, by most standards, chemical remover is thought to be fully adequate. If a blow torch is used care should be taken not to fire or over-scorch the woodwork. After wiping-up, using coarse damp paper, allow a short time for drying and then apply the first coat of oil-based primer. This latter is usually a light grey or some other neutral colour and seals the pores for taking a second coat of the same shade and texture. Cracks should now be filled, using knifing putty, plastic wood and—for the larger cracks—epoxy resin compounds. Five more coats are now laid and allowed to dry out, some of the best and most durable at this stage having a base of finely powdered slate.

After the fifth coat there should be a good rub down with sand paper of fine to medium grain. During this process surfaces should be kept moist with the aid of a large sea sponge and soapy water. Try to prevent water from entering deep cracks, wherever possible, and make sure to dry thoroughly with a good quality leather.

The next application is a half-and-half mixture of the oil-primer with the final top colour. This is rubbed down, but not too rigorously. The first and second colour coats are then added with a third coat containing enamel paint to improve the flow. The top or glazing coat contains a fair quantity of varnish. A second glazing coat is often advisable but not always necessary.

It may be noted that rustic or country cars and carts were often left unpainted in the colour of the natural wood, although protected by layers of varnish. This looks highly effective on the float and governess car but less so on some of the more elegant types. Avoid any attempts at false graining or staining.

Lining-out or striping

For lining-out the areas concerned are flattened and rubbed down with fine grade sandpapers. Colours are taken from sealed tubes and are the types favoured by sign-writers and decorative artists. They are usually thinned with pure turpentine only, avoiding-substitute turpentine and petrol-based thinners. Once the lining has dried out it is wiped over with a damp or tack rag to clear off any dust or foreign matter. The pattern of lining is then covered with extra coats of pale body varnish, sometimes three but more frequently two in number. Gold leaf for striping and other decorative work is applied by pressing the leaf from a sheet or strip on to a prepared surface of size. This is now very expensive and a satisfactory substitute is obtained from a mixture of powdered bronze and varnish, sometimes mixed or thinned with a dash of turpentine. Too much turpentine, however, imparts a grey and lifeless appearance.

There are several types and thicknesses of stripe or lining-out, ranging from the hair-line through fine, stout, round, narrow and heavy stripes to broad line. These are also used in combinations of double fine lines, double stout lines, double round lines and fine line centre, narrow stripe and parallel fine lines, full stripes, divided stripes and divided stripe with distance fine lines. Brushes for lining are known as pencils, there being two main types or larger and smaller, also known as swords and daggers. The dagger has all its hairs or bristles of two

A newly-restored gig (M. Williams).

inch length mounted in the quill of a feather, while the sword has hairs of graduated lengths attached to a wooden handle by wires or a ferrule. Some painters now use a striping or lining wheel, in which paint flows on to a revolving wheel from saturated fabric contained within a well of the handle. These latter, however, are difficult to use in certain restricted areas.

Lettering on vehicles

This is seen at its best on early farm wagons, in a tradition later adopted for use on canal boats and river barges, known as 'shadowgraph'. Many carts and wagons had the name of the owner and farm address displayed on the front or headboards, each letter with a depth of shading which accounts for its style and title. These are generally in a bold sans-serif style without finials, although sometimes one sees debased forms of Roman lettering such as Ionic or Egyptian with square serifs or finials. The gothic or black letter form, although sometimes appearing on both wagons and stage coaches, was a mid-Victorian innovation or revival and often looks out of place on horse-drawn vehicles.

Names and destinations frequently appeared on the sides of stage coaches. Larger letters were usually outlined rather than shaded although shading was also used, often applied with gilding to smaller names and words. Where shading was used this was of a shallower depth than on wagons. The most familiar style of coach lettering was the block form in which there is equal thickness of both cross and down strokes. Cyphers or monograms appeared either as round-hand letters or Roman capitals. Lettering was far more discrete on mail than on stage coaches and usually in a better style.

The much-neglected art of the sign writer should always appear bold and flowing, as though conscious of scale and space, all of which harmonises with the sweep and freedom of long haired brushes and well-diluted (but not over-diluted) colours of normal practice. While the use of a chalked snapline, to keep a level, and a cushioned mahlstick to steady the wrist (rather than the hand) are permissible, tracings and templates should be avoided as too mechanical, also the immature niggling which implies lack of decision or a cautious, untrained approach. Sign-writing is at its worst when over-ornate or imitating the comparatively cramped, confined qualities of letterpress, the latter being adequate and desirable in its own sphere, but unsuitable for large-scale work. It is, above all, a form of painting rather than printing.

Chapter 9

Acquiring the right vehicle

An obvious precondition in choosing a vehicle is the activity in which the would-be owner wishes to engage. Apart from those kept for exhibition and in private collections, the choice—at least from the period shortly after the Second World War—has its limitations, although gradually improving with the increase of makers and repairers. Unfortunately large numbers of privately owned vehicles were sold either for scrap or to overseas buyers, many of the more interesting types finding their way to the United States. Magnificent examples of the coach-and carriage-builder's craft changed hands at unrealistic prices, more than a few ending on mass bonfires as the quickest way to salvage metal for re-sale. During the 1950s very few were able to foresee the revival of interest in horse-drawn vehicles, which only began seriously ten or twelve years later, to which increasing scarcity may have partly contributed. Ever since the 1920s a number of old vehicles from Broughams to bakers' vans, especially the headed types, ended their days as chicken coops or garden tool sheds, surviving a number of years in their less dignified role as a tribute to the soundness of their construction. The author recollects seeing one particular coach, at a hotel in the West Midlands, fitted up as a telephone box for guests and patrons.

The position has now changed for the better as more individuals and firms are becoming interested in the restoration of old vehicles and even the introduction of new types. With the increased value and appreciation of older vehicles there is also less likelihood of seeing works of fine craftsmanship smashed-up in cross-country activities or by the inexperienced and over-enthusiastic novice. Strong but lightweight vehicles for eventing and the more practical side of training and competitive driving have at last become a reality, some firms and individual makers specialising in their construction.

Those wishing to drive for pleasure over park roads or in quiet lanes, usually country dwellers or those with access to the right locations, have far more scope than either the collector of older types or the more active enthusiast. Yet however personal and intimate such interests may be, driving is bound to have its public side, with the increasing lure of group or club activities and the need to show, if only at local level. This makes it advisable to choose something both strongly made yet elegant, acceptable as a piece of solid craftsmanship while respecting the demands of taste and tradition. These types may include several varieties of gig and dogcart, the ralli car, float and governess car, also a fairly wide range of phaetons. There is no reason why some lighter vehicles used by tradesmen for delivery purposes, until the 1950s, should not be revived—at least

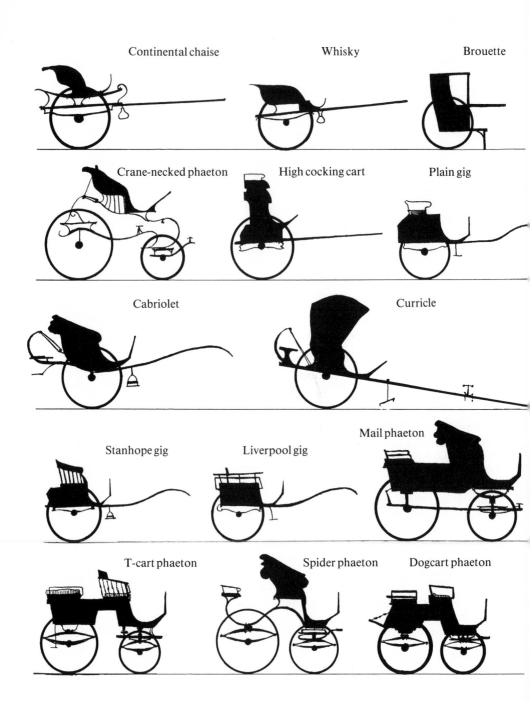

Sketch silhouettes of notable vehicles I

as a private interest—as many of these were pleasing, almost sporting in appearance—especially the lighter weight, two-wheeled types. These, however, may raise a few eyebrows among the pundits and would be difficult to place in show classes.

Before deciding on the exact vehicle to buy it may be a good idea to browse through some of the more recent catalogues of coach and carriage makers, a number of which are now available as reprints. Mention has already been made of the majority of better-known types in earlier parts of this text, while there are a number of other books and pamphlets worth consulting, if only to increase breadth of knowledge and appreciation. It is soon realised that there are numerous variations of the same vehicle, some of which have only minor differences, causing endless confusion even in the heyday of driving. For the novice this tends to be daunting, although learning to recognise the key types is all that really matters—a skill soon acquired through interest and intelligent observation. Popular types were often named after their designer or builder, especially the former, who may have been a person of perception, with an interest in driving for its own sake and even a scientific bent to improve existing standards. Such men were either of independent means or involved in professions or trades far removed from coach building, passing on their ideas— with notes and perhaps sketches—to the actual makers. In this way the Brougham was named after Lord Brougham and Vaux, mainly interested in education and legal reform; the Hansom cab was named after a famous architect, while the Stanhope gig and phaeton were named after the Hon Fitzroy Stanhope, a notable amateur whip of the period but far from being a practical craftsman. One reason for such diversity of types is that in a world of versatile craftsmen and numerous small firms employing them, the prospective buyer could walk into almost any workshop and suggest a custom-made model with special fittings according to his whim, some of which took the public imagination and were ordered by other clients, spawning a new breed.

Not so many years ago, it was possible to find the type of vehicle most desired without too much trouble. Some were jacked-up or hanging from the rafters of coach houses at private residences, or even in farm sheds and barns. Yet by the 1980s many of these survivals, both urban and rural, have been cleared out and either demolished or modernised. It is still possible to find the odd treasure in a cart lodge, but no longer rightfully expected, even the buildings—in some areas—being under threat of destruction.

Advertising and answering advertisements in local papers, especially those of country towns and rural areas, is one of the ways to make a purchase by private contract, to which all the rules of ordinary purchase should apply, plus extra caution from the novice's viewpoint. There is also a range of magazines and journals either relating to horse matters or country-sporting interests, in which there may be classified sections devoted to the sale of vehicles, more reliable than ordinary newspapers. A list of such magazines may be found in the bibliography.

An inexperienced person should always be prepared to take a more knowledgeable friend to view the object of purchase, even to rely on the judgment of a qualified agent or go-between. It is also sensible to get in touch with a local wheelwright, finding his address in a trade guide or the yellow pages of the telephone directory. When involving oneself with a third party, however, always make sure in advance of any fees or commissions expected for services rendered. While inspecting a vehicle or making a purchase ask sensible questions but normally speak as little as possible, looking, listening and touching within the bounds of common-sense. Beware of dealers touring the country on a 'here-today-and-gone-tomorrow' basis, many of whom are eager to batten on the novice as an easy victim. There are still such people about, although declining in numbers, against whom the main line of defence is to insist on credentials and a permanent address. It is perhaps needless to say that a thorough inspection and even a trial run, wherever possible, are essential parts of the sale procedure. Buying through the post on the evidence of a few snapshots alone, faded or otherwise, is far from desirable. At all times try to establish, with as much tact as possible, the background and reliability of the vendor and need for disposal. In all cases the old saying 'let the buyer beware' should be uppermost in the mind of any would-be purchaser.

Many vehicles and items connected with horses are sold at long-established horse fairs such as Appleby and Stow-in-the-Wold, to name but two of the more outstanding. These places, however, are not recommended to any but old hands and those experienced in the arts of dealing. Only go to such places, if determined to purchase, in the company of a friend and witness.

A further alternative is to attend sales by public auction either in established markets or at farms and country houses 'under the hammer'. Sadly, there are times when even a large and well-known collection has to be reduced, dispersed or abandoned, for a number of genuine reasons, the fairly recent sale of the Royal Umpire Exhibition at Croston, Lancashire being a case in point. There are many auctioneers in country towns dealing with such goods and properties and it is possible to have one's name added to their regular mailing lists. Some of the better-known collections, however, may be sold by London auctioneers with household names. When attending an auction always allow plenty of opportunity to view the goods offered, well in advance or on the special viewing day. Keeping a cool head and not being carried away by excitement of the moment is an obvious precaution, not always remembered, despite the hard-learnt lessons of a more conventional British up-bringing and education.

The main auctioneers for horse-drawn vehicles, are now the Reading firm of Thimbleby and Shoreland, by whom sales of vehicles, horses and livestock have been held on a monthly basis for over a century, also holding—in recent years—at least three annual sales of carriages and harness. Do not expect vehicles or other items at these sales to exchange hands at knock-down prices, much depending—especially for the home buyer—on the relative strength of the pound sterling. The Reading sales of the above firm are now something of an international event, with dealers and private buyers from countries as far apart as Holland, France, Spain, Scandinavia, the United States and Australia. It is still possible, however, for the knowing person to acquire a sound vehicle of the unrestored type—at reasonable prices—with only minor faults which may be corrected to make it a real bargain. At such sales the antiques and museum pieces fetch the best prices, especially if they are in good condition. At the May Sales in 1978 one of the top prices in the four-wheeled section, was £6,300 for an unusual type of town coach used by the Stonor family for several generations, being something of an heirloom. Lower down the scale an Irish gig sold for £260, while exercise carts went for between £120 and £60 each, the cheaper ones being of modern design and recent construction but well-used. At the September sale for 1979 there was an entry of 132 vehicles, with 1,500 lots covering

Britschka

Dress chariot

Barouche

Square landau

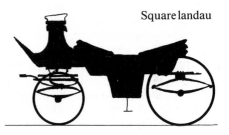

Brougham

Victoria

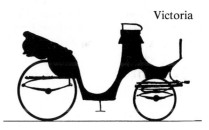

Brake

Wagonette

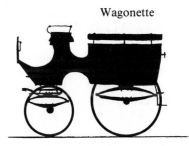

Sketch silhouettes of notable vehicles II

vehicles, harness and spares. At this sale the top price was £9,500 for a park drag or private coach, previously owned by Edward Slater-Harrison Esq, in need of repainting, which appears not to have left the coach house since the late 1930s. This was bought by a west country interest against stiff competition from Dutch, French and German bidders. A louvred or slatted tandem cart, being a form of dogcart for show purposes, went for £2,600, bought by a member of the British Driving Society, again in the teeth of strong overseas competition. A hearse was sold for £435 and drays or trollies, as used by street traders, for £600 each. It may be noted that a hearse was always well looked after and seldom over-used, well-horsed and with a light load, so that survivors are usually in good condition and suitable either for conversion or to cannibalise for spares.

One of the most popular two-wheeled vehicles for amateurs or the novice is the governess car, of which large numbers were still being made up to and even during the Second World War. Some sell for well over £300 each, but those in need of repainting and repairs may cost less than £100. Popular or fashionable names of London makers such as Offord or Mills, help to raise the price of these or other vehicles. When purchasing, however, do not be deceived by trade names stamped on the metal hubcaps, as these are interchangeable and not always the originals.

Advice is no substitute for experience but the following remarks may at least serve as a guide to help avoid the worst errors and pitfalls of purchasing. The first part to inspect and judge is the framework and undercarriage of a vehicle on which the body rests. Second to this may be the wheels, followed by the shafts (if a shafted and single-horse vehicle), and later the body or upper works. Wood rot may be one of the worst, yet least obvious, dangers, especially with older vehicles, working from the inside of the fabric to the outside and not always visible. Even when on or near the surface it is a common trick to disguise it (as much as possible) beneath layers of new paint and putty, although it is amazing how many beginners are deceived by even the most sketchy patchwork. For this reason the safest vehicle to buy is the unpainted but merely varnished rustic cart. Test surfaces by pressure of the hand, patting and pressing wherever unsound work may be suspected. The pointed blade of a pocket knife or even the finger nails may be useful in this context, but not always to the liking of the vendor. It was an old Romany ploy to buy a vehicle only at dusk or after dark, as lamplight often shows imperfections much better than the variable light of morning and early afternoon. Beware of recently or badly painted vehicles, where third-rate craftsmanship may hide a multitude of sins. Most genuine workers are far from eager to be involved in a swindle, while the insincere vendor is likely to be unskilled and greedy.

Worm holes are often seen in old or neglected vehicles, as in antique furniture and picture frames. The importance of these is sometimes exaggerated as the worm may have long become extinct. This is, however, a relative matter and too many wormholes are obviously an unsightly imperfection. Yet as long as there are only a few holes and the worm has ceased its activities, they may be ignored. If the worm is still alive and active this may be tested by finding a powdery substance in one or more of the holes. There are several firms able to treat this condition at reasonable costs, although the need for such trouble should greatly influence the asking price. Worm-eaten wheels and shafts, in particular, if untreated, may lead to serious accidents.

When examining wheels make sure that each set matches-up as a pair, even the slightest difference between opposites making for serious trouble when driving, also lowering the value of the vehicle for showing, exhibition or resale. Examine for loose or ill-fitting spokes which may prove dangerous, unless receiving immediate attention.

Iron tyres should fit snugly on the felloes or wooden outer parts of each wheel, again a matter of possible danger and trouble, if unchecked. Where rubber tyres are used (solid rubber), these may be either perished or badly worn down especially on a well-used but neglected vehicle, distorting the iron channels in which the rubberwork is fitted. Wheels which seem to shake and wobble, when the vehicle is man-handled or pushed about, are a sure indication of wear but may be adjusted by fitting extra washers, usually of leather. Where there are doors, lockers or tailboards make sure these open properly, opening and shutting them several times, to judge the soundness not only of the woodwork but of handles and hinges.

Although some vehicles have adjustable shafts it is essential to consider all types in relation to the animal intended to work between them. The height of the vehicle may be raised or lowered by at least four inches by the introduction of special blocks of wood, set in or drawn out from the space between leaf springs and axles. Shafts that are too long and large or far too short, make for difficulties in harnessing (putting to), further imparting too much sway to the bodywork and unsteadiness of motion to the wheels. On the other hand, tight, stubby shafts may annoy the horse through over-tight fitting and lead to kicking, fretting and a general unwillingness to face work. Narrow shafts may chafe and gall the flanks, while short, badly-formed shafts may bring the hindquarters too near the dashboard and bodywork, also bruising the upper hocks. A minor detail, although leading to some annoyance, if unchecked, is the soundness and security of brass ferrules on the tips of the shafts which sometimes fly off and get lost even during man-handling. These are frequently loose or damaged if the shafts have been dropped a few times on hard surfaces or in any way abused. In this connection it may be noted that a vehicle should always be man-handled in and out of its coach house or lodge, as driving horses into buildings can lead to all kinds of nasty accidents.

Of the five or six main types of vehicle for driving purposes in modern conditions, the float and the governess car or tub cart are the least suitable for anything beyond road work, as these are low-slung and often fitted with cranked axles, bringing them near the surface of the ground. The seating is fairly low, either sideways-facing or far back in the body of the vehicle, making the keen observation necessary in obstacle tests and cross-country work difficult. For cross-country driving and eventing it is an advantage for the driver to be fairly high at the front, but not too high, as near the horse or team as possible and square-on to his work. Most varieties of phaeton, dogcart and gig are suitable for eventing, unless it is an international contest, although—to some ways of thinking—these are better preserved for sedate driving or exhibition purposes, especially when attractive for their own sake. It may be noted that vehicles for international events under official rules, must have four wheels with seating for a driver, travelling referee and up to two grooms or assistants. The brakes may be either of the hand lever or foot pedal type, operating on the rear wheels. The weight must be a minimum of 600 kg with no part of any vehicle more than 1.6 m in width.

One of the better types of small vehicle now used in competitive driving, especially for ponies, is known as the Fenix phaeton or Fenix dogcart, made by the firm of G.P. Worsley and Co of St Helens, Merseyside, now very popular in the North of England. This is a small-sized dogcart phaeton, minus the inner compartment for gundogs and external slats of the original type, suitable for either a pair or team. It has all-welded steel underworks or chassis, metal-spoked wheels and wooden upperworks. The under-lock or turning circle, positioning of the wheels and adequate braking (contact by foot pedal), makes this both safe and swift-moving for even the roughest terrain. It is also available as a do-it-yourself kit, at reduced cost, although some models are given the luxury treatment, finished and lined-out in the best traditions.

A further range of vehicles of modern design and sturdy construction are John Willie carts, originally named after a Shetland pony owned by the founders of the firm responsible for their design. These were originally pony-sized exercise carts on tubular steel frames with rubber or pneumatic tyres, selling—in the smaller versions—for about £50 each, but now retailing, after a decade or so, in the region of £200. A later and larger type now closely resembles the Cape Cart on wooden spoked wheels, first appearing in 1974, followed by versions of the dogcart phaeton and an up-dated governess car.

Some firms are also producing four-wheeled vehicles of a larger type, suitable for international events at all levels, one of which was shown on the BBC programme 'Tomorrow's World'. This is the Daresbury phaeton (named after the celebrated amateur whip Lord Daresbury), produced by Messrs Crofords, having a unique spare wheel, shock absorbers (coil springs) and hydraulic disc-brakes, the chassis being of hollow steel section throughout, although the upperworks are of wood finish in a traditional style. The larger vehicles of this type are made only to order. The Harewood Carriage Co, mentioned in an earlier chapter, have also made outstanding contributions to the design and safety of larger vehicles for eventing.

There are still a number of firms in Britain able to repair, renovate or construct horse-drawn vehicles, working to the highest standards, including a few individuals with small yards working on a semi-professional or part-time basis. These seem unlikely to decline in numbers, according to current trends.

In November 1979 a leading maker quoted in the region of £1,500 for a two-wheeled dogcart (to order) and between £2,000 and £3,000 for a four-wheeled dogcart phaeton, all in the larger horse sizes.

Buying and selling as an investment

The horse-drawn vehicle is often a sure hedge against inflation, as there is little reason to doubt that prices are likely to rise or remain stable within the foreseeable future. Apart from other motives, including sentiment, the investment angle of all purchases of a capital nature must now be faced as a reality. This may be deplored by some, but their consolation should be that vehicles are at least kept in circulation to be appreciated by as wide a range of people as possible.

In general terms it is better to acquire vehicles of British rather than foreign origins. Numerous continental vehicles were recently imported into this country for sale purposes, some of fine workmanship, but large numbers either badly put together or in second-rate condition through botched repairs. Former commercial prosperity in Britain, during the period when large numbers of carriages were still being used in daily life, often promoted a better state of

Left *A stage coach in Bakesley Hall Birmingham Branch Museum. Note the steps for reaching the roof seats* (K. Bennett). **Right** *An open lot gypsy living van from the collection of the Hereford and Worcester County Museum* (M.H. Brindley).

finish and soundness of workmanship than in countries undergoing internal revolutions, economic depressions and a subsequent decline in standards of living. As the standards set for traditional quality and appearance of horse-drawn vehicles, especially of the later types, were also dominated by British taste and enterprise, even good continental vehicles are a sounder proposition if they look as British as possible.

Those which are intended for resale should be essentially of a type for which there is a general demand. A fire engine or station bus is not so likely to find a ready buyer as a gig or phaeton which may appear in the show ring or be used for combined driving events.

Make sure, when offering vehicles for sale through public auction, that all information and catalogue descriptions are as helpful and accurate as possible, which may need some research into origins, but avoids both doubt and confusion. Those who sell to a disappointed or unsure customer may find it difficult to sell a second or third time. In the large, modern sales of the 1980s, it may not always be possible for the auctioneer or his agents to examine every item with the thoroughness it may deserve, putting the vendor on his personal honour.

A basically sound type of vehicle should not require a great deal of restoration and repainting, but whenever this is done make sure that it is up to the most acceptable standards. Obviously botched handiwork is likely to make the better-informed purchaser suspicious, even to a point where faults may be exaggerated, or suspected where they never existed. The cheaper vehicle, however, needs less attention than the more elegant and expensive types as the

A farmer's float in the Hereford and Worcester Museum (M.H. Brindley).

cost of repairs and repainting might be almost the same for both while the margin of profit on luxury items may be very much higher in proportion. Without scratching and skimping, try to put a realistic limit on the amount of time and money spent on renovation. Buyers down-market are also more interested in the do-it-yourself angle than those with a longer purse, so that cheaper vehicles such as the tub cart or float do not greatly benefit from too elaborate or expensive a treatment.

Valuable hints for repainting should always include the following. It is unwise to overpaint with synthetic or modern cellulose paint over a basis of traditionally-treated coachwork. The pigments blended with linseed oil do not mix with synthetic paints and may eventually curdle, causing cracks and lumps like the hide of a reptile. It is also unwise to spray-paint any part of a vehicle with iron or steel tyres, especially the wheels, as this leads to cracking and flaking through vibration, often in a very short time.

Always ensure that a vehicle offered for sale has sound wheels, while for the more expensive types the original upholstery, or something as near like it as possible, is a great asset. When renewal of interior trim is essential, keep as much to the original style as possible, which also applies to other fittings, avoiding the appearance of a second-rate hybrid. Most vehicles intended for export should be more carefully restored than those for local or home sale, as repair and restoration costs may be even higher in countries abroad, especially in the United States.

Most vehicles sell reasonably well throughout the year, although it is generally better to offer show types early in the season, such as spring or early summer, rather than in autumn or during the winter months.

Chapter 10

Harness and driving

Horses are harnessed and driven in different teams according to the draught of their vehicles and the type of presentation. A single horse is usually within shafts, except for the native Ekka cart of India, with its single pole above the back and hind quarters of the draught animal, or chain gear for hauling certain agricultural implements. The single horse and vehicle is obviously more economical to keep and easier to drive than a pair or larger team, associated with smaller types and the owner-driver rather than with stately carriages kept more for display than utility. From the late 18th century a number of more daring people have driven tandem, either horses or ponies, but this is not a practical proposition in modern traffic and far from efficient as a means of draught. It is, however, a fine sight in the show ring and has also been adopted in some cross-country events, with variable success. When heavy farm or commercial horses are used in tandem this is a far different matter as slower teams are easier to control and often needed in certain combinations for space

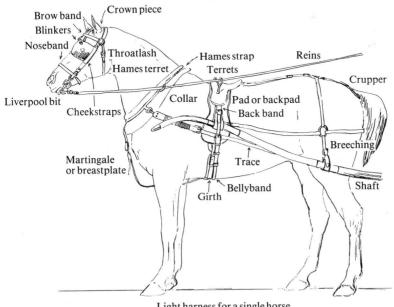

Light harness for a single horse

144   *Collecting and restoring horse-drawn vehicles*

saving and general economy. Double shafts were infrequently seen, except in East Anglia. Three horses in line are sometimes wrongly described as tandem but are more correctly in trandem, and rarely seen at any period.

Shafts usually project from the front of two-wheeled vehicles, fitting inside, outside or under the bodywork according to the type encountered. Exceptions are found with certain floats and cab-fronted vehicles on which supporting brackets—at the front—may be used. With four-wheeled types they are hinged or pivoted, attached to special futchells, loops or rods.

Two horses side-by-side are known as a pair and harnessed to a coach, carriage or wagon pole, apart from those in plough gear. Horses three abreast are now a rarity, seldom popular in Britain, although once commonplace in Russia, where they were known as a troika, also in France, for hauling buses and street cars. Some British fire engines were drawn by three horses abreast. During the second half of the 19th century there was a short-lived craze in Europe and America, but especially in the United States, for driving a version of the cocking cart to three horses abreast.

A pair next to the vehicle and one ahead is known as driving unicorn, while a single horse in the shafts and two or more ahead is known as pickaxe. Heavier vehicles may be drawn by teams of four or six, while at one period eight horses and upwards were not unusual for certain loads. The leading horses of large teams were controlled by men on foot while with a coach or carriage the lead horses, of a team of six or more, were usually ridden and driven by postillions. The legendary forty-horse hitch was sometimes driven in American shows and circus parades, although similar large teams were also used to draw the first combine harvesters in the wheat belt of the Middle West, before the introduction of tractors and self-powered machinery. The terms shaft- and thill-horses relate to those in shafts, while leaders are at the head of a team and wheelers next to the vehicle. An extra horse used on a steep gradient is a cock-horse, when ridden, and a chain-horse when worked in chain gears and not ridden. At one period extra horses were often kept at the foot of a hill, some-times hired out by their owners, provided by charitable institutions interested in animal welfare (Our Dumb Friends' League), or by commercial firms with vehicles in regular operation over that route.

The main elements of harness would be bridle, draught collar, pad saddle or ridge pad—secured by girth and bellyband, and the rear part or breeching holding back the load on a steep hill. For leaders of teams and the gear of plough horses, also for reasons of fashion and display, breeching was not always worn, especially during the second half of the 19th century. A crupper or looped strap enclosed the tail, joined to the pad saddle by a meeter strap, while on some forms of harness a false martingale (the true martingle is worn by saddle horses) passes between the fore-legs from the girth and attaches to the lower part of the collar, sometimes ornamented with brasses, especially on horses drawing wagons and commercial vehicles.

The bridle is used to support the bit, with loop or ring attachments for the reins, as a means of control. It encloses the head and sides of the face with a number of narrow straps and lashings, most of which are self-explanatory, such as brow band, nose band and throat lash. Straps under the chin and above the nose are not always present, especially on heavy horses for farm work and in the United States or Canada. Heavy draught or cart horse harness is much heavier and broader than for lighter work and smaller draught animals. Blinkers or

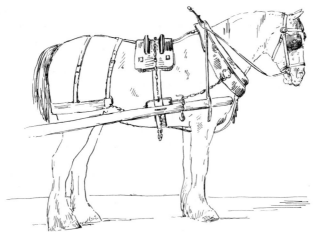

Heavy harness for a single horse

winkers, both correct but the former at least sounding more sensible, are worn by most draught horses in Britain, these being square or rounded leather guards projecting forwards from cheek straps but further held in place by leads from a V strap above the head or poll. Blinkers prevent the horse from seeing the following vehicle or load which might cause alarm, especially in a younger horse. As a grazing animal of the plains the horse relied very much on seeing both forwards and backwards—ever on the look out for a concealed hunter or beast of prey—without moving its head too far in either direction, for which the position of its eye-sockets (partly at the front and partly at the side of the head) was ideal.

The neck collar or draught collar with its curved bars or hames, fitting into grooves or depressions on either side of the neck, formed attachments for rein rings (territs) and traces or tug chains, leading back to either shafts or the actual vehicle. The metal fittings are essentially part of the hames rather than the leather collar, although fitting together like hand and glove. Neck collars were always made by a specialist craftsman and considered ideal for the British draught horse with its high neck and shoulders, but had to be an individual fit to avoid making sore places or neck galls. The collar is put on upside-down before the rest of harness, with its wider or lower part at the top, turned to the correct position at the base of the neck. An alternative is the easier-fitting breast collar or harness, more suitable for lighter draught and conditions in warmer climates, also favoured for military harness since the turn of the century and still used in

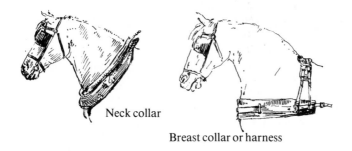

Neck collar

Breast collar or harness

gun teams of the Royal Horse Artillery (King's Troop). Breast harness had the advantage of being easy to fit and change, often necessary in wagon or gun teams when a horse might be killed or injured and its replacement needed at short notice.

The pad saddle or ridge pad lies in the centre or slight hollow of the back, just behind the shoulders (withers), having a cross strap (for heavy draught horses a ridge-chain or ridger), holding up the shafts on either side of the body. The crupper links with the pad saddle to prevent it sliding forwards, also supporting the rear-side straps or hip and loin straps which hold the broad, horizontal band or web of the breeching. Breeching was of great assistance to a horse both in backing and holding on steep and slippery surfaces. In later years it was more evident with commercial horses and shunned by the more snobbish Victorians for this reason, being partly a whim of fashion. With the harness of the royal state coaches a heavy form of breeching was retained even for the leaders.

With a pair of horses on either side of a pole the fore-end or head of the pole was attached to loops known as kidney links, on the draught collars, by means of chains and straps, rearward traces being attached to upright rollers or roller bolts on the splinter bar or to horizontal bars or swingletrees. Traces of the leaders led back to swingletrees joined to a double tree, in turn hooked to the head of the pole. It may be noted that swingletrees are also known as whipple, wipple or whiffletrees and such an arrangement for leaders as 'a set of wiffletrees'. On the type of vehicle (having reliable brakes) drawn by a four-in-hand team, at least in more fashionable circles, breeching was not always considered suitable or necessary. Reins for a pair or team are crossed, split and coupled between horses so that the driver may control each and all with a single hand. Back reference should be made at this point to a section of chapter three, dealing with private coaching. Bits worn by horses driven in teams usually have long cheek pieces and horizontal bottom bars under the chins, to keep the reins from being confused or tangled with those of their partners. Leaders do not usually wear breeching, while their reins also pass through rings on the bridles and saddle or ridge pads of the following pairs. In the old days the reins passed through a ring or loop on top of the head.

With tandem harness the wheeler is attached to the shafts in a form of so-called gig harness with a single, rearward trace-carrying strap or kicking strap in place of full breeching. There are also split rein loops or territs on the ridge pad, reins from the leader passing backwards through the upper half. A buckle on the hame tugs or straps leading to the shafts, accommodates the traces of the leader. The fore-horse is always without breeching, its traces carried on a single loin strap.

In unicorn teams the fore-horse is attached in front of the pair by means of a swingletree, while with pickaxe teams there is a set of swingletrees preceding the harness of the rearward or wheel horse.

Curricle gear, as previously discussed, involves the joining together of a pair by means of cross or T bars attached to both pad saddles and draught pole. The main draught effort, however, is through leather traces between collar and swingletree.

Some farm vehicles and implements have chain gear or traces and, in using such items as ploughs or harrows, frequently dispense with saddle pad or cart saddle (the pad is known as a cart saddle or saddle for heavy horses), breeching and crupper.

Harness can be either black or brown, which is largely a matter of taste, although at one time brown was considered more fashionable. Black patent leather is mainly used for more formal coaches and carriages. Reins are always brown or a natural colour, whatever the colour of the harness. An effort should be made not to combine plain with patent leather or brown with black. When in doubt aim at something neat, although darker rather than lighter, with matching parts.

Harness in greater detail

The preceding part of this chapter was mainly a general description of harness, now followed by more detailed comments.

Bits: There are a great number of bits used for different purposes but the main driving type is now the Liverpool bit, with cheek, middle and lower bars. This should be a good individual fit and neither too large nor too small, both the latter tending to bruise the mouth or pinch the lips and sides of the mouth. The exact position of the mouthpiece is variable, depending on the type of horse but usually said to have two inches above the corner tooth for a mare and one inch for a gelding. The average Liverpool bit has four possible adjustments or positions, which are further listed as plain cheek, half—or 'rough'—cheek, middle and bottom bar. With plain cheek the rein is merely buckled to the ring of the cheek piece. With half cheek the rein is buckled round the bar of the bit, under the mouthpiece and inside the ring, giving the driver better control than with plain cheek. The middle bar imparts additional driving control—this can be increased either by lowering the bit in the mouth or by tightening the curb chain under the chin. The lower or bottom bar is seldom used and mainly reserved for horses which try to gain control by pulling and boring. In the hands of a novice or unskilled driver it may cause both unnecessary pain and damage to the mouth.

Curb chain: This is a single chain fitting under the chin which has to be twisted from left to right before fitting, so that the links lie flat in a chin-groove under the lower jaw. When the end link had been placed on the curb hook of the bit, adjustments are made by taking up the slack and tightening or loosening link-by-link. In a correct or average fit it should be possible to insert two fingers, side-by-side and edgeways-on, between the chain and the lower jaw of the horse.

Bridle: This is a complex of straps named after their position and functions. The cheek straps/pieces are known collectively as a headstall, the main pieces of which should be in a parallel and upright position on either side of the face, a little behind the cheekbone and not too far forward. The throat lash or latch, fits under the lower jaw near its junction with the neck in a diagonal position, tight enough to check the headstall and prevent this from slipping either backwards or forwards, but not being too tight. The nose band is at right angles to the cheekstraps, about three fingers' breadth above the nostrils. Blinkers should be fairly tight and even, preventing the horse from glimpsing its rearward load, but not too close to the eyes. Those that are too tight tend to gall and cause general irritation.

Reins: These are the main form of control and communication between driver and horse. They may be wide or narrow according to taste and the size of the driver's hands but, for general purposes, are about an inch across. Thick reins are harder to control than thin reins, but very thin reins soon become soft and slippery, tending to stretch in wet weather conditions. Bearing reins are often less severe than they at first seem, essential for a horse with poor head carriage or one which bores and constantly lowers it head. They are, however, frequently an adjunct of fashion and display—sometimes abused—and should never be worn by horses pulling a heavy load. Use and adjustment is always a matter of experience and should not be considered the domain of the novice.

Coupling reins: These are used for pair-horse driving and consist of two parts per rein. They are the long draught rein forming direct control between the driver and horse and the short or coupling rein, adjusted by a buckle to different lengths, branching from the draught rein to the bit of the second horse.

Collar: This must lie flat on the shoulders of the horse and should always be of sound leather, well lined. Galls on the neck are caused either by too loose or too tight a fit. With a loose or over-sized collar this tends to rock about and chafe the skin, while looking clumsy and unsightly. The hames should fit neatly and snugly into their grooves, buckled at the top, as tightly as possible, by means of the hame strap or toplatch. To prevent hames from being knocked out of position, which sometimes happens when a sudden stop is made, a false martingale is often fastened over the links at the bottom of the collar. It is more essential to ensure a correct fit with a set or pair of team harness than for a single horse.

Breast collar: This ensures greater freedom for the horse but many drivers claim that it is impossible to get as much solid work out of an animal harnessed in this way, compared to the neck collar. Much, however, seems to depend on attitude and individual choice. Ideally the breast collar should be fairly high and the breast strap—though its centre—as near horizontal as possible.

Traces: These should be neither too long nor too short. A horse too far from its work on long traces is not so well able to pull as those on a shorter trace, although it is equally unsound to have the rear parts of the animal too near the dashboard.

Backband, bellyband and girth: These must be adjusted to prevent the shafts appearing too high or too low. Those which are too high are awkward and unsightly, while those which are too low pull down extra and unnecessary weight on the back of the horse. Bellybands are usually looser on double than on single harness, allowing a width of at least three fingers between girth and bellyband.

Pad saddle: This should be fairly light and not too tight fitting, well-padded on the underside. It should be well-placed in the centre of the back. When going a long distance down hill or on a steeply falling gradient it may be better to tighten the pad, especially if no breeching is worn, to prevent it slipping forward, which may chafe and gall the elbows of the fore-legs.

Crupper: This should be just tight enough to prevent the pad saddle from slipping forwards. Make sure that the leather is at all times fairly pliable or supple and that all hairs of the tail are passed through the hole or tailpiece together and in the right direction.

Breeching: This is necessary in steep and hilly country. It should hang about 13 inches from the dock of the tail, in a horizontal position. There are several types of breeching but the most commonly used fastens to slots in the shafts, about half way down their length.

Brasses: These are ornamental, worn mainly by commercial and heavier draught horses. Of pagan origins they were said to ward-off the evil eye and ensure a good harvest. The more traditional type are found as a facepiece between the eyes or on the martingale between the fore-legs. They range from geometrical motifs to stars, faces, horse-shoes, windmills, leaping horses and even railway locomotives. Some are commemorative.

The technique of driving

There are two main ways in which a novice may learn to drive, although it is an advantage to have had some previous knowledge of horses before embarking on either course. One method is to take instruction either at a school of driving or from a friend already driving, while the other is to make a study of various books, pamphlets and articles which have been published during the past few years. Try to make initial experiments in traffic-free areas or on private roads. Wherever possible use an older and fully experienced horse, which has been driven by a number of different people. This latter is as much for the sake of the horse as for the driver or passenger. There are now several schools and similar places, in different parts of the country, running courses for driving and other branches of horse-mastership, some on a residential basis.

It is better to drive in the traditional English manner as this is more elegant than other styles and provides better control over the horse or pony. This is to hold the reins in the left hand and the whip in the right, both of which are used for guiding and as aids. Some Americans, including the stage coach drivers of the old west, used the reins with both hands, as did many British tradesmen and country folk. The safest and most acceptable method, however, is a hand for the reins and a hand for the whip.

The right hand is essentially for the whip, which is used not only to touch the horse but to make hand signals to other road users. If, when learning to drive, a whip feels too heavy and clumsy, it is better to use a light stick, at least for the first few lessons. The whip should be well-balanced in the palm of the hand, pointing in the direction of the left or near-side of the horse, but carried well up and away from its hind quarters. The only part to strike is between the collar and the pad and never on the hind quarters or behind the pad, which latter may encourage backward kicking. Make a definite stroke rather than a flick, the weight behind the blow depending on the temperament of the horse. A horse which is lazy and lethargic needs a much stronger blow than one which is lively and high-spirited, but never strike too hard or use the whip as an instrument of dire punishment. Always remember that a touch with the whip may steady a confused or distracted animal, in moments of crisis, as though bringing it to its senses.

The reins should be held as described below, taken up before mounting the vehicle and transferred to the left hand on sitting down. The left-hand or near side rein is placed over the forefinger while the off side or right hand rein is under the middle or second finger. The thumb should not be pressed on the reins except when looping (of which more later) and is normally kept fairly straight, well to the right or off side. In the meanwhile the forefinger is also pointed to the right-rear, keeping the rein close to the knuckles, moving the horse to right or left by turning the hand either up or down. The main grip on the reins is via the third and little fingers, which should be tight enough to prevent them slipping.

The first lesson, on reaching the driving seat, while having full control of reins and whip, is to judge the correct pressure which may be brought to bear on

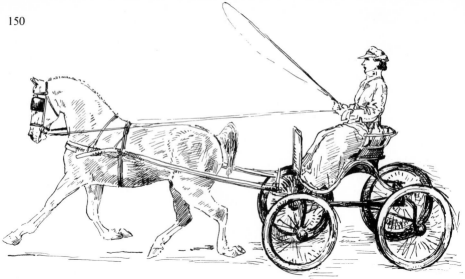

Hackney pony

the mouth of the horse, known as 'feeling' or 'giving the office'. It is through this feel or contact that the driver learns to gauge the reaction to his control and powers of communication. Although at one time drivers of professional status seldom spoke to their horses from the box, but made clacking and champing noises, which every child soon learned to imitate, the modern instructor now encourages use of recognisable language. The first command is to 'walk on', accompanied by a slight squeezing or pressure of the reins. If there is no response a touch with the whip near the withers or shoulders is in order. A hard-mouthed horse which may have been spoilt through ill-usage may need a tighter, firmer pressure than a well-schooled horse with the right responses. Once the horse has moved forward a pace or so the reins are slightly relaxed by dropping the hand, otherwise the horse may stop again, thinking it is being held back. Early stopping and starting is likely to lead to the bad habit of jibbing.

Increasing the pace to a trot, once the horse is walking firmly and freely, is further encouraged by tightening the reins with the words 'trot on'. Bringing the horse to a stand requires a steady, backward pull on the reins, without the driver leaning too far back, accompanied by the words 'whoa' or 'whoa-there'.

A well-broken animal with a light mouth, which is ideal for any form of driving, should be held with the left hand only. Increased control, however, is acquired by placing the right hand on the reins, about four inches in front of the left hand, the near rein between the second and third fingers while the off rein is under the little finger only. Try to keep both hands fairly level and not let the right hand drop far below the left.

Always keep the reins as near to the same length as possible. A slack off-side rein in the right hand tends to look sloppy and unbusinesslike, but was a common fault even in the days of unlimited horse traffic. To shorten the reins the right hand should be placed in front of the left hand, with the off rein under the little finger and the near rein between second and third fingers of the same hand. Complete the movement by sliding the left hand upwards towards the right hand. To lengthen rein hold in the same manner as above with the right hand, but slide the left hand slightly forward.

In changing direction, slacken the pace and give sufficient warning to other road users. Turning to the right entails placing the right hand on the left rein some distance in front of the left hand. Turning to the left or near side is done in the reverse manner, but always giving a little with the left hand to aid or emphasise the message from the right hand. Never jerk a rein, which at one time was known as 'ringing the bells', a slack and careless habit. A steady pressure and a slower but determined movement is always preferable to quick, jerky movements. Looping is rarely done when driving a single horse or pair and is mainly reserved for tandem work. It has the advantage of always leaving the right hand free to use the whip and is sometimes necessary with a young or green horse. To make the loop, the rein is pulled up and placed under the left thumb, which is pressed well-down against the joint between knuckle and forefinger. Keep the hand steady throughout but release gradually when a turn has been made.

A hard driver will pull too strongly on the horses mouth and retain a firm but over-strong contact throughout the journey, although holding the reins in a sloppy manner makes the animal loose its concentration so that it may stumble through boredom. A skilful driver learns to vary the pressure and is said to play with the reins. The whole point is to keep both driver and horse fully awake and aware of what is happening. Both lapsing into boredom or an inflexible routine are signs of the driver's lack of true awareness, and may be highly dangerous.

Most horses should be discouraged from cantering or galloping in harness and although this may be done in certain events it is not desirable for normal road work or in the show ring. A cantering horse is soon out of control in these circumstances, and may cause accidents, requiring greater driving skill than merely trotting. As considerable damage may be done by the odd accident or run-away it is advisable to invest in third party insurance, especially when showing and driving in public on a regular basis.

Further mistakes to avoid concern: (a) Turning too sharply without warning. (b) Turning or stopping without proper signals. (c) Taking off the bit and bridle while the horse is still in the shafts. (d) Not taking sufficient care when over-taking other vehicles, especially in the show ring. (e) Driving either too quickly or too slowly and not keeping to an even, level pace. (f) Not ensuring that harness is properly adjusted or the vehicle sound and road worthy. (g) Driving directly into a coach house or cart lodge. The horse should always be unharnessed and led away from its vehicle, which is manhandled to its resting place.

Chapter 11

Events, presentation and ringcraft

The range of events

One of the most popular show classes concerning light draught horses is for hackneys, divided into separate groups for horses and ponies. It is essential, however, that entrants are owners of animals registered with the Hackney Horse Society. Many of the larger shows, especially those at national level, have hackney classes, but these are not always in evidence at smaller shows, unless there is a local tradition of hackney breeding. There are sub-divisions of classes for horses and ponies of pure breed, driven single, in pairs, tandem or unicorn. During the Victorian era the hackney was a smart delivery horse for better class tradesmen, with special commercial classes at the majority of shows. It is only in comparatively recent years that it has been bred almost exclusively as a show animal.

Classes for single hackneys are now the most widely supported, at all levels, horses and ponies being shown to a Mill's wagon or show wagon. This vehicle has descended from an earlier American exercise wagon with the driver's seat mounted above wire-spoked, bike wheels on a tubular frame. Classes for pairs, unicorn and tandem are driven to more conventional vehicles, the tandem always to a dogcart or gig with two wheels rather than four. Ideally the correct vehicle for a pair of hackneys would be a small version of the phaeton, accompanied by a liveried groom at the rear. Many of the competitors in these

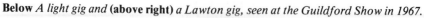

Below *A light gig and* (**above right**) *a Lawton gig, seen at the Guildford Show in 1967.*

classes are professional hackney breeders, dealers and showmen, emphasis being on the horse or pony rather than the vehicle. With other classes road work may be involved but the hackney horse or pony is kept to the ring and collecting paddock.

The classes for private driving are usually under several headings, competitors displaying vehicles which are driven by themselves or their friends, rather than by coachmen or hired drivers, and not having the high box-seats of many professional turnouts of the larger type. Hackney show wagons and business or trade vehicles are not acceptable in private driving classes, under any consideration. There may be further divisions between hackney and non-hackney horses drawing the vehicles (the hackneys usually known as hackney-type), also between singles, tandems and pairs, but a great deal depends on the type of show and the probable number of entries. With the smaller shows there are more likely to be general classes to avoid the disappointment of only one or two arriving for each class or the entire class having to be scratched through lack of support. Singles are usually, but not always, driven to small two-wheelers, while four-wheeled vehicles are the domain of pairs and larger teams. With private driving classes the interest is centred on the vehicle and skill in driving rather than conformation of the horse or pony, although the size and appearance of the animal between the shafts, relating to cart, gig or carriage, is of the utmost importance. Marks are also gained for smartness of turnout and good manners both in and out of the ring. There is nearly always an additional road test, with private driving classes, away from the show ring and grounds.

Coaching classes for four-in-hand teams were formerly very popular at the larger horse and agricultural shows and are now undergoing a revival of interest during the late 1970s and early 1980s. These are sub-divided between road coaches, private coaches or drags and regimental coaches. Road coaches are the former stage coaches, or identical with them. They are of a type seen on most trunk routes of Britain during the first half of the 19th century, although some were revived for sightseeing purposes or amateur driving, at a later period. They

Private coach

retained their bright colours and names such as 'Red Rover', 'Tally Ho' and 'Nimrod', being strongly built and slightly larger than private coaches. They were essentially utility vehicles, in their original form, used by fare-paying passengers and a limited parcels traffic. While there were two or more persons to act as grooms on a private or regimental coach, the road coach has only one servant—apart from the driver—this being the guard, who was technically in charge of the vehicle and looked after the interests of the passengers. In the time of accident or flood he would ride ahead on one of the coach horses, to bring help or give warning. In the show ring the guard wears a frock coat of scarlet and gold with a top hat of the old-fashioned beaver type, similar to the livery of the mail coach guards, men at one time considered to be at the head of their profession. Most guards carry a strongly made case or pouch in which is stored a carriage clock by which coaches were officially timed. On mail coaches this was known as the king's or queen's time, delivered to the guard of the Irish Mail, by a post office courier arriving at Euston on horseback, even in the days when the mail service had been transferred from road coaches to steam trains. The stage and mail coach guards sounded warnings on their coach horns, although on stage coaches tunes were often played on a key bugle to entertain the passengers, the most popular being Pop Goes the Weasel', a drinking song of the London tailors. The container for the horn on a road coach was a solid affair of wood or leather, while on a private coach it was made of basketwork. Harness tended to be heavier and less elegant on a road coach with the pad saddles comparatively large. The collars were also of a more elastic type, sometimes of plaited straw, so that they could be interchangeable for short distances, a spare being carried at the side of the vehicle. The colour of the harness could be black or brown, while the horses were rarely a good match and off- or odd-colours such a piebalds (black and white in patches) were frequently seen. Some road coaches in modern classes often have teams of piebalds, which are showy and great favourites with the spectators. Although once condemned as circus horses these latter are often of good conformation and temperament.

Trade class, a pair of Shires

Skewbalds, or brown and white horses, are considered less reliable. Other teams may be made up of combined greys with piebalds and skewbalds. In the old days, however, a gentleman whip or wealthy amateur preferred to drive a matching team and disdained odd colours.

Private and regimental coaches tended to be lighter and more elegant than road coaches. They were also known as drags or park drags, sometimes confined to the private or park roads of a large country estate. While private coaches would be painted in more sombre or family colours, regimental coaches were in the colours of their regiment or corps with the regimental badge on the door panels and rear boot. Private coaches never carried inside passengers and always drove with the windows firmly closed. Those sitting on the box and gammon boards were limited to twelve in number. Two of the latter, however, were liveried grooms, as near identical as possible in height, age and weight, wearing top hats, breeches, boots and short frock coats—the latter in family colours to match the coach.

In coaching events, at horse shows, the teams and their vehicles are first sent on a road tour or marathon of any distance up to twelve miles, although rarely more than six miles, representing a drive between stages. On returning to the show ring they are marked for appearance, harnessing and smart action.

Trade classes

Trade turnouts or commercial horses and vehicles may be shown in either classes for light or heavy horses. The heavier classes sometimes appear with a mixed range of horses, as in a general class, or limited to a specific breed such as shires or Clydesdales. At some shows, in the London area and Home Counties, there are classes for costermongers and street traders, usually having their trollies or small drays loaded with flowers, fruit and fresh vegetables.

As with the private driving classes, trade classes may be sub-divided between singles, pairs and four-in-hand or unicorn. They include conventional trade carts and vans, usually of the delivery type, and sometimes the wagons and carts of farmers and millers. In recent years there have been special classes, at some country shows, for agricultural vehicles and implements, attended by carters and waggoners in old style costume, with Billycock hats, smock frocks and gaiters. Vehicles have to be driven rather than led in all classes, although some classes have single horses not in vehicles, judged for the beauty and novelty of their harness, brasses and general decoration. Apart from the cockney classes with their fruit and vegetables, trade vehicles are always shown empty and unadorned. Emphasis in judging is on appropriate vehicle and matching horses, correct harnessing and smartness of turnout, also skill in driving. Drivers following a trade which has a traditional style of uniform or livery are expected to appear in this type of dress, a custom not always followed in recent years when inverted snobbery drives so many into a neutral zone of cloth cap or battered trilby with crumpled sports jacket and flannel trousers, to say nothing of an open-necked shirt. At one time butchers and fishmongers wore striped aprons with straw hats of the boater-type, while dairymen and laundrymen wore white coats with peaked caps of the military type. The coat of the dairyman was fairly short and more like a jacket, while that of the laundryman was at least knee length. The baker often wore a brown or green knee-length coat. A brewer's drayman had a three-quarter length driving or box coat in a double-breasted style with a high-crowned hard hat, not as tall or imposing as a top hat. The drayman's mate or trouncer also wore a hard hat but often a bowler, with a knee-length leather or canvas apron and short jacket. Both wore leggings or gaiters, although in later years these were worn only by the actual drivers. Railway drivers or van and carmen, wore dark uniform jackets and breeches with peaked caps and leggings. Cockney drivers, usually self-employed men in a small line of business, were more informal, except when appearing in special outfits as pearly kings, their coats and trousers smothered in pearl buttons.

Light commercial classes are now mainly the preserve of either hackneys, hackney types (with some hackney blood) or the Welsh cob. The latter was formerly a great favourite with London dairymen, many of whom were themselves of Welsh descent.

Other driving events

From the spectators' viewpoint some of the most exciting events are the so-called scurry classes. While turnout and attention to detail are not so important as in private driving and similar classes, great skill may be involved in the management of either pairs or single horses. The aim is to drive between obstacles without touching or dislodging them, often as time trials, good timing being a deciding factor. In some classes the horse also has to be ridden for part of the course and jumped over low fences, as a combined riding and driving class, with appropriate changes of harness.

What may be termed combined driving, apart from the mixed riding and driving mentioned above, was introduced to this country in fairly recent times and is of continental origins. The first and most dedicated patron and practitioner in Britain was, and still is, HRH the Duke of Edinburgh. There are now many combined events held in Europe, the United States and other parts of the world, rapidly increasing in popularity with both competitors and spectators. International trials and events are frequently held on both sides of the Iron Curtain. The first essential, however, is a large area of unspoilt parkland or open country, beyond the built-up zones. Perhaps the most

Above *The dressage section and* (**below**) *cross-country driving at the three-day event held at Howker Hall, August 1978* (M.H. Brindley).

attractive venue in Britain is at Cirencester on the borders of the Cotswolds (Cirencester Park), although other important events have been held at Eaton Hall, Lowther Castle, Windsor Great Park and Scone Castle in Perthshire.

The sport is now governed through a code of rules drawn up by Colonel Sir Mike Ansell, accepted by the *Fédération Equestre Internationale*, covering the entry of four-in-hand teams, pairs and singles, although in international driving events only four-in-hand teams are allowed to compete.

On the first day of a three-day event there are usually dressage tests with an inspection of horses, carriages, drivers and grooms, judged for general turnout, smartness and deportment. Horses are tested in all their paces, which includes trotting, walking and inscribing circles or figures of eight. There is also a test for standing immobile for at least fifteen seconds. All this may be done within a

fairly limited space such as a paddock or show ring. The second day is devoted to cross country driving or a marathon, which may be eighteen to twenty-six miles. These follow surfaced roads to a limited extent but are mainly over open fields or parkland, along woodland tracks and sometimes through open water such as ponds, lakes and shallow rivers. There are also a number of specially constructed or arranged hazards, while on some courses the vehicles have to weave in-and-out between tree trunks, hurdles or large boulders. Hazards encountered at a combined event in Poland included a high girder bridge, unfamiliar cobbled streets and the distraction of a railway marshalling yard with clanking goods trucks. In Hungary foreign horses were expected to drive with composure past a country wagon with its unhitched team of long-horned oxen, perhaps larger and more formidable-looking than any other cattle of this type in Europe. On the third day there is a further obstacle driving test, in the show ring, not unlike the scurry races mentioned above. These demand great control, driving between twenty pairs of conical plastic uprights spaced only an inch or so wider than the vehicles. All types of horses are used, the most popular in Britain being Cleveland bays, hunters broken to harness, Welsh cobs, hackneys and even Shetland ponies. Continental competitors arrive with Gelderlands from Holland, Holsteins and Oldenburgs from Germany and Lippizaners from Hungary. It is essential not to confuse the British Shetland pony with the American Shetland, the latter now being much taller and a distinctive type of pony in its own right.

American classes

Driving classes in North America, especially during the past decade, are a rapidly increasing growth area of the equestrian scene. Most of the larger and more popular events are now controlled by the American Horse Show Association, the rules of which may be obtained from the Secretary, AHSA, 598 Madison Avenue, New York City NY 10022. These are subject to annual changes and additions so that it is always an advantage to have the latest copies. There are still, however, many local and smaller shows, in different states, which remain unaffiliated.

Harness classes are often for special breeds and types of horse or pony, some of which are rarely seen in Britain or Europe, such as the spotted horse or Appaloosa of the far west, the American Shetland, the Morgan and the saddle-bred. There are both formal and informal or pleasure classes for most types.

Formal classes can be either Park Driving or Fine Harness Driving, the latter limited to a special vehicle known as the fine harness buggy, designed for the show ring. Informal or pleasure classes are judged on manners and temperament of the horse rather than on its quality, breeding or outstanding features of the vehicle. Park driving is highly formal and now has the highest possible standards of any class.

It is widely accepted that in America and Canada most horses are dual-purpose. Members of the American Saddlebreed Association are mainly responsible for producing a particular type of riding horse but train these for driving, so that there are also saddle-bred classes for two- and four-wheeled vehicles in junior drivers, lady drivers, amateur drivers and classes for young horses (aged four years old and under), in addition to fine harness and pleasure driving events.

Morgans are also treated as multi-purpose horses, popular in all states of the

Union. They have, in common with other outstanding breeds, what are known as Roadster classes, these being for swift, adaptable light-harness horses appearing not only in the ring but in modern traffic. To make matters even more complicated there is a Roadster Division open to all draught horses, usually dominated by the Standard Breed, which is the American trotting horse of the big national and international race meetings (harness racing). Such horses are driven, for show purposes, either to a fairly heavy road wagon or to a smaller 'bike' wagon, according to size. Drivers in these classes dress like jockeys in stable colours, with peaked caps, and tour the ring in a clockwise direction, while most of the other classes drive in an anti-clockwise manner, starting from the right rather than the left. Roadster classes are first judged for road gait and later for racing paces, often making several laps of the ring at full tilt.

Hackney horses and ponies have a great following, especially in the Atlantic Coast, Middle States and New England. They are very similar to British classes although sometimes having events for collections of three or more, shown in identical single harness or as singles plus a pair. There are both park drag or coaching events with a section for drags drawn by pure-bred hackneys only. Park drags in the four-in-hand classes must be of a solid or single colour with liveried grooms, while road coaches have a driver and guard usually in traditional scarlet and gold. Road coaches are in two or more colours.

Some of the more colourful classes, especially those for Morgans, are shown with their drivers, grooms and passengers in historical costumes or the dress of ethnic and minority groups such as Mexicans from the borders of Texas, early settlers or the Pennsylvanian Dutch, these being known as Cavalcade American groups. Appaloosas, although seen to better advantage under saddle, are usually hitched to buckboard or buggy and known as 'Appy classes'.

Combined riding and driving events are sponsored for both Arabs and Morgans, known in America as combined events. Quarter horses are frequently shown and raced with chuck wagons, while teams of eight or more draught horses (of the heavy type), compete for trophies in heavy draught classes. Some heavy draught horses also take part in weight pulling matches or 'pulling bees', first popular in New England.

In addition to traditional horse shows and combined driving events there are two less formal types of activity, which deserve passing mention. One of these is the rodeo, a display of horsemanship dating back to the days of early Spanish settlements, still strongly supported in some of the western states. Over the border in Canada a similar type of show is often known as the stampede, the most important of which is the annual event at Calgary in Alberta. These often feature chuck (food) wagon races with strongly-built, open wagons of the agricultural type driven to four-in-hand teams, escorted by outriders. The outriders start the race by loading the wagons with stores and equipment, including a portable kitchen stove. Wagons and outriders have to cross the finishing line together, after making a circuit of the track, part of which is an obstacle course between crates and barrels. After the din of loading, the outriders find it difficult to mount their excited horses to follow the chuck wagons, adding a thrill of pursuit to that of racing. This is one of the most exciting equestrian spectacles since Roman chariot racing, and possibly even more dangerous!

The racing of trotting horses and ponies is also a popular activity in most parts of the United States, using the two-wheeled sulky with its wire-spoked wheels, light metal construction and woven canework seats. For many years harness racing was better known and appreciated in the New World than racing under saddle, except in parts of the deep South where traditions were more akin to those in Europe. It developed from buggy and road wagon racing between pioneer farmers and early settlers, but is now strictly controlled and highly formal, representing large sums of capital investment. Although there are many permanent race tracks at which trotting and pacing may be seen, the most exciting events—with authentic atmosphere—are held at the State and County Fairs in the fall or autumn period after the harvest has been gathered-in. Pacing, in which both legs on the same side of the horse move together, is often slightly faster but less tiring to the horse than natural or square trotting, but requires special harness and training. It tends to make the body of the horse or pony roll from side-to-side like a camel, which latter moves naturally in the same gait, while square trotting is much nearer the true poetry of motion.

Preparation for a show

Planning and preparation for an important show means hours of work, long before reaching the show ground. This applies to horse, driver and vehicle but, in the correct order of things—at least show-wise—the vehicle needs prior attention.

First wheel the vehicle into an open space for a thorough examination and airing, at least several days before the event in which it is to appear. Hose off any dirt, grime or dust and sponge well into cracks and apertures, making sure to dry-off with a leather and later with a soft rag or cloth. Make sure that leatherwork has the full treatment, with plenty of saddlesoap and elbow grease to make it soft and pliable. After a thorough cleaning and polishing push the vehicle back under cover throwing dust sheets over bodywork, wheels and shafts. Burnish and polish the metal fittings at the last possible moment, seeing that surrounding areas of coachwork are protected from stains and splashes with layers of absorbent paper (newspapers are excellent).

To clean harness properly it should be taken to pieces, as much as possible, and every part treated individually. If liquid metal polish is used this should be kept well-clear of the bit, which enters the horse's mouth. Ordinary leather harness may be blackened with boot or shoe polish (or brown polish, as the case may be), but reins should be left brown in their natural colour. Lamps must be well-cleaned, especially the lens, and new candles fitted, as these may be inspected by the show judges. The whip should have the stock or handle well-polished, while the thong is normally treated with an application of mutton fat for greater suppleness and durability. Never whiten or colour the whip thong in any way. When all this has been done the lamps and harness should be wrapped in lengths or layers of cloth such as old towels or curtains for storing away, in a damp-proof room or chest, until needed.

To prepare the horse both tail and mane should be thoroughly washed and rinsed out. Spare or over-long hairs must be trimmed from the heels and jawline, while the hooves are well oiled or blackened. During transit it is advisable to cover the horse with a cloth or blanket, keeping the tail in bandages to avoid unnecessary staining. At the show everything necessary and portable should be stored in large suitcases, old laundry baskets or handy wooden boxes which may be up-ended and opened outwards like miniature wardrobes, clearly labelled on the outside with a list of the contents. On arriving at the ground make sure the vehicle has its final check and polish, while the coat of the horse may have a final touching-up with a stable rubber.

Do not use patent leather harness, or anything too showy, with a rustic or country turnout. Both brass and silver or white metal mountings are correct but brass—made to gleam like silver—is always preferred. Colours of vehicles should complement the horse as far as possible, the main colours being restrained rather than bright and fanciful. Yellow, as favoured by the late Lord Lonsdale—once known as the 'Yellow Earl'—is the only strong colour appearing in this connection, although stronger or brighter colours are sometimes used in lining-out or striping.

Transport

While horses or ponies are transported in a variety of boxes and trailers, the vehicles may either be carried on a low-loader, well lashed-down and protected from the weather, or included in the body of a large horse box, with the horses. When lowering the carriage down ramps from a higher level make sure the right winching or pulley gear is available, also willing assistants to ease it up or down. Even a phaeton of moderate size needs about four people to man-handle it into a box, without risk of damage. A Land-Rover makes an ideal towing vehicle for both trailers and low-loaders. In using the larger horse box it may be necessary to have a special licence for a heavy goods vehicle. Make sure, with the larger type, that there is an exit for emergency unloading—at the side—and plenty of room both for personnel and spare gear.

It may be possible to hire transport for certain events, from concerns dealing with these matters, traced through the yellow pages of a telephone directory. Yet while this may be better for casual showing, those with a full programme may find it even more expensive than owning the right box or box and trailer.

Presentation

Everything should be well-cleaned, groomed and burnished, but without an air of over-dressing or exaggeration. There has been much recent controversy on the subject of plaiting of manes for shows, rules for which tend to vary on a regional basis. The tail, however, should never be plaited or decorated in any way, except with heavy draught or farm horses in agricultural classes. If the mane does not lie flat enough and looks scrubby, however, plaiting may well be the only reasonable solution. Avoid a mixture of too many strong colours and the whole range of dyed strings and ribbons used by travelling shows and gypsy folk frequenting horse sales.

Grooms may be necessary in some classes and it is always an advantage to have a passenger to help balance the vehicle or run to the horse's head in time of need. The groom, however, should not wear full livery unless attending the larger and more formal type of coach, carriage or phaeton. Boots and breeches look better, in all cases, than slacks, trousers and ordinary walking shoes. Avoid the temptation to wear any form of historical or fancy-dress costume, unless taking part in a pageant or special class devoted to that sort of thing, more popular in America than in Europe. Over-dressing and too colourful a costume usually detracts from horse and vehicle. Men should wear a bowler hat for most classes, black or grey rather than brown, while women should wear neat and close-fitting hats unlikely to blow-off and cause alarm. Gloves look better than bare hands, especially on a cold day, and make it easier to control the reins, especially in cold or wet weather. Women in driving classes usually look more dignified wearing skirts rather than trousers, although boots and breeches are preferred to slacks or even jodhpurs. Jeans, beret-type headgear (once very popular during the 1930s) and flimsy headscarves of the '50s and '60s should be avoided at all costs. If the weather is inclined to be wet and showery there is no substitute for a good quality riding mackintosh, certainly not a transparent plastic mac or greasy trenchcoat, however waterproof.

Once in the show ring the competitor may be said to have 'come under starter's orders' and the control of the ring stewards. Attention should be paid to their advice and instructions at all times. Always keep a look out for oral and hand signals from both judges and stewards.

It is not thought advisable to give the horse or pony a good feed of corn before entering the ring as this makes him too active and likely to hot-up (especially ponies), in the atmosphere of a busy show ground. Be ready well in advance of schedules and take advantage of this to warm up the horse and loosen his joints and sinews, which may be stiff after a long road journey in a confined space. Trotting up and down in a clear space, not too far from the ring, certainly not too fast and avoiding other events and displays, may also ease the nerves and make the horse less chary of unfamiliar crowds. In such circumstances talking quietly to the horse and leading it about for a short time, may be of considerable help.

Shortly after entering the ring a general class may be divided into pairs or singles and further sorted out—in line or double lines—according to size of horse or pony and type of vehicle, as though on parade. The driver may be kept waiting for some time at this stage but must remain still and straight, especially during the preliminary examination of harness, grooming and turnout, although ready to lead-off for an individual drive or tour of the ring at the first signal. Never appear to lean too far forward or slump over the reins.

Judges look for a variety of things but most would agree over cleanliness, an alert appearance, firm yet free action and boldness or courage allied with obedience of the horse to its driver's touch and command. Some judges always insist on inspecting the candle lamps and deduct marks if these are not ready for use. This could mean either that they are burnt too far down in their sockets or that the wick is unsinged, it being harder to light a new wick than one which has burnt for only a few seconds. Such neglect may not seem very serious but betokens lack of attention to detail on the part of the driver. Other judges may expect to find a fully stocked first aid box or kit of repair tools, along with a coil of rope, a coil of wire, a hoof pick and even a note pad and pencil, the latter for sending messages in time of accident or breakdown. All this is a far cry from the days, before the First World War, when a driver was allowed to pass out with a penknife, a length of string and a shilling-piece. In other words, the less horses are seen on the roads and in public places the greater the necessary precautions to be taken against anything going wrong.

It may be noted that the road test comes shortly after the first inspection, during which the judges may be well-hidden, somewhere along the prescribed route. Back in the ring, following the road test, horses are examined for soundness and general condition. Those which appear strained, nervous or sweating too much are usually marked-down at this stage. After a further tour of the ring the possibles are called in for final judgment and awards are soon made. Sometimes the reasons for certain placings may be explained but it is unwise to challenge a decision either through judges or stewards. On leaving or entering the show ring gentlemen should transfer the whip to the left hand and raise their hats in the direction of the Royal Box or President's Box, perhaps towards a guest of honour by whom the show may have been opened. Lady drivers bow and raise their whips to a horizontal position on a level with the brow or forehead. Men, especially coachmen and professional drivers, may also hold the whip in this way with a slight upward tilt of the elbow, but raising the hat is considered more correct and stylish. To wave or flourish the whip or hat for any other reason may be considered ridiculous.

After the event a horse should be returned to its box or temporary stable, offered both consolation—if not in the ribbons—and a good rub-down or strapping. Unharness in the open with plenty of elbow room. The normal procedure is to start with the breeching or rearward straps, then to unbuckle the traces and loosen the bellyband or girth, gradually working forward. Having removed the body harness the horse should be led well clear of its vehicle, especially the shafts or pole, and a halter substituted for the bridle. The bridle and bit should only be taken off when the rest of the unharnessing has finished. Leaving an unbridled horse between shafts is asking for trouble, as a frightened animal still attached to its vehicle may cause untold damage.

Chapter 12

Running a commercial stable

Although the role of the draught horse now seems secure in the immediate future there are still impediments to a full-scale revival of its use. One of the main drawbacks concerns lack of stabling, while in some areas there is also a shortage of the heavier and more suitable types of horse. With redevelopment plans and large-scale demolitions, the former stabling is rapidly disappearing while new buildings have to comply with a whole range of planning requirements which may well daunt all but the most enthusiastic. There is still, however, a wide area of possibilities in the use of prefabricated structures— supplied by several firms—if only as a temporary measure. The breeding and supply question is very much a case of demand and now rapidly improving, for which thanks are due to a small group of people retaining faith in the draught horse breeds even when some lines were rapidly nearing extinction. In this the larger breweries have greatly assisted, recognising that the universal interest in horses as a talking point may be good for business in a number of ways.

It is said there is no room in modern commercial life for sentiment, certainly not as an end in itself, and horses are expected to prove their worth, demonstrated in the most scientific terms possible. It is now several years since time and motion study experts, employed by a firm of Lancashire brewers, worked out that barrels of beer, within a short radius of the depot, were delivered far more cheaply by horse than by motor lorry or any other form of mechanical transport.

Everything today has to be streamlined and efficient in order to survive, including the horse department. The highest cost factor is labour or manpower and, as so much depends on this, it is vital to have both reliable horses which are seldom under the vet or eating their heads off in a loose box, and also vehicles which are sturdy enough to withstand long running with the minimum out-shopping or maintenance. In the latter case iron and steel must predominate over wood and although it may be hoped that some of the more traditional types are reserved for shows, the modern delivery wagon should be cheap and both easy to make and repair (as a matter of comparisons), running on pneumatic tyres. There has been endless discussion and argument on the latter subject and few people would agree that pneumatics, especially the larger balloon types, do much for the aesthetic charm of a turnout, while in the context of certain farm carts they were often too small and the vehicle too low-slung to be of much use. However, taking all factors into account, they seem to have proved their worth in most spheres. A number of the larger firms still using horses on a regular basis, including Messrs Whitbread of London and Messrs Vaux and Company of Newcastle-on-Tyne, seem to prefer them for beer deliveries after prolonged experience of both types. All thing being equal the disc-type wheels, as seen on motor lorries, which accompany pneumatic tyres, are easier to supply and need less attention (especially with a shortage of trained wheelwrights) than wooden-spoked wheels with iron-shod tyres. It has also been proved by the above firms that the most efficient delivery routine is through pairs with a well-balanced load on pneumatics, rather than by a single horse. In this context tare and load weight drawn by a single are shared through pairing, which increases the overall weight. Larger teams are no longer practical in modern traffic conditions, economics apart, but ideal for showing and publicity. Deliveries from the average large business concern should be within a radius of four or five miles, allowing for a minimum of at least twice per day, amounting to about six tons. It is significant that a higher capacity is often expected of a modern wagon on pneumatics than with the older wooden types on spoked wheels, with a mainly wooden bodywork.

Coping with the problems of staffing and manpower is essentially a matter of leadership, plus administrative ability. There is apparently no shortage of younger people willing to work with horses, either heavy or light, even in cities and built-up areas. Weekend work, however, must be arranged on a fair rota basis—which is seen to be fair—with guaranteed overtime for routine duties on Saturday mornings. There must also be adequate relief systems to cover manpower in time of accidents and holiday periods. Horses must be fed and mucked-out, even while resting, covering the run of weekends and public holidays. In such cases it may be necessary to divide Sunday and Bank Holiday work between morning and evening shifts. Much of the half day or Saturday work, when deliveries are normally suspended, must be devoted to general maintenance on the wagons and about the yard. While heavy horses for harder physical work often rest throughout Sunday and most of Saturday, lighter horses may need special exericse stints on Saturday mornings.

Brewer's show dray

The average heavy horse in regular work needs about 8½ lb of oats per day with chopped hay and bran, also additional quantities of hay at which to pull when he feels hungry. This should be supplemented by two good mashes per week, the latter given both at mid-week and the weekend.

In times past commercial stables were often out-of-bounds to the public, while it was difficult to view them even for those with the right background and sound reasons for entry. This must now change as the horse becomes increasingly important as a publicity factor. Any large-scale stable must be willing to accept outside interest, even organised visits and school parties or student study groups, all of which help to keep the draught horse alive in the public consciousness. Winning over public sympathy may be half the battle in any commercial enterprise.

Unfortunately, despite initial enthusiasm, there are now fewer young people with past experience, or even from families with the right background of horse knowledge, applying for stable jobs. Everything has to start that much further back and horses with sound temperament, easy to handle both in and out of stables, are a necessary prerequisite. Yet this may be a double advantage as such animals are nearly always better behaved than their less reliable compatriots, both in traffic and in shows. The Percheron, Suffolk Punch and Welsh cob all fulfill these requirements and have better health records than most breeds. The Welsh cob, although capable of hauling good weights and up to the heaviest possible work for its size, is much smaller than the Percheron or Punch but ideal for lighter delivery work and once much sought after to pull milk and bread carts, although now regarded as an excellent dual-purpose, ride or drive animal, especially for showing and eventing. All these animals are both able to walk and trot with a fair load and having less feather or fetlock than some heavy breeds are not so likely to suffer from complaints of the limbs and feet. A docile but willing nature makes them easy for the novice or untrained older person to control, while their sound, firm legs and glossy coats put them in a superior category for show turnouts, also making the right impression for public contacts both on the streets and at stable inspections.

It may be further noted that an economical stable of any size needs a resident shoeing smith or farrier-cum-blacksmith, able to help as much as possible in renewing the metalwork of wagons and for general repairs.

Chapter 13

Horses for draught

Perhaps the most outstanding of British light draught horses was the Yorkshire coach horse, unfortunately extinct from the period after the Second World War. A similar type, however, still flourishing (thanks to support from the Royal Mews), is the Cleveland Bay, also from Yorkshire. Mainly bred in the Cleveland hills, large numbers were also found in the south-eastern corner of County Durham. The height is fifteen hands three inches to sixteen hands (one hand = four inches) but although of good presence it may lack something of the Yorkshire coach horse, being slightly longer in the back and loins. It is always a shade of bay, as might be expected from its name, with thick black mane and tail, some having a black list or dorsal stripe along the centre of the back. According to Lady Wentworth, an authority on the British breeds of horse and pony, the bays were originally crossed with Spanish horses during the 17th century and a century later with English thoroughbreds. These were the two main breeds of English carriage or coach horses of which only the Cleveland Bay now survives into the 1980s. There were and are, however, numerous other animals pulling vehicles of all types, including many crosses with infusions of carthorse, thoroughbred and foreign blood. Light and heavy horses of the Irish draught breed are certainly worthy of an honoured place in such lists, the breed

Cleveland Bay

now undergoing a revival of interest, officially sponsored by the Department of Agriculture of the Irish Government.

Other breeds of fairly recent introduction to England are the Gelderlands of Holland, which are large horses but of good action, the Holsteiner and Oldenburger of Germany and the Lippizaner of Hungary. All these are dual-purpose horses, up to a good height and with excellent conformation. The Oldenburg has the added advantage of reaching early maturity.

There are a great many smaller horses and ponies for harness work, the most outstanding being hackneys. The breed is now divided between hackney horses and hackney ponies, the horse being up to sixteen hands but rarely more than fifteen hands two inches while the pony is under fourteen hands two inches. Although a well-established breed, recognised in its present form for over two hundred years, it is only since the turn of the present century that it has been widely exploited as a show animal. There are even references in 19th century literature to the common or humble hackney. Its early ancestry depended on a cross between warm-blooded or Eastern types with English trotting horses, especially those bred in Norfolk for road work. It is reputed, like the even earlier roadsters, to 'go on for ever', with great stamina, although not perhaps with such great hauling power for its size as some types. Some larger hackneys have been driven as teams of coach horses, in private drags, but most are now shown in special wagons. Their showy paces, partly the result of training, are perhaps too exaggerated for some tastes and should be judged by their own, unique standards. Colours are bay, brown and the chestnut, although medium bay now seems to predominate.

Welsh cobs are some of the finest dual-purpose animals in Britain, strong yet graceful and easy to handle, with a temperament almost beyond reproach. They are bred in the grazing areas of West Wales and the foothills of the Cambrian Range, mainly in Cardiganshire, and may be used for a variety of purposes. In the old days they were often riding animals used to round up cattle and sheep on rough hill pastures, but also driven to market and church or chapel. Until the 1930s it was recognised that breeding stock of Welsh cobs was always part of the dowry of a farmer's daughter, especially on hill farms of the south and west. Between fourteen and fifteen hands, they look well in a gig or dogcart but are

Welsh cob

now finding favour as teams for cross-country events and combined driving. Their action is naturally high, yet powerful, while most examples have a good head and tail carriage. They have more hair or fetlock than the English or standard cob, but not excessive enough to cause weakness in this area. Colours are bay, brown and grey, odd colours sometimes appearing but always discouraged. There are two sections for Welsh ponies with the smaller or mountain pony, now mainly a child's mount, at about twelve hands and the larger cob-pony at twelve to fourteen hands, the latter similar to a smaller version of the Welsh cob. They both appear well in harness, drawing the smaller type of vehicle which might be shown by younger people.

The English cob resembles the Welsh cob in many ways but is more phlegmatic and not such a showy performer. Often more a size and type than a breed, it has short but sturdy limbs and a strongly built or compact and 'cobby' appearance. Between fourteen and fifteen hands, it is half horse and half pony, useful for riding and driving, being of no particular colour range.

The Connemara is the only true Irish pony now bred, but sometimes included amongst English breeds, as large numbers have been bred and reared in England for a considerable period of time. Its ancestors are from the extreme West of Ireland, some claiming that its stock was crossed with Spanish horses swimming ashore from the wreck of the Armada. It stands between thirteen and fourteen hands high and is usually grey, although black, brown and bay are by no means uncommon.

The Dales pony of north-west Yorkshire, formerly the North Riding, is a fairly large animal for its type, often compared with a miniature carthorse, used on moorland farms for riding and driving. It has a short neck but good head carriage, with a short, strong back and fair amount of feather on its lower limbs. The height should be fourteen hands two inches or slightly below. Colours are bay, black, brown and grey with darker colours tending to predominate.

Fell ponies are from Lancashire and the Cumbrian side of the Pennines, thoroughly at home in wild fell country bordering the Lake District, being smaller versions of the Dales pony with less feather or fetlock and longer, leaner heads. They are about thirteen hands two inches and black or brown with a few white markings. Greys appear from time to time but are not liked or encouraged. Like the Dales pony they were widely used in agriculture and as pack horses, especially in connection with the Cumbrian lead mines. As pack animals they ambled in droves or strings of twenty and upwards, led by a bell horse or mare, usually the latter, chosen for its cunning in knowing the best path and hung about with chiming bells. Each pony carried upwards of sixteen stone of lead in panniers, over 240 miles per week.

Highland ponies used by Scottish deer stalkers to carry their equipment and the bodies of slain stags, are of two main types, both suitable for harness work. The sturdier but smaller breed is found in the Western Isles and known as the 'barra', from which the mainland 'garron' is descended. It thrives on a sparse quantity of grazing, in its natural habitat, and may find a living where even sheep or mountain deer might starve. Smaller 'barras' are between twelve and thirteen hands, while 'garrons' are up to fourteen hands two inches. They are compact and close coupled, with small heads but strong-deep necks. Colours are brown, dun and grey, some with attractive silver manes and tails.

There are several breeds of native pony from the south and west of England, all of which may be ridden by children and appear well in shafts. The largest and perhaps the most uncouth, is from the New Forest area, although a hardy and willing type. The head is often on the large side, inclined to be somewhat out of proportion with the body, for real beauty. The normal height is about thirteen hands.

The Exmoor pony from the borders of Devon and Somerset is a smart-looking pony between twelve hands and twelve hands three inches. The colours are mouse brown, bay and dun with a light or mealy-coloured muzzle. It is well up to either carrying or drawing a good weight.

Dartmoor ponies are up to twelve hands two inches and are bay, black or brown. While clean-limbed and hard, they do not seem as distinctive as the Exmoor breed, but usually have a look of great alertness and intelligence.

Shetland ponies should not be underrated or dismissed as suitable only for very small children or circus and pantomime acts. The smallest of the British native ponies, they are between thirty-six and forty-two inches at the withers or shoulders, although normally about forty inches. Height with this breed is always measured in inches rather than hands. They are of remarkable intelligence, especially the stallions, and are frequently driven to small phaetons—in pairs of teams—for cross-country driving or scurry events. In the early days they frequently worked as pack animals in the Shetland Islands, although later down coal mines in shafts which were too cramped and low for larger ponies. Colours are dun, black, cream and odd colours, nearly always with a dark list and black points. They have a small head and dished, or Arab, profile. The body has a sturdy, compact appearance but without stuffiness, on short, hard legs. Mane and tail are luxuriant while the hoofs are small, well-shaped and hard.

Among the various foreign ponies introduced to Britain, mainly for driving, during the past few years, is the golden-chestnut Haflinger of Austria and the Tyrol. The height is just under fourteen hands. In Austria and Germany they were used for forestry work on steep slopes and for military pack-work in mountain warfare.

The Norwegian or Fjord pony is now fairly popular for cross-country driving in pairs and teams. It is about fourteen hands and appears in two main breeds, almost identical to laymen. There are duns, bays and browns but mainly the former with a high-standing dark mane and proudly arched neck. Some have a dorsal or eel stripe on the back and withers. The earlier breed survived from shoreline settlements of the north-west providing the pack horses of the Vikings, known as the *fjord-hest*, while those of the south and further inland, perhaps slightly larger, were the valley horse or *doele-hest*.

Arab horses are now widely used for draught and show purposes, especially in the United States, although little seen in this role in Britain. The conformation of this excellent riding animal does not suit the vehicles and harness of European tradition, although many experts consider they are seen to better advantage under saddle than between shafts. They are a hardy breed in a wide range of colours, with a dished profile, small muzzle, fine but firm bone structure and elegant head and tail carriage. Seldom more than fifteen hands, although the mares are often much smaller. Considered the oldest pure-breed in the world, they originated in the northern part of the Arabian peninsula, but are now mainly bred in Europe and North America. Arab blood has been used

Shire horse

to improve and up-grade many breeds in all parts of the world and is the foundation stock of the English thoroughbred.

British heavy horses, seen in both agricultural and commercial or trade classes, are the shire, Clydesdale, Suffolk Punch and the Percheron. The largest and most powerful is the shire, between sixteen and eighteen hands, the stallions often slightly larger than the mares and up to a ton in weight. Its main characteristic is the large amount of feather on its heels, some of which is nearly always white. Although of good temperament it tends to be a slow and deliberate mover. Its lips are well together and its ears long and fine, although the nose tends to be convex and slightly Roman. The general appearance is

Clydesdale

Suffolk Punch (mare)

commanding and of great dignity, but not always of refined equine type or beauty.

The Clydesdale is the heavy draught horse of Scotland and the Border country, although large numbers were also found in Northern Ireland (before farm mechanisation) and in colonial territories with many settlers of Scottish descent. Slightly smaller and more active than the shire, but less placid and docile. It has an appearance of better breeding than some draught horses, but may degenerate to an awkward legginess in the wrong type. Colours are bay, brown and black with splashes of pure white on head, legs and body.

The Suffolk Punch is essentially a farm horse of the Eastern counties, noted for its hardiness and longevity. Like the shire, its ancestry may be traced back to the Middle Ages, although greatly improved during the mid-18th century. The modern punch is a chestnut of a docile temperament, sometimes with a flaxen mane and tail. Until recent years there was also a much darker, near-bay breed, which seems to have died out. There is very little feather on the legs, while the body is compact and the neck deep but well-arched, with a small head. The term 'punch' means something firm, rounded yet compact, like a balled fist. It is about sixteen hands and wide at the fore-end, unlike the much narrower Clydesdale and modern shire. It may be noted that the shire was originally more like the punch but through cross-breeding and fashion, during the past seventy years, it is now more like the Clydesdale. The punch can haul well at the trot (which is an advantage over a good many other heavy breeds), and was sometimes used, in hilly districts, as a heavy-weight coach or carriage horse. Short legs, allied with a low-slung body, give it extra purchase for its loads.

The Percheron is usually a grey but, less frequently, a black or slate-grey horse. It came to Britain during and shortly after the First World War having made a favourable impression on the War Department as a transport and artillery horse in the French Army, an enthusiasm soon shared by farmers and land-owners serving with the British Expeditionary Forces. It is normally about sixteen hands three inches, with the mare a trifle shorter. There is considerable Arab blood in its veins, dating back to the Arab and Moorish invasion of France

Percheron

from Spain during the Middle Ages. In later years this type was fused with some of the better draught and post horse stock of northern Europe so that it may be said to represent the best of both worlds. It is almost clean-limbed, short-coupled and with a small Arab-like head on a deeply arched and crested neck. The skin and silken coat are of exceptionally fine quality. Large numbers were at one time exported to all parts of the world, especially to the United States and Canada, but in later years to Japan. This is arguably the most attractive and versatile of all the heavy breeds, combining willingness and spirit with strength and docility.

Appendices

1 Places to visit

The most outstanding place to visit in Britain, for anyone interested in horses and carriages, is the Royal Mews at Buckingham Palace, London. This has the advantage over many museums and show places of still being in daily use, the living embodiment of a proud tradition. It is open to the public on Wednesday afternoons throughout the year between 2 pm and 4 pm and on Thursdays at the same times between May and September, except during Ascot week, or on state occasions, when horses and vehicles are needed in processions. There is a special visitors' entrance from Buckingham Palace Road, the visitors' exit being a Doric arch designed by John Nash as the official or carriage entrance.

A tour of the main yard and buildings, keeping to the left, takes the visitor past the Gold Coach House, in which the State Coach of England is kept, then past the Coach Houses and the State Carriage House, continuing past the stables, State Harness Room, Saddlery Exhibition Room and finally into the souvenir shop in the Old Carriage House near the exit. The Coach Houses contain among other things a pony phaeton of Queen Victoria, a wagonette, single Brougham, bow-fronted Clarence and a covered brake. The State Carriage House is slightly larger with about twenty vehicles including the State Landau, the Irish State Coach, the Glass State Coach, a Victoria and the original charabanc presented to Queen Victoria by the King of the French. The State Harness Room displays much of the harness and accoutrements for the royal coaches including the harness for the State Coach or Golden Coach of England. The stables may be inspected and house a mixed stud of Windsor Greys (horses originally kept at Windsor) and Cleveland Bays. There is also a special display of saddlery used by the Queen at the Trooping of the Colour ceremony, on her official birthday, and numerous items of harness and saddlery presented to the Royal Family by foreign heads of state and other distinguished visitors.

Other places of interest are listed below although opening times and admission fees are subject to fluctuations and should be checked well in advance of an intended visit.

2 Carriage museums and collections

THE BRITISH ISLES

London area   (1) Hampton Court Palace, Hampton, Middlesex.
                               (2) The Science Museum, Exhibition Rd, SW 7.

	(3) London Passenger Transport Collection, The Old Flower Market, Covent Garden, WC 2.
Avon	(1) Bath Carriage Museum, Circus Mews, Bath.
	(2) Bristol City Museum and Art Gallery, Queen's Rd, Bristol.
	(3) Dodington Park, Old Sodbury.
Bedfordshire	(1) Shuttleworth Collection, Old Warden, Biggleswade.
	(2) G.C. Mossman, Bury Farm, Cuddington, near Luton. (By appointment.)
Cheshire	(1) Eaton Hall, near Chester.
	(2) Gawsworth Hall, near Macclesfield.
Cleveland	(1) Stockton Transport Museum, Preston park, Yarm Rd, Stockton.
Cornwall	(1) Camborne Carriage Museum, Lower Grillis Farm, Treskilland, Redruth.
Derbyshire	(1) Red House Stables, Old Road, Darley Dale.
	(2) The Tramways Museum, Crich. (For horse cars.)
Devonshire	(1) Arlington Court, Barnstaple.
	(2) Buckland Abbey, near Yelverton, Tavistock.
Durham	(1) Open Air Industrial Museum, Beamish Hall, Stanley.
	(2) Raby Castle, Stainsdrop, Darlington.
Hampshire	(1) Breamore House, near Fordingbridge.
Hereford-Worcester	(1) Hartlebury Castle, near Kidderminster.
Humberside	(1) Hull Transport Museum, 36 High St, Kingston-on-Hull.
	(2) Scunthorpe Museum, Oswald Rd, Scunthorpe.
Kent	(1) Tyrwhitt-Drake Museum, Archbishop's Stable, Mill St, Maidstone.
Lancashire	(1) City of Liverpool Museum, William Brown St, Liverpool.
Leicestershire	(1) Museum of Transport and Technology, Corporation Rd, Leicester.
Lincolnshire	(1) Mawthorpe Collection, Woodlands, Mawthorpe.
Norfolk	(1) Cockley Cley, near Swaffham. (Sir Peter Roberts.)
Nottinghamshire	(1) Industrial Museum, Woollaton Park, Nottinghamshire.
Shropshire	(1) The Whitehouse Museum, Aston Munslow, near Ludlow.
	(2) Weston Park, Shifnal.
Staffordshire	(1) Cheddleton Flint Mill, Cheddleton.
	(2) County Museum, Shugborough Hall, near Stafford.
Suffolk	(1) Museum of East Anglian Life, Stowmarket.
Surrey	(1) Transport Trust Library, Guildford. (Books and documents only.)
Scotland	(1) Hamilton District Museum, 129 Muir St, Hamilton.
	(2) Old Blacksmith's Shop, Gretna Green.
	(3) St. Cuthbert's Co-operative Society, Edinburgh.
	(4) Social History Museum, Kirsidy, Fife.
	(5) Transport Museum, Glasgow.
	(6) Transport Museum, Leith Walk, Edinburgh.

Ulster	(1) Transport Museum, Witham St, Belfast.
Warwickshire	(1) Charlecote Park, near Stratford-upon-Avon.
West Midlands	(1) Black Country Museum. Tipton Rd, Dudley.
Yorkshire	(1) Castle Howard, North Yorks.
	(2) Castle Museum, Tower St, York.
	(3) Sibden Hall, near Halifax.
	(4) Yorks Mills, Aysgarth Falls, near Hawes.
Isle of Man	(1) Manx Museum, Douglas.
	(2) Rushen Abbey, Ballasalla. (Walter Gilbey Esq.)

OVERSEAS

Australia	(1) El Caballo Blanco, Bodeguera Stud, Waraloo.
Austria	(1) Kunsthistorische Museum (Wagonburg) Monteurdepot, Buring 5, A-1010 Vienna 1.
Belgium	(1) Musée des Carrosses, Brussels.
	(2) Château de Nokere, Gent. (Appointment with Baron Casier.)
Bermuda	(1) The Carriage Museum, Water St, St George's.
Canada	(1) The Horseman's Hall of Fame, Calgary, Alberta.
Czechoslovakia	(1) Hippological Museum, Slatinany Castle.
Denmark	(1) 4684 Holme Olstrip, Sparresholm, Sjelland, Copenhagen.
Eire	(1) Guiness Museum, St James' Gate, Dublin.
	(2) Luggala, Roundwood, Co Wicklow. (Appointment with the Hon Garech Browne.)
France	(1) Musée de la Voiture, Château de Compiègne.
	(2) Musée des Voitres, Versailles, near Paris.
Germany	(1) Celle, near Hanover.
	(2) Marstall Museum, Schloss Nymphenburg, Munich.
	(3) Marstall Museum, Thurn and Taxis, Regensburg.
	(4) Town Palace, Darmstadt.
Holland	(1) Agricultural Museum, Heille, Zealand.
	(2) Boerwagenmuseum. Achter Bonenburg, Buren.
	(3) Het Loo Palace, near Apeldoorn. (Royal Carriages.)
	(4) Koninklyk Staldepartement, The Hague. (Royal Carriages.)
	(5) National Country Museum, Arnhem.
	(6) National Rujtuigmuseum, Nienoord, Leek, near Groningen.
	(7) Stichting Rijtuigenmuseum, 'Duinrell', Wassenaar. (Appointment with Mr R. Mutter.)
	(8) Wagenburg 'de Waal', Island of Texel.
Italy	(1) Leonardo da Vinci Museum, Milan.
	(2) Museo delle Carrozze, Palazzo Pitti, Florence.
	(3) Museo delle Carrozze, Macerata.
Poland	(1) Carriage Museum. Lancut Castle. (SE Poland.)
Portugal	(1) National Coach Museum, Lisbon.
Spain	(1) The Royal Mews, Madrid.
Sweden	(1) Vagn Museum, Malmo.
Switzerland	(1) Eidg Militarpferdeanstalt, Bern. (Appointment with the Commanding Officer, Cavalry School.)

(2) Kutschensammlung Robert Sallamann, St Gallerstr 12, 8580 Amriswil.

(3) Museum of Transport, Lucern.

USA   (1) El Pomar Carriage House, Colorado Springs.

(2) Hawthorn-Melody Museum, Libertyville, Illinois.

(3) Henry Ford Collection, Edison Institute, Deerborn, Michigan.

(4) John Pollinder, Pollinder Rd, Lynden, Washington.

(5) Kentucky Horse Park, Lexington, Kentucky.

(6) Mission San Joan Bautista, Cal.

(7) Morven Park, Leesburg, Virginia.

(8) Ringling Circus Museum, Sarasota, Florida.

(9) Seely Stables, Old Town, San Diego Historic Park, 2725 Congress St, San Diego, Cal.

(10) Shelburne Museum, Vermont.

(11) Smithsonian Institution, Washington DC.

(12) Studebaker Collection, Century Centre, South Bend, Indiana.

(13) Suffolk Museum, Stony Brook, Long Island, New York.

(14) The World Circus Museum, Baraboo, Wisconsin.

3   Builders and restorers of horse-drawn vehicles in Britain

George Amos and Sons, Lion Works, 26, New End Square, Hampstead, London NW3.

James Asridge Ltd, 77, Christchurch Way, London SE10.

L.W. Ballard, Chants Cottage, Angmering Village, Sussex.

Henry Bowers and Co, Chard, Somerset.

Richard Brereton, Wern Newydd, Painscastle, Powys, Wales.

Crofords Limited, Dover Place, Ashford, Kent.

George Darley, Coniston, Near Hull, Humberside.

Fairbourne Antiques, The Oasthouse, Fairbourne Mill, Harriestsham, Kent.

A. Hales, The Hackney Stables, Manor Rd, Wales, Near Sheffield, Yorks.

Harewood Carriage Company, Dobles Lane, Holsworthy, Devon.

Eric Homewood, Mill Farm House, Arlington, Barnstaple, Devon.

M.A. Horler, The Old Malt House, Radford, Timsbury, Near Bath, Avon.

A.H. King, Grangefield Smallholding, Woking Road, Guildford, Surrey.

Mart Coachbuilders, Sparrow Lane, Long Bennington, Newark, Nottinghamshire.

D. Morgan-Davies, Newtown House, Ravenglass, Cumbria.

Gordon Offord, 264, Brompton Road, London SW3.

Philip H. Pickford, Fontmell Magna, Shaftesbury, Dorset.

Pilgrims, Old England Yard, Shillinstone, Near Blandford, Dorset.

George Pycroft, Kiln Cottage, Butser Hill, Burton Petersfield, Hampshire.

Replica Carriage Co, Hayden House, High Street, Somersham, Huntingdonshire.

J. Richards, Gawsworth Court, Near Macclesfield, Cheshire.

F.J. Stubbings, Biscombe, Stapeley, Taunton, Somerset.

Wellington Carriage Company, Long Lane, Telford, Salop.

Wheels and Shafts, Poole House, Castle Street, Nether-Stowey, Bridgwater, Somerset.

John Willie's Saddleroom, Burley Ringwood, Hampshire.

G.P. Worsley and Company, St Helens, Merseyside.

4   Societies and associations

American Driving Society, Hastings-on-Hudson, NY 10706.

American Horse Show Association, 598, Madison Avenue, New York NY 10022.

British Driving Society, Mrs P. Chandler, 10, Marley Avenue, New Milton, Hampshire.

Carriage Association of America, H.K. Sowles Jr, 885, Forest Avenue, Portland MA.

Cleveland Bay Society, J.F. Stephenson Esq, MA, York Livestock Centre, Murton, Yorkshire.

Combined Driving Committee. The British Horse Society, National Equestrian Centre, Kenilworth, Warwickshire.

Dales Pony Society, Sec G.H. Hudson Esq, Ivy House Farm, Yarm-on-Leer, Yorkshire.

Dartmoor Pony Society, Sec D.W.J. O'Brien Esq, Chelwood Farm, Nutley, Uckfield, Sussex.

English Connemara Society, Mrs Barthorp, The Quinta, Bentley, Farnham, Surrey.

Exmoor Pony Society, Mrs J. Watts, Quarry Cottage, Sampford, Brett, Williton, Somerset.

Fell Pony Society, Miss P. Crossland, Packway, Windermere, Cumbria.

Hackney Horse Society, National Equestrian Centre, Kenilworth, Warwickshire.

Haflinger Society of Gt Britain, Her Grace The Duchess of Devonshire, Chatsworth, Bakewell, Derbyshire.

Highland Pony Society, Miss D. MacNair, Beacon Corner, Burley, Hampshire.

Norwegian Fjord Ponies, The Hon Mrs Kidd, Maple Stud, Ewhurst, Surrey.

Shetland Pony Society, D.M. Patterson Esq, 8, Whinfield Road, Montrose, Angus.

Welsh Pony and Cob Society, T.E. Roberts Esq, 32, North Parade, Aberystwyth, Wales.

Heavy draught breeds

British Percheron Horse Society, A.E. Vyse Esq, Owen Webb House, Gresham Road, Cambridge.

Clydesdale Horse Society, S. Gilmore Esq, 24, Beresford Terrace, Ayr, Scotland.

Shire Horse Society, R.W. Bird Esq, East of England Showground, Alwalton, Peterborough, Northamptonshire.

Suffolk Horse Society, c/o Church Street, Woodbridge, Suffolk.

5   Major English shows at which there are driving and harness events

April   London Harness Horse Parade Society. Regent's Park, London. Easter Monday. (An amalgamation of the cart horse and van horse parades of former days).

May	Newark and Nottinghamshire Agricultural Society Show.
	Chelmsford (Essex) Horse Show.
	Royal Windsor Horse Show.
	Northern Counties Pony Association, Shropshire.
	Shropshire and West Midlands Agricultural Society Show.
	Devon County Show.
	Horley Riding and Driving Club Harness Show.
	Aldershot Horse Show.
	Heathfield and District Agricultural Show.
	Hertfordshire Show.
	Bromham Horse Show, Wiltshire.
	Royal Bath and West Show.
June	City of Worcester Show.
	North Somerset Annual Agricultural Show.
	Watford Horse Show.
	Derbyshire County Show.
	South of England Show, Ardingly (Sussex).
	Sherborne Heavy Horse and Driving Show.
	Leicestershire Agricultural Society's Show.
	Essex County Show.
	British Driving Society Show. Smith's Lawn, Windsor.
	Lincolnshire Agricultural Society Show.
	Royal Norfolk Show.
July	The Royal Show. (Royal Agricultural Society) Stoneleigh, Kenilworth, Warwickshire.
	Steeple Barton Shetland and Driving Show.
	Northleach Welsh Pony and Cob Show, Cheltenham, Gloucestershire.
	Royal International Horse Show. Wembley, London.
	Royal Welsh Show.
	East of England Show, Peterborough.
	Northampton Show.
	New Forest Agricultural Show, Brockenhurst, Hampshire.
	Abergavenny and Border Counties Show.
August	National Pony Show. Malvern, Hereford-Worcester.
	Rutland Show.
	Essex Tradesman's Show.
	New Milton Horse Show, Hampshire.
	Witney Driving Show.
	South East Essex Riding and Driving Club Show.
	Pembrokeshire Agricultural Show.
	Denbighshire and Flintshire Agricultural Show.
	Ponies of Britain Summer Show, Peterborough.
	Skelton Agricultural Show, Cumbria.
	Mid-Somerset Show.
	Gillingham and Shaftesbury Show.
	British Timkin Show, Northampton.
	Greater London Show, Clapham Common.
	Ashby Agricultural Show. Ashby-de-la-Zouche, Leicestershire.
	City of Leicester Horse Show.

September Dorchester Agricultural Show, Dorset.
Romsey, Agricultural Show. Hampshire.
Northern Driving Championships, Holker Hall, Cumbria.
Brockham Harness Driving Club Driving Show. Surrey.
October Horse of the Year Show. London.

6   American shows with driving events

May   Dressage Show. Shone's Driving Establishment, Millbrook NY.
Carriage Marathon. Children's Services Horse Show,
   Framington CT.
Carriage Drive. Farmington CT.
Annual Marathon Drive. Devon Show, Devon PA.
Driving Classes. Bath Saddle Club Show, Prattsburg. NY.
June   Hunterdon Driving Show. Hickory Run, Califon NJ.
Hunterdon Horse and Pony Club Show. Hickory Run, Califon. NJ.
Pleasure Driving Clinic. Shone's Driving Establishment,
   Millbrook NY.
Olney Driving Meet. Olney Pony Farm, Joppa MD.
Mid-Hudson Driving Club Picnic Drive. Mohonk Mountain House,
   New Paltz NY.
Mid-Hudson Driving Club Pleasure Driving Competition.
   Dutchess County Fair Grounds, Rhinebeck NY.
Harford County Equestrian Centre Pleasure Driving Show.
   Bel Air MD.
Myopia Driving Events. Topsfield MA. Three-day event.
Driving Classes. Auburn District Fair, Auburn CA.
Rose Hill Manor Driving Show. Frederick MD.
July   Annual Stonybrook Driving Competition. North Shore Horse
   Show Grounds, Stonybrook LI.
Carriage Days Driving. Owls Head Foundation and
   Transportation Museum, Owls Head ME.
'Old Roxbury Days' Wagon Rally and Driving Contest. Booth,
   Roxbury CT.
Driving Classes and Marathon. Warrington PA.
Menlo Circus Club. Park Carriage Drive CA.
Lorenzo Driving Meet. Lorenzo State Historic Site. Cazanovia NY.
Annual Old Chatham Hunt Driving Meet. Old Chatham NY.
August   Fairfield Hunt Club Driving Competition. Westport CT.
Harness and Draft Class, Midland Empire State Fair, Billings
   MONT.
Driving Division. Delaware County Fair, Walton NY.
Walnut Hill Driving Competition. Pittsford Driving Club NY.
September Driving in Connecticut Weekend. Pleasure, cross-country,
   dressage, etc.
Driving Classes, California State Fair, Sacramento CA.
Gladstone FEI Driving Event, (three phases, five divs).
New England Draft and Carriage Horse Days. Obstacle course
   and over-night cross-country drive.

Annual Driving Clinic and Weekend. Green Mountain Horse
Association. Woodstock VT.
Second Annual Teams Competition. Shone's Driving
Establishment. Millbrook NY.
Mid-American Coaching and Driving Competitions.
Humphrey Equestrian Centre, Mentor OH.
Annual Marlboro Marathon. West Brattleboro (Marathon) VT.
Meeting and Weekend of Driving. American Driving Society,
Mohonk Mountain House, New Paltz NY.

October   Dressage Competition, Shone's Driving Establishment.
Millbrook NY.
Annual Fall Foliage Drive, Shone's Driving Establishment.
Millbrook NY.
Fall Carriage Rally. White Memorial Foundation, Litchfield CT.
Myopia-Ledyard Four-in-Hand Driving Event. FEI rules.
Hamilton MA.
Annual Driving Meet. Leesburg VA.
Annual Oakdale Driving Meet, Rockville MD.
Yosemite National Park Drive, Stockton CA.

November Sebastopol Drive, Sebastopol CA.
Royal Winter Show, Toronto, Canada.

7 Bibliography

A Book About Travelling Past and Present by Thomas A. Croal. William P.
Nimmo, London and Edinburgh 1877.
All Drawn by Horses by James Arnold. David and Charles, Newton Abbot
1979.
American Horse-Drawn Vehicles by Jack D. Rittenhouse. Crown Publishers,
New York 1958.
An Assemblage of 19th Century Horses and Carriages by Jennifer Lang, with
illustrations from the original sketches by William F. Freelove. Perpetua
Press, Farnham 1971.
A Practical Treatise on Coach Building by J.W. Burgess, London 1918.
Army Service Corps Training, Part III, Transport HMSO, 1911 (reprinted with
amendments 1915).
A Romany Rye George Borrow, London 1857.
Black Beauty by Anna Sewell (for details of cabs and cab-horses). London 1877.
Boswell's Life of Johnson London 1791.
Buses Trolleys and Trams by Charles A. Dunbar. Weidenfeld and Nicholson,
London 1967.
Carriage Building in England and France by G. Hooper, London 1890.
Carriages by Jacques Damase. Weidenfeld and Nicholson, London 1968.
Carriages to the End of the Nineteenth Century by Philip Sumner.
Science Museum Booklet, HMSO 1970.
Discovering Carts and Wagons by John Vince. Shire Publications, Princes
Risborough (sec ed) 1974.
Discovering Commercial Horse-Drawn Vehicles by D.J. Smith. Shire
Publications Ltd, Princes Risborough 1977.
Discovering Horse-Drawn Carriages by D.J. Smith. Shire Publications Ltd,
Princes Risborough (sec ed) 1980.

English Horse-Drawn Vehicles by David Parry. Frederick Warne, London 1979.

Farm Waggons of England and Wales by James Arnold. John Baker, London 1969.

Guide to the Transport Museum, Hull by J. Bartlett MA, FSA, FMA
City of Hull Museums, Kingston-upon-Hull 1971.

Harnessing-Up by Anne Norris and Nancy Pethick. J.A. Allen, London and New York 1979.

Horse-drawn Heavy Goods Vehicles Compiled and Introduced by John Thompson. John Thompson, Fleet 1977.

Horse Power by Marylian and Sanders Watney. Hamlyn Publishing Group, London, New York, Sydney and Toronto 1975.

Horses and Saddlery by Maj G. Tylden. J.A. Allen, London and New York 1965.

Kilvert's Diary 1938-40 (mid-19th century).

Making Model Horse-Drawn Vehicles by John Thompson. John Thompson, Fleet 1976.

Manual of Horsemastership, Equitation and Animal Transport HMSO 1937.

Pepys Diary 1825 (mid-17th century).

Quick Silver by R.C. and J.M. Anderson. David and Charles, Newton Abbot 1973.

Roads and Vehicles by Anthony Bird. Longmans, London and Harrow 1969.

Road Vehicles of the Great Western Railway by Philip J. Kelly. Oxford Publishing Company, Ltd, Oxford 1973.

Saddlery and Harness Making Edited by Paul N. Hasluck. J.A. Allen, London and New York (reprinted 1962).

Salute the Carthorse by The Rev Philip A. Wright, Ian Allan 1971.

Show Driving Explained by Marylian Watney and William Kenward. Ward Lock, London 1978.

Single and Pair Horse Driving Maj Gen Geoffrey H.A. White CB, CMG, DSO. The British Driving Society.

Stage Coach by John Richards. Watmoughs Ltd and Horse Drawn Carriages Ltd, in collab. with the BBC 1977.

The Art and Craft of Coachmaking by John Philipson 1897.

The Driving Book Maj H. Faudel-Phillips. J.A. Allen, London and New York 1965.

The Elegant Carriage by Marylian Watney. J.A. Allen, London and New York 1961, reprinted 1979.

The English Farm Wagon by J. Geraint Jenkins. Oakwood Press, for the University of Reading 1969.

The English Gypsy Caravan by C.H. Ward-Jackson and Dennis Harvey. David and Charles, Newton Abbot 1972.

The English Pleasure Carriage by W. Bridges Adams, London 1837. Reprinted by Adams and Dart, London 1971, with introduction by Jack Simmons.

The History of Carriages by Laszlo Tarr. Vision Press London and Corvina Press, Budapest 1969.

The History of Coaches by George Thrupp, 1877.

The History of the Horse Bus as a Vehicle by Charles Lee. British Transport Commission, London 1962.

The Horse in Art by David Livingstone-Learmouth. The Studio, London and New York 1958.

The Horse World of London by W.J. Gordon. David and Charles (reprinted
   1978).
The Royal Mews, Buckingham Palace Official Guide. Pitkin Pictorials Ltd
   1964.
The Shell Book of Country Crafts by James Arnold. John Baker for Shell 1968.
The Wheelwright's Shop by George Sturt (George Bourne). Cambridge
   University Press, Cambridge 1963.
Thy Servant the Horse by Lionel Edwards RI. Country Life Ltd 1952.
Walter's Horse Keepers Encyclopedia W.H. Walter. Andrew Elliot (Right Way
   Books), Kingswood.

Magazines and Journals
Carriage Journal, The Quarterly (obtainable only by subscribing members of
   the Carriage Association of America).
Country Life 2-10, Tavistock St, Covent Garden, London WC2E 9QX. Weekly.
Country Quest Caxton Press, Oswestry, Salop. Monthly.
Field, The 8, Stratton St, London W1X 6AT. Weekly.
Horse and Driving Watmoughs Ltd, Idle, Bradford, West Yorkshire BD10 8NL.
   Quarterly.
Horse and Hound 189, High Holborn, London WC1V 7BA. Weekly.
Horse and Pony Scottish Farmer Publications Ltd, 39 York St, Glasgow C2.
   Monthly.
Horse World 17, Fleet St, London EC4 1AA. Monthly.
Light Horse, The 19, Charing Cross Rd, London WC2H 0EY. Monthly.
Pony 19, Charing Cross Road, London WC2H 0EY. Monthly.
Riding: The Horselover's Magazine 189, High Holborn, London WC1V 7BA.
   Monthly.
Scottish Field 70, Mitchell St, Glasgow. Monthly.

Glossary

Anchor head bolt   The projecting head of a bolt with a slit to receive a spring.
Angle iron or bar   Roller bar of iron with L section, used for connecting side plates, etc.
Apron   Waterproof or leather covering at the front of a carriage to protect the driver or passengers in wet weather.
Archibald wheel   Patent, iron-hubbed wheel, invented by E.A. Archibald in 1871. Used on military wagons of the US Army from 1880.
Arch panel   Rounded panel fitted to the underside of a luggage boot or container.
Arm rail   Piece of wood or metal forming the shaping line on the lower quarters of a carriage body.
Axle   Bar of wood or metal forming the spindle or axis on which a wheel turns.
Axle arm   The end of an axle penetrating the centre of a hub or nave.
Axle, cranked   Axle made in the form of a crank, at right angles to the body of a vehicle, to support a low-slung cart or float.
Belt rail   Same as an arm rest or rail.
Bent timber   Wooden member bent by artificial steaming and manipulation.
Blocks   Wooden or iron blocks used above or under leaf springs of a vehicle to raise the level of the body.
Body   The main part or bodywork of a vehicle above the springs and axle.
Body brace   Iron support for the side of a wagon.
Body plate   Iron plate fitted to the inner side of rockers or under supports of a coach or carriage.
Bolster   Wooden, crosswise member of an unsprung wagon, between the axle-tree and main bodywork. Also a crosswise block or support on a timber carriage.
Bolster plate   Iron plate fixed to the underside of a wagon bolster to receive weight and friction in pivoting.
Bond   Circular hub band.
Book step   Folding understep of a carriage.
Boot   Receptical on a coach or carriage for luggage.
Bottom bars   End bars holding longitudinal rockers of a coach body together.
Box   Seat on which the driver of a coach or carriage sits. Formerly a tool box. Also an axle box, being part of the hub penetrated by the axle arm.
Boxing on   Fitting a hub or axle box.
Brace   Strap or stay used to effect greater rigidity.

Bracket   Bent or cranked iron to support a lamp, shaft or footboard.

Brad   Small sprig or nail used to attach beading.

Brake   Instrument used to retard a vehicle in motion.

Brake beam   Wooden beam supporting brake blocks.

Brake block   Also known as a brake shoe or slipper. Portion of the brake that brings pressure to bear on a tyre.

Brake lever   Rod, pedal or crank used in moving the brake blocks.

Branch   Stay used in carriage constuction to connect two or more parts.

Breeching hook   Hook on a shaft to which the breeching straps of harness may be attached.

Breeching loop   Metal loop sometimes used as substitute for a breeching hook.

Bush   Cylindrical lining to receive the wear of pivots and journals.

Butt bend or band   Hub band on the rear end of a hub, next to the wheel.

Canopy   The standing top of certain vehicles, supported by corner or side pillars.

Cant rail   Protective top rail or guard.

Carriage bolt   Long bolt with a square shank below the head or between head and thread, used in coach and carriage construction.

Carriage part   Any part of a carriage except the bodywork.

Cart shaft hook   Hook, on cart shafts, used as a connection for traces.

Cart shaft rod   Rod on a cart shaft used to support hooks.

Chair   The combination of platform bars and fifth wheel on certain heavy vehicles.

Channel tyres   Solid rubber tyres fitted into metal frames or channels.

Cleat   Winged iron at the side of a wagon to receive the lashing-down ropes. Also known as a roping point.

Closed top   Carriage with a falling hood or head, but having permanently raised side quarters.

Club Handle   The T-shaped handle of a coach or carriage door.

Collar   Projecting ring or rim on the inner side of an axle arm.

Collet   Axle band or washer.

Cork ledge   Strip of cork attached to the footboard of a vehicle to afford a better grip for the driver.

Corner pillar   Corner support for the body of a vehicle.

Coupling pole   The perch of a timber carriage between fore and hind parts. Also the under-perch of a wagon.

Crab   Socket at the side of a coach pole with loops on either side to receive the pole straps.

Cradle   Skeleton rear body of a vehicle to receive luggage.

Crane or craneneck   Curved irons to support the bodywork of a carriage while allowing underlock of the forebody.

Crawl   The wrinkled surface of paintwork or varnish on the side panels of a neglected vehicle. Also the wrinkling of varnish above paint.

Crest panel   Panel under a door or window of a coach on which a crest or monogram may be painted.

C spring, also **cee**   Curved body spring in the shape of a letter C.

Curled hair   Animal hairs twisted and curled but later unpicked, used for stuffing carriage cushions.

Curtain   Top piece to enclose the upper part of an open carriage, which may be rolled-up.

Cut-under   Part of the bodywork cut away to allow the fore-wheels a full turning-circle.

Dashboard   Protective board at the front of a low vehicle to shield the driver from splashes.

Dash rail   External rail fitting round the sides of the dashboard.

Daumont, à la   Carriage drawn by horses which are ridden and controlled by postillions, rather than driven from the box.

D link   D-shaped link used in securing cross springs.

Dennett springs   Patent springing of the early 19th century, with two length-ways and one cross spring.

Dish   The outward cant of wheel spokes above the axle.

Dogstick   Prop under the rearward part of the vehicle to prevent it rolling backwards on a slope.

Door crest   The upper part of a coach or carriage door.

Door stile   Framing of a carriage door, forming the recess into which a drop light is lowered.

Double suspension   Combined elliptical springs and C springs.

Double tree   Connection for two swingletrees. Also known as an evener.

Dowel pin   Pin or plug of wood or metal used as a connection in place of a tenon.

Dragshoe or drugshoe   Wedge or skid used as a brake iron under the rear wheel of a wagon or coach.

Dragstaff   Same as a dog stick.

Drawbar   Attachment for traces, same as a splinterbar.

Drayel   Iron staple at the end of a shaft for the attachment of trace harness.

Drip moulding   Concave guttering on a coach roof to prevent rain water entering the interior of the bodywork.

Drugbat   Country name for a drag or drugshoe.

Drunken wheel   A badly set wheel.

Dummy board   Platform at the rear of a coach on which a footman rides. Also a luggage rack.

D wheel   Fifth wheel of a wagon in the form of a letter D.

Ear   Forged plate projecting from the side of a vehicle, with holes drilled to receive bolts.

Earbreadth   Projection at the side of a wagon to support a stay or stanchion.

Elbow spring   Steel spring, slightly curved, pivoted on loops at one or both ends.

Elliptical spring   Steel springs invented or perfected by Obadiah Elliot in 1804. Made of curved leaves or plates in elliptical form, hinged together at the extremities.

End bar   Cross-bar forming an end to the framework of a carriage body.

End board   The crosswise rearboard of a wagon or cart. Also known as the tailboard or tailgate.

Ex-bed   The same as axle-bed. Term mainly used in rural England.

Falling top   Carriage top or hood that can be raised and lowered.

Felloe   Pronounced 'fellie'. The segment of a wheel rim.

Fifth wheel   Horizontally placed wheel of the fore-carriage, on which axle and carrying wheels pivot in full lock.

Folding top   Same as a falling hood or top.

Footman holder   Loop or pendent to which a footman might cling when riding the dummy board.

Fore-carriage   The under-gear at the fore-end of a vehicle.

Front pillar   Upright fore-pillar of a vehicle to support the bodywork.

Futchell   Horizontal, forward-pointing member which supports the fore-carriage and swaybar.

Futchell bed   Stout wooden member fixed to the top of the futchells, through which a pivot or kingbolt passes.

Gammon boards   Outside or roof seats on a stage or mail coach.

Garden seats   Forward facing seats on the upper deck of an omnibus.

Garnish rail   The inner wooden framing of a coach window.

Gather   The forward position or set of an axle.

Gauge   Width of track between opposite wheels.

Gear   Under part of a vehicle, including wheels, axles and springs.

Glass frame lifter   Strap or cord for raising a coach or carriage window.

Glazed leather   Patent leather, used in coach making.

Half patent axle   Axle deriving from the patent axle but have a single nut at the termination and a collar at the back of the wheel, sunk into the hub.

Hammer cloth   Ornamental cloth with deep fringes, draped over the box-seat on certain carriages and coaches.

Hanger, body   Iron fitting or loop to hang or secure under-springs.

Hanger, brake   Connecting rod attaching a swinging brake beam to an upper bar.

Harness leather   Leather used for both harness and the falling hoods of certain carriages.

Head   The top or roof of a vehicle.

Head block   Block of wood on a fore-carriage, forming a still point or pivot on which the axle turns. Also a resting place for the perch into which it is morticed.

Head block plate   Metal plate used in fixing the perch to the head block.

Head board   The front end of a cart or wagon, opposite the end or tail board.

Heel bar   Bar or block on which a driver braces his feet.

Hind-carriage   The rear underpart of a coach or carriage.

Hinge pillar   Pillar on either side of a coach door in which the hinges are set.

Hold back   Loop on the under-side of a shaft to which breeching straps are fastened.

Hood   Top or head of a carriage, also protective covering above the driving seat of an otherwise open wagon.

Hoop   Tyre of a wheel. Also a curved iron supporting a hood.

Hound   Futchell on a farm wagon.

Hound bar   Rear bar attached to hounds, on which the hangers of a brake beam may be fitted.

Hound pin   Securing pin for a hound, fitted at the rear of an axle.

Hub   The turning centre of a wheel into which the lower ends of the spokes are fitted. Also known as a nave.

Hub cap   Plate fitted over the face of a hub for decorative purposes or to keep out dust and dirt.

Hug   Part of the hub bearing, fitted against the collar of an axle arm.

Imperial   Roof seat on a coach or omnibus.

Iron   Protective side rail on the seat of a vehicle.

Ivory trim   Ornaments and accessories of a coach made from ivory, such as card-cases, studs, door-handles, etc.

Jack   (1) Windlass device for raising a carriage wheel clear of the ground.

(2) Upright support at the corners of running gear to contain the end of a thoroughbrace.

Jockey   Slang term for a postillion.

Journal   The rotating part of an axle arm which turns in the box or bearings.

Journal box   Either an axle-box or the bearing in which the roller of a brake roller-bar turns.

Jump seat   Folding seat which may be slid forwards or jumped to conserve space in a carriage interior.

Keyhole strap   Tapering strap at the end of a swingletree, helping to keep the traces in place.

Keystaff   Staff passed through loops at the front end of a tipcart, turning or removing which enables the body to dump.

Kingbolt   Also known as the kingpin. Pivot passing through or secured to the front axle on which the fore-carriage turns.

Knee boot   Knee flaps at the front of a carriage, usually made of wood, used as a form of protection.

Knifeboard   Longitudinal seating on the upper deck of an early omnibus. Passengers sat back-to-back, facing outwards.

Lamp   Lamp or lantern hung from brackets or sockets on the outside of a vehicle, illuminating the road ahead and making its presence known to other road-users.

Lamp barrel   The stem or lower part of a coach lamp by which it may be fitted into a slot or socket.

Leader doubletree   Doubletree at the head of a coach pole, to which the leaders of a team are attached.

Light   Glass window of a coach or carriage.

Limber   Fore or hind part of an articulated military vehicle, especially of a guncarriage.

Linch pin   Wedge-shaped iron pin used in securing a wheel to its hub or nave.

Lining   The trim or internal upholstery of a coach.

Lining-out   Painting lines or decorative stripes on the wheels or bodywork of a vehicle.

Lock   The turning circle of a vehicle, often described as a half-lock, full-lock, etc, according to extent.

Locking stop   Projection of the fifth wheel to prevent it turning too far under the bodywork.

Long staple   Form of shaft-rod for harness connections.

Mail patent or **mail hub**   Axle and hub in which the hub is secured by three long bolts.

Mail spring   Platform springs for stage and mail coaches, also known as Telegraph springs.

Main brace   Straps for connecting springs to bodywork.

Mat   Pad or rug covering the floorboards of a coach or carriage.

Monkey board   The rear platform of a horse bus.

Nave   Alternative name for a wheel hub.

Neap   Wagon pole and futchells made from the same piece of timber, split at the ends.

Neck yoke   Bar attaching a horse to the front end of a pole, in double harness.

Nutcracker springs   Combination of springs in which a pair of half elliptical springs are attached to crosswise dumb springs.

Nut washer   An axle washer.

Outrigger   Side projection at the front of a vehicle to which an extra horse may be attached.

Oval light   Carriage window of an oval shape.

Oxford bounder   High-wheeled dogcart of the mid-19th century.

Pad   Centre part of a carriage step on which the foot is placed when mounting a vehicle.

Perch   Longitudinal pole or bar connecting the front and rear parts of a carriage as a means of support.

Perch bolt   Similar to a kingbolt or pin on a fore-carriage.

Perch brace   Iron brace extending from the rear axle to the fore-part of the perch, which it meets at an acute angle.

Perch carriage   Vehicle using an under-perch or perch.

Perch wing   Type of hound or futchell of the fore-carriage, used with or under a perch.

Picking out   Painting fine lines or ornaments on the side panels of a vehicle.

Piecing out   Extending parts of metal or wood such as axle arms.

Pillow   English country name for the front bolster of a wagon.

Pillow spring   Wasp-waisted interior spring of a pillow or cushion.

Pin   Slender bar of wood or metal used in coach- or carriage-making as a support or connection.

Platform bar   Transverse wooden member on the fore-carriage of a vehicle with a fifth wheel. These combine with the wheel, on a platform-sprung vehicle to form the chair.

Platform springs   The low-slung combination of crosswise and lengthwise springing.

Play   Movement of an axle in its bearings.

Point bend   Metal band used on the front or face of a hub.

Pole   Long bar or beam to which horses are hitched for double harness work. The carriage pole has end loops, while the coach pole has an extended hook. Also known as a tongue.

Pole bridge   Iron bridge or bar to hold the rearward end of the pole and prevent it from lifting or slipping.

Pole cap   Iron fitting at the fore-end of a pole to which the chains are connected.

Pole chains   Chains attached to pole gear as a connection with harness straps.

Pole circle   Member in the form of a bent wooden ring to which the rearward end of a pole is secured. Used to convert a shafted vehicle to pole draught.

Pole collar   Metal fitting securing pole to axle.

Pole crab   Socket at the fore-end of a pole having two eyes for straps.

Pole eye   Part of the coupling gear through which a bolt passes to secure a pole to the fore-carriage.

Pole pin   Securing pin at the end of a pole, used to prevent it becoming detached from the vehicle.

Pole pin strap   Short leather safety strap for securing a pole pin.

Pole plates   Metal plates on the rearward end of a pole to prevent it wearing against the futchells.

Pole socket   Metal socket of a transom on front gearing, through which the pole passes.

Postillion   Mounted driver usually in charge of a pair of horses, riding one and driving the other.

Pump handle   Rearward support—in a transverse position—at the ends of coach rockers, to support the dummy board.

Quarter   (1) Section of a coach body. The body is divided into four quarters. (2) Side sections or parts of a falling top. (3) The rearward part of a carriage top on either side of the curtain.

Quarter light   Small window in the upper part of a coach body.

Quarter panel   Thin, board panel used to cover the quarters of a coach body.

Rein rail   Support for driving reins on the top of a dash-board.

Riser   Block used to raise the bodywork of a vehicle.

Rocker   Curved under-support beneath the body of a heavy coach, fitted with a lining of steel rocker plates.

Roller bolt   Vertical, large-headed bolt on the splinterbar, to which traces of the wheel horses are attached.

Roller or **scotch roller**   Small roller under the near-side rear wheel of a vehicle to prevent it running backwards on a steep hill.

Roof   The fixed or standing head of a covered vehicle.

Rumble   Rear seat on a coach or carriage, usually open.

Sand board   Sturdy wooden member across the hounds or futchells of a vehicle, through which the kingpin passes and on which the bolster rests.

Sarven wheel   Patent wheel invented by J.D. Sarven in 1857. Spokes screw or rivet together within double hub plates.

Sash   Lower part of a coach or carriage window frame.

Screwing-up   Tightening nuts on a carriage wheel.

Scroll springs   (1) Springs in the form of a scroll. (2) Alternative name for C springs.

Set   The angle of an axle arm. Downward set is 'swing' and forward set is 'gather'. Necessary for well-dished wheels which would otherwise bear too much weight on hubs and linch pins.

Shackle   Staple to receive a suspension brace or to couple springs together.

Shackle barrel   Spring shackle used to fasten together ends of platform springs.

Shackle eye   Aperture through which a shackle bolt passes. Known as 'eyes-up' or 'eyes-down', according to position.

Shafts   Bars or thills used for attaching a horse to its vehicle. Either single or double but usually the former.

Sill   Bottom timbers of a carriage to which other parts are fitted.

Skeleton boot   Carriage boot or box-seat not fully panelled, often made of iron stays.

Slider bar   Alternative name for a sway bar.

Spindle   Side supports of a wagon body. Also the rods supporting the back rest of a driving seat.

Splinterbar   Crossbar at the front of a vehicle to which harness traces are attached.

Spoke   Wooden part or bar of a wheel, forming connection and attachment between hub and rim or tyre. There are seven parts. (1) The tenon or tongue entering the hub or nave. (2) The shoulder directly above the hub. (3) The front side near the hub. (4) The throat, changing from square to oval section. (5) The back or rear side near the hub. (6) The body or oval part forming two-thirds of its length. (7) The point which enters the felloes.

Spoke dog   Lever with a hook, used in drawing spokes together when driving-in the felloes.

Stagger Placing wheel spokes at alternately different angles for extra strength and security. Also known as dodge and strut.

Stake Upright iron or stanchion at the side of a wagon to help contain or protect the load

Standing pillar Upright to support a coach roof.

Stay Form of metal arm or support.

Strake (1) Iron plate fixed to a wheel before the introduction of band tyres. (2) Alternative name for a stake.

Sway bar Bar at the rear end of futchells used to retain and steady tne under-carriage.

Swing The dip necessary for downward set or dip of a dished wheel.

Swingletree Short, horizontal bar to which traces are attached with certain forms of pair harness or in teams. Two mav be united by a doubletree. Also known as a whippletree or whiffletree.

Swing pole Detached pole between the second pair of a team of six. Also known as a swing or swinger.

Sword case Narrow box at the rear of a travelling coach or carriage to contain dress swords (formerly worn by gentlemen with full evening dress).

Syssing The crawling or crazing of paintwork, known in America as alligator.

Tailboard Same as backboard or tailgate.

Tail pegs Wedge-shaped or conical pegs used for holding a tailboard in position. Secured by means of short chains.

Telegraph springs Platform springs on stage coaches. An alternative name for Mail springs. First used on a coach named the 'Telegraph'.

Thoroughbraces Longitudinal strap suspension for coaches and carriages.

Transom Bar to which the forward end of a perch is usually attached.

Tug iron Same as hold back.

Turtle boot Also known as a turtle-backed boot. Fore-boot of a heavy coach or carriage, shaped like the upper shell of a turtle. Detached from the main bodywork and hung on iron hoops or loops.

Umbrella top The top of a light carriage in the form of an umbrella or parasol.

Under-carriage The supporting, undergear of a vehicle.

Wagon standard Upright post supporting the fore-end of a wagon body.

Wagon standard brace Iron or steel brace supporting a wagon standard.

Washer Flat ring intended to prevent or reduce friction.

Wheel Circular disc or spoked framework on which a vehicle rolls. Also a horizontal member for pivoting.

Whiffletree Same as a swingletree.

XC plate Metal parts which are tinned to prevent rusting or corrosion.

Yandell top Forward or downward curving roof or top on certain types of American buggy, named after its inventor. Similar to the later autotop.

Yard of tin Slang name for a coach horn.

Yoke tip Metal socket of a neck yoke for pole straps and chains.

A list of British terms with their American equivalents

British	American
Axle-box	Bush
Bolsterplate	Lockingplate
Bond	Hub-band

British	American
Buggy (two-wheeled gig)	Buggy (four-wheeled vehicle)
Carriage or under-carriage	Gearing
Carriage rug	Lap rug
Dash or dashboard	Splash or splasher/splashboard
Dirt iron (projection over a hub)	Sandband or false iron/box
Dogstick	Dragstaff or mountain point
Dragshoe or drugbat	Shoe or slipper
Dustcart	Trash or garbage wagon
Float (low-loading vehicle)	Light wagon or floater
Footboard	Toeboard
Footwarmer	Carriage heater
Foreway (set of an axle)	Gather
Gammon seat or gammon board	Top seats
Head	Fixed top
Headboard	Top-rail
Head collar	Halter
Hood	Bonnet
Horsebox	Horse-trailer
Limber (forebody of an articulated military vehicle)	Caisson
Lining-out	Striping
Lockingplate	Bedplate
Mudguard	Fender
Oilcloth	Oil carpet
Patent leather	Glazed leather
Pillow	Front bolster
Pole	Tongue
Tailboard	Tailgate or endboard
Telegraph springs	Mail springs
Timber carriage	Lumber buggy
Trim or trimming	Lining
Waterproof cloth	Rubber duck
Wingnut	Thumbnut